The Song of the Cathar Wars

The Song of the Cathar Wars

A History of the Albigensian Crusade

WILLIAM OF TUDELA

and an

ANONYMOUS SUCCESSOR

translated by

JANET SHIRLEY

Ashgate

Aldershot • Burlington USA • Singapore • Sydney

Published by
Ashgate Publishing Limited
Gower House
Croft Road
Aldershot
Hants GU11 3HR
England

Ashgate Publishing Company
131 Main Street
Burlington, VT 05401-5600 USA

Ashgate website:http://www.ashgate.com

Paperback edition published 2000

Janet Shirley has asserted her moral right under the Copyright, Designs and Patents Act 1988 to be identified as the author of this work.

British Library Cataloguing in Publication Data

William, of Tudela
   The Song of the Cathar Wars: A History of the Albigensian Crusade.
   1. Narrative poetry, Provençal—translations into English. 2. Narrative
   poetry, English—translated from Provençal. 3. Provençal poetry—to
   1500—translations into English. 4. English poetry—translated from
   Provençal. 5. Albigenses—poetry.
   I. Title. II. Shirley, Janet.
   841´.03´0901

Library of Congress Cataloging-in-Publication Data

Guillaume, de Tudèle, fl. 1210–1213.
   [Chanson de la croisade albigeoise. English]
   The song of the Cathar wars: a history of the Albigensian Crusade/
   William of Tudela and an anonymous successor: translated by Janet
   Shirley.
      p. cm. Includes index. (Cloth)
   1. Albigenses—Poetry. 2. France—History—Philip II Augustus,
   1180-1223—Poetry. 3. Languedoc (France)—History—Poetry.
   I. Shirley, Janet. II. Title.
   PC3340.G84C413   1996
   849´12—dc20   96-12313
                                                                          CIP
ISBN 1 85928 331 4 [hbk]
ISBN 0 7546 0388 1 [pbk]
Printed in Great Britain by MPG Books Ltd, Bodmin, Cornwall

Contents

List of maps and figures

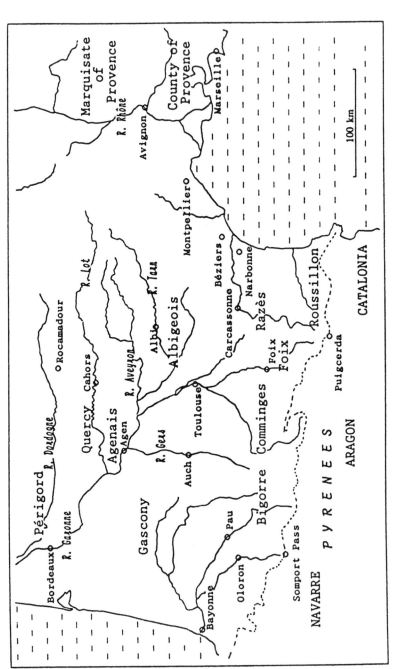

1 General map for *The Song of the Cathar Wars*

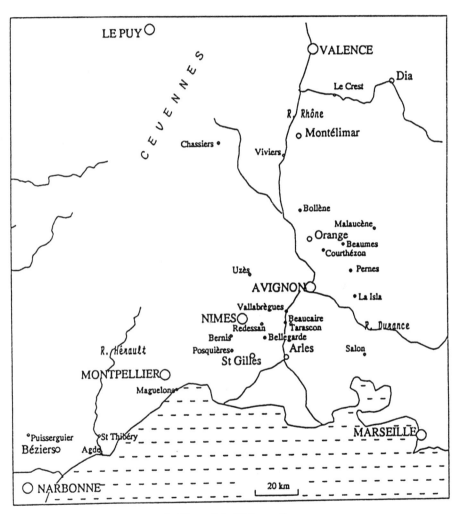

2 Map of the Rhône valley

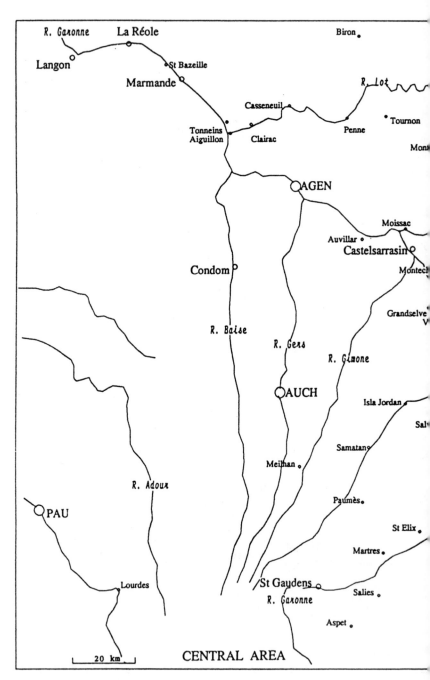

3   Detail of the central area

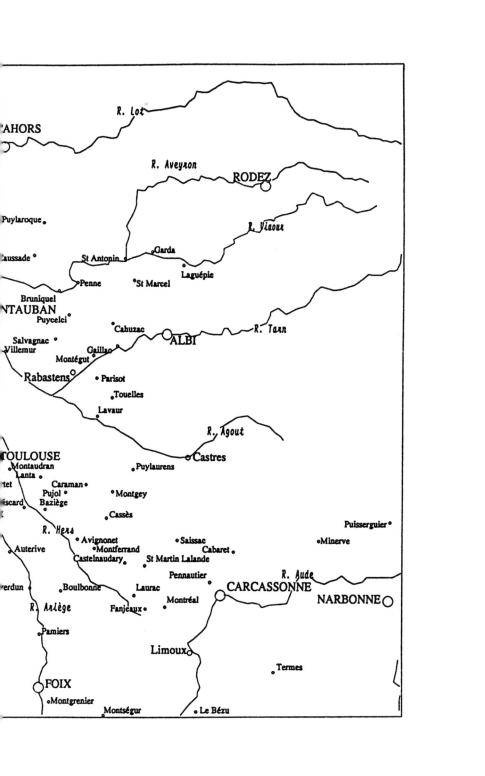

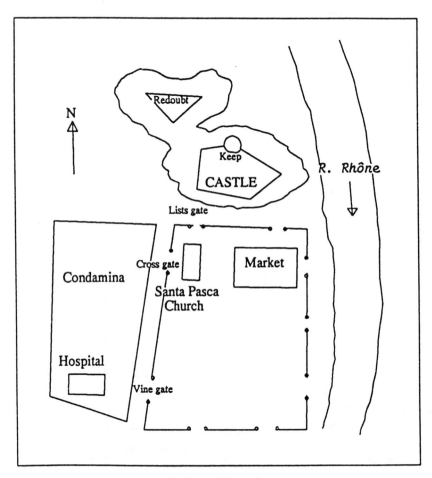

4 Plan of Beaucaire

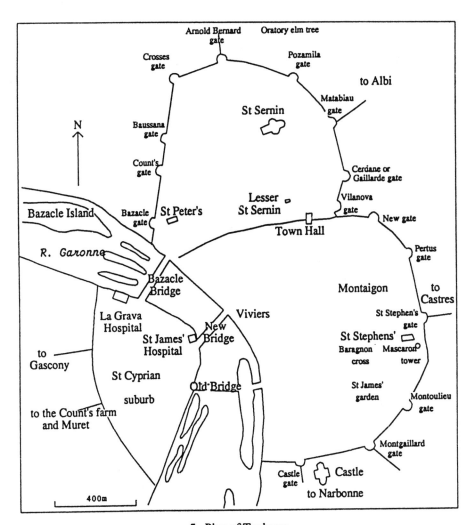

Arnold Bernard gate

Oratory elm tree

Crosses gate

Pozamila gate

to Albi

Matabiau gate

St Sernin

N

Baussana gate

Count's gate

Cerdane or Gaillarde gate

Vilanova gate

Lesser St Sernin

New gate

Bazacle Island

Bazacle gate

St Peter's

Town Hall

R. Garonne

Pertus gate

Bazacle Bridge

Montaigon

to Castres

La Grava Hospital

Viviers

St Stephen's gate

New Bridge

St Stephens'

to Gascony

St James' Hospital

Baragnon cross

Mascaron tower

St Cyprian

Old Bridge

St James' garden

suburb

Montoulieu gate

to the Count's farm and Muret

Montgaillard gate

400m

Castle gate

Castle

to Narbonne

5 Plan of Toulouse

Introduction

The *Canso* and its authors

The poem offered here in translation tells the story of events in Languedoc between the years 1204 and 1218, events known to us as the Albigensian Crusade. Exhorted to do so by the Church, warriors from the Ile de France and northern Europe rode south in order to exterminate heresy and acquire wealth, and were vigorously resisted by men and women of Languedoc, now often called Occitania. This was not yet part of France, and much of it had closer links with the realms of Aragon or Navarre than with the small French kingdom far away in the north. In August 1209 a French baron, Simon de Montfort, was chosen to command the military attack. His principal opponent was Raymond VI, count of Toulouse.

The crusade was launched and strongly supported by Pope Innocent III in order to stamp out the dualist heresy then flourishing in Languedoc. Most writings by these heretics have long since perished, so that the surviving evidence is mainly provided by their enemies, but it seems clear that Cathars believed in the existence not of one supreme God but of two gods who were equally powerful, one good and one evil; that they regarded everything physical as belonging to the evil god, and therefore to be abstained from wherever possible - no wealth, no sexual intercourse, no eating of meat and as little as possible of any other food. They also held that 'the Roman Church had been founded by the evil god to frustrate the work of Christ' (Bernard Hamilton, *The Albigensian Crusade*), and that Christ did not really die on the cross and therefore did not need to rise from the dead. Their own name for themselves, 'Cathars', meant those who are pure, cleansed, and their preachers went about from place to place not only teaching but demonstrating a Christ-like love of poverty and abstention from worldly lusts. It was in response to this challenge that St Dominic began his great career, himself adopting a life of poverty and preaching. Here too are the origins of the Inquisition, for in the early 1230s the Church established this tribunal as a more systematic means of heresy-hunting.

This account of the crusade against the Cathars or Albigenses - people of Albi, a stronghold of the heresy - has no surviving title, except that in his opening lines the first author refers to *la cansos que maestre Guilhems fit*, 'the song which Master William made'. There were two authors, William, who tells us something about himself in his opening lines and in laisse 9, and a man whose name we do not know who picked up William's work almost in mid-sentence and carried it magnificently on from an entirely different point of view. The change-over occurs between laisses 131 and 132, after about one third of the text.

William of Tudela, the first author, supported the papacy and the northern French and their allies, although with some qualms now and then at particular acts of cruelty. His anonymous continuer, however, is whole-heartedly on the side of the southerners. This does not mean that he supported heresy; on the contrary, he indignantly denies that any of his heroes were guilty of such an error and asserts their orthodoxy. So did they, and it is noteworthy that the most frequent accusation brought against Raymond of Toulouse was not that he was himself a heretic, but that he was not sufficiently hard on heretics among his vassals.

William and the Anonymous differ in other ways as well. There are, of course, similarities - both wrote in forms of Provençal, that of William being less southern and more French than that of his successor. Both wrote a historical narrative in alexandrine verse, the lines being rhymed in groups of irregular length now called 'laisses'. Both included plenty of direct speech and gave the performer of the verses good scope for dramatic presentation and lively effects. Both used a literary device to help the performer carry over from the end of one laisse to the beginning of the next: William rhymes throughout each laisse on one sound, but ends his final half line with a new rhyme, the one that he will use all through the following laisse. His successor does not change the rhyme like this but instead ends each laisse with a resounding phrase, which he then repeats as the first words of the next laisse.

But there are other differences between the two men, and these are striking. One is their point of view: William is emphatically a loyal Catholic who deplores *la fola erransa* of the heretics and thinks it an unfortunate necessity, indeed their own fault, if they are slaughtered. The Anonymous is a passionate opponent of the crusade, thinks no villainy too evil to be ascribed to its commander, Simon de Montfort, and shouts for joy at each success won by Count Raymond or by his son, 'the brave young count'.

Another and considerable difference between these two authors, one that is all but lost in translation, is that William was a good competent writer but his successor was a man of genius. William can tell a good story and is careful to leave us in no doubt that he was a well educated literary man ('Never in the host of Menelaus from whom Paris stole Helena were so many tents set up on the plains below Mycenae ...'). The Anonymous, however, can toss showers of words into the air and catch them again, can make the morning air shimmer before our eyes as the knights ride to war along the riverbank with the sun glinting on their armour and on the waters of the Garonne. More than this, he has great economy of style, never any hint of long-windedness or padding, and his command of dialogue is such that we read on in amazement, thinking, for example, 'How brave of that man to speak to Count Simon like that!' before we catch ourselves up and remember that the whole conversation can only be invented.

Outline of historical events

The dualist heresy flourishing in Languedoc did not originate there, but survived there when it had vanished from other parts of Europe. It is thought to have come perhaps from Bulgaria as early as the tenth century, and then spread widely, prospering as commerce prospered, following trade routes and growing as towns grew. Ideas can be exchanged as well as goods. In many places the authorities were glad to co-operate with the Church in putting down dissent, but the situation was different in Languedoc, where there was no general system of primogeniture. Inheritances were normally shared out between all the surviving offspring of the deceased, so that fiefs were sub-divided and power dispersed. In such a situation subversive doctrines were less easily checked.

In the early years of the thirteenth century Pope Innocent III sent legatine commissions into Languedoc to combat heresy, but without much success. Most zealous of his emissaries was Arnold Amaury, abbot of Cîteaux and head of the Cistercian order. He and his subordinates used the Cathars' own methods of poverty and preaching and at this stage avoided harsh measures. But in 1207 the pope's legate Peter of Castelnau excommunicated Raymond VI, count of Toulouse, and in January 1208 one of Raymond's men retaliated by murdering Peter. Pope Innocent now abandoned peaceful means and ordered a crusade against Toulouse. Raymond, however, asserted his innocence of the murder and asked for an impartial investigator. Innocent sent his notary, Milo, but told him privately to take orders from Arnold, abbot of Cîteaux. Negotiations dragged on. In June 1209, with the crusade already on its way, Raymond VI was formally reconciled to the Church and accepted all the required conditions.

He then immediately took the cross himself, thus putting all his own lands out of bounds to the crusade, as the property of an active crusader was under the protection of holy Church and could not be attacked. Instead the crusaders made war on the lands of Raymond Roger Trencavel, viscount of Béziers and Carcassonne, Count Raymond's nephew. On the day of St Mary Magdalene, 22 July 1209, Béziers fell to the abbot of Cîteaux and its inhabitants were massacred. The Jewish community, interestingly enough, had already left the city, accompanying its viscount Raymond Roger, who had gone to organise the defence of Carcassonne.

Before long Carcassonne also fell, on less harsh terms than Béziers, and Raymond Roger, surrendering on safe-conduct, was put in prison in spite of the personal intervention of his overlord, Peter II, king of Aragon. There he died in November of the same year.

The crusaders, meanwhile, had - not without difficulty - found in Simon de Montfort, titular earl of Leicester, a leader to take command of military operations. (It is his fourth and youngest son, also Simon, who is famous in English history as 'the father of parliament'; he died at Evesham in 1265.) There was considerable unrest throughout the winter, but gradually Count Simon won control of Trencavel lands and ousted such local lords as did not co-operate with him. In the summer of 1210 he took the rock-perched castle and fortified village of Minerve and burned alive 140 Cathars who refused to recant.

Fresh moves were made against Raymond VI. Arnold of Cîteaux excommunicated him again; Simon de Montfort did homage to Peter, king of Aragon, for the Trencavel fiefs; Raymond refused to help the Church stamp out heresy among his vassals. The crusaders besieged and took Lavaur, throwing its Lady down a well. They failed to take Toulouse but subdued most of the rest of Raymond's lands. In 1212 Simon summoned a *parlement* to Pamiers and drew up a new code of laws for the lands he had conquered.

Simon's supremacy became more than the king of Aragon could tolerate. His fresh intervention on behalf of Raymond VI and young Raymond (VII) led eventually to conflict with the abbot of Cîteaux, with the pope, and to war between the crusaders and Aragon. Peter II was defeated and killed at the battle of Muret on 12 September 1213.

Yet Simon still could not take Toulouse. Pope Innocent sent a new legate, Peter of Benevento, to Languedoc. He absolved Raymond, who placed Toulouse provisionally in the custody of the Church. Simon retained control of the territories he had conquered.

At Easter 1215 Louis, heir to the crown of France, came on crusade to Languedoc, and as overlord of Toulouse ordered the legate to hand the city over to Simon, who dismantled its defences. In November the same year the

Fourth Lateran Council met. Innocent ruled that Simon should continue to hold his conquests, that Raymond VI should receive a pension, and that his son, young Raymond, should hold the marquisate of Provence when he came of age.

In 1216 the Raymonds, father and son, arrived in Provence where they found strong local support. Young Raymond captured Beaucaire, while his father was in Spain recruiting help. In September 1217 Raymond VI retook Toulouse, except for its fortress, the Narbonnais castle. Pope Honorius III, who had recently succeeded Innocent, ordered a new crusade, and the city was besieged in the spring of 1218. On June 25 Simon de Montfort was struck and killed by a stone from a siege engine.

Although Amaury de Montfort was immediately chosen as count in place of his father, and in 1219 summoned a crusade from France to help him, he made no progress, and in 1224 he went home to Paris and made over his claims to the king of France.

But heresy still flourished in Languedoc, and in 1226 Honorius III excommunicated Raymond VII and called a new crusade from the north. Eventually Raymond VII was forced to acknowledge that he could no longer fight the united strength of the French crown and the Roman Church, and in 1229, stripped to his shirt-sleeves, accepted the peace terms offered him in Paris.

In 1219 these events and others such as the disastrous Trencavel war of 1240, the fall of Montségur in 1244, and the transfer of the county of Toulouse to the French crown when Jeanne, daughter of Raymond VII and wife of Alfonse de Poitiers, died without heirs in 1271, still lay far ahead, and our Anonymous could finish his *Song* on a hopeful note. The Virgin Mary, St Sernin, God and his saints will come to the young count's help, he says, and will save Toulouse.

Reliability and value of the text

The Song of the Cathar Wars was written in verse to be sung, an entertainment in a baron's hall, but this does not mean we should regard it as fiction. Both authors were concerned to present a true picture. William of Tudela used eye-witness testimony when he could, and quoted his sources, as for instance Pons of Mela (laisse 5), Isarn, prior of Vielmorès (laisse 84), and Count Baldwin's bailiff and provost who told William how well the count ate during the siege of Moissac (laisse 119). He also points out that he could have made his song much better if he had been able to ride with and get to know the crusaders listed in laisse 36. (His line-filling phrases 'as the song says', 'as the book tells you', however, are not a reference to other sources, only variations on the theme of 'as I was saying'.) William's chronology lacks detail, but the only inaccuracies scholars have found is that he transposes the dates of the fall of Termes and the council at St Gilles (laisse 58) and exaggerates the duration of the siege of Termes. He also locates at Arles a council which is probably but not certainly the same as one that took place at Montpellier (laisse 59). All the other events he describes are correct, in so far as they can be checked from other sources. This means that we can trust him when he mentions events not recorded elsewhere, such as the crusade from Quercy and the Agenais (laisses 13 and 14), and the attempt made by Peter II of Aragon to achieve a settlement during the siege of Carcassonne (laisses 26-32).

The anonymous author who wrote the larger part of the *Canso* proves equally reliable. Where he can be checked against such texts as the *Hystoria albigensis* of Peter of Les Vaux de Cernay (a pro-crusade chronicler from the north; see bibliography), he is accurate, and where he is the sole authority to mention the presence of individuals at such-and-such a scene, he is often supported by charter evidence. His narrative is, however, to some extent uneven. Some events, such as the siege of Beaucaire, are told in great detail, others are skated over or omitted. E. Martin-Chabot, most recent editor of the *Canso*, claims that this unevenness indicates our author's presence at some events and absence from others and that this is in itself good evidence of his reliability (M.-C., ii, p. xxi).

The lively speeches the Anonymous puts into his characters' mouths are of course not meant to be taken literally; they serve to set differing points of view before the audience in a vivid way and to keep the action of the poem moving. Some of them also enable the partisan author to depict Simon de Montfort in a thoroughly repulsive light - here are all these admirable crusaders, we think, great men from the north like the count of Soissons, telling the wicked count to behave better, and yet he persists in his cruel ways! It is easy to forget that these are literary devices and that in all probability the count of Soissons and the others never dreamed of uttering such remarks.

It is important to remember that this text was meant to entertain as well as to inform, and to earn money. It was not going to be read in studious silence but out loud, declaimed, sung, it would be watched and listened to. Auditors would be eating supper, drinking, chatting with friends and family after a hard day in the saddle, criticising the performer's shortcomings or applauding his skill, his command of pathos, irony or horror, and, 'for those who can use it' of melody. Nobody was going to toss a coin to an entertainer who failed to keep his audience awake or forgot to flatter the hearers or their relatives. There are several asides in the text expressing gratitude to generous donors, as for example the reference by the Anonymous in laisse 194 to Roger Bernard, son of the count of Foix, *que m daura e esclarzis*, 'who gave me gold and glory'. The last few laisses, too, display an astonishing command of adjectives: not one of the lords mentioned but is valiant, heroic or generous, and never does the Anonymous repeat himself; he has several new epithets ready every time. Surely this gives us a clue to the likely composition of his audience, among whom he intends shortly to be passing round his hat.

As well as a description of events as they occurred, the *Canso* offers modern readers insight into the world-view of thirteenth-century men and women, into their likes and dislikes and unconscious assumptions. Blinkered as we cannot fail to be by assumptions of our own, we may never fully understand our predecessors, but it is a step towards doing so if we can directly encounter the kind of writing they themselves enjoyed. Again and again, for instance, we notice that rank, inherited status, was of absolute importance. So too was the display of wealth, for wealth equals power. We have only to observe the archbishop of Reims in his furs on a particularly hot day in the scorching summer of 1212, when warriors with any sense were in their shirt-sleeves (laisse 118). Vital too was the ownership of land; this thread runs through the whole story and references are many. One example is the passionate bewilderment expressed by Raymond VI in the court of Rome (laisse 151): how can anyone expect him to become a landless man, with no base, nowhere to lay his head? Another essential element, linked closely with land-ownership, was family solidarity. The more we study the text, the more we realise what near relatives many of these warriors were - fathers, sons and sons-in-law, brothers and cousins; and their wives and daughters played a greater role than is sometimes perceived. These are family feuds and family disputes.

Yet another difference we encounter is a matter-of-fact reliance upon God - he was expected to take a direct hand in events, and that not just by devout persons but by bloody-minded soldiers. So too were the saints, and it was important to have good strong saints on your own side. Toulouse, our author clearly felt, was fortunate in having the body of St Exupéry to put on display in time of danger (laisse 213).

Delight in warfare is very clear, and so are other aspects of war - it was not all glitter and heroism. 'Go for the backs of their knees', advises Bernard of Cazenac (laisse 205), and in laisse 211 we see foot-soldiers coming onto the battlefield at Baziège to finish off the fallen. War was a professional and profitable business - plunder and ransoms formed an essential part of it. Pay, except for mercenaries, is usually referred to discreetly as 'gifts'. Several times Simon de Montfort is shown at his wits' end because, he says, his companions want to leave him as he has no funds left and no gifts to give them. (Crusaders also, of course, go away when they have done their forty days' duty, *la carantena*, as the count of Soissons does in laisse 208.) The professional attitude to war is also very clear in Count Simon's repeated fury at his defeats by mere amateurs, 'unarmed men' who have had the temerity to oppose him, 'as if the hare were to turn on the hounds!' Similarly the French knights are horrified at the deaths of the German crusaders so shamefully killed by villeins at Montgey (laisses 69 ff.).

Another striking feature is the importance of daylight and nightfall, and of the onset of winter and the fresh green of spring. No one can mount a campaign until there is enough grass for the horses, and the Anonymous can find no better imagery to describe the joy felt at the arrival of young Raymond of Toulouse than to say that 'he brought us light, he gave colour back to us'. With sunrise, the grey shapes of early dawn take their own colour again and return to life.

Translator's comments

Translations, it is said, are either beautiful or faithful, never both. This one aims at accuracy but is not literal. Readers who compare it with the Occitan text will find, for instance, that at times the author uses three verbs for emphasis ('they killed, slew and slaughtered ...') and I have used only two or perhaps one, to avoid heaviness. Very often, too, I have introduced proper nouns where the text uses common nouns or pronouns, so that instead of 'the count ... the count ... the count ...' I have 'Count Raymond ... Count Simon ... the count of Foix', and so on. I have also added the word 'young' now and then, to distinguish Raymond the son from Raymond his father.

Various expressions

The term *paratge* has proved untranslatable. In derivation it is the same word as our 'peerage' and has a general meaning of 'equality', of being level with one's peers, that everything is all right because rank and order are decently observed, just as in cases of 'disparagement' (once meaning 'to marry out of one's class') rank is put under threat and society de-stabilised. P.T. Ricketts defines *paratge* as 'le droit territorial et l'honneur de celui qui le revendique', rights over land and the personal honour of the lord who claims them (see bibliography). *Paratge*, then, is seriously threatened by the disinheriting of the counts of Toulouse. But the word contains further nuances: Freda White says that in twelfth-century Languedoc 'life was illumined by a quality the troubadors called *parage*. That word ... included food for all, festal games and dances, fine clothes and good manners, kindness and the sweetness of life. Above all it meant poetry' (Freda White, 1964, *West of the Rhône*, Faber, p. 64.). William and the Anonymous might be slightly surprised by this definition, but they would recognise 'illumined' and agree that *paratge* was a rich and joyful word.

Pretz, often appearing in conjunction with *paratge*, is another awkward word. It can mean: 'price, money, payment, value, glory, reputation' or 'worth'. I have usually translated it 'worth', sometimes 'glory'.

The word 'Saracen' occurs both as a noun and as an adjective - *Sarrazinis*, *Sarrazinal*. Massacres are more terrible than any 'since the days of the Saracens', that is since the Moslem invasions in the eighth century and later; see laisse 21, n. 3. 'Saracen' walls or ramparts, however, are those of great antiquity, in fact likely to be Roman or Visigothic.

Personal names

These I have usually put into the form most familiar to English readers, for example Theobald not Tibaut, and Peter, king of Aragon, not Peire. Some names are nicknames, and are translated where possible, such as the Wolf of Foix. The *Tinhos del Juratz* (laisse 211) remains Tinhos but the word probably means 'scabby'. Guy *Cap de Porc*, pig-head, is not translated. Generally 'de' is translated as 'of', except where habit makes 'de' more appropriate in English, as in 'de Montfort' or 'de Lucy'.

Place names

Some place names which in this text occur in their Occitan form, such as La Isla Jordan or Rocamaura, will be found on modern maps in their French form, L'Isle-Jourdain, Roquemaure, because in the end the French won this long war. I have kept some of these in their southern forms, but consistency is not possible: Masselha appears as Marseille, and so on.

As in all writings of this period, the word 'France' does not refer to the whole country which now bears that name, but to the comparatively small kingdom in the north, the Ile de France and its appurtenances.

Money and horses

The phrase 'thousand-shilling horse' that occurs several times translates the word *milsoldor*, a 'thousand-shillinger'. *Livres, sous* and *deniers*, £.s.d., relate to each other as English pounds, shillings and pence used to do: twelve *deniers* = one *sol* or *sou*; twenty *sous* = one *livre*. A thousand *sous* horse will have cost fifty *livres*, whether this was actual coin or money of account. In laisse 97 Bouchard rides a horse worth over a hundred *livres*; no doubt an exceptional animal. What coins themselves were worth depended where they were minted - at Tours, Paris, Le Puy or elsewhere. See, for instance, laisse 57 where we are told how well the count de Montfort behaved at Termes in not robbing the ladies of even the worth of *un poges*, a tiny coin from Le Puy.

Dates and times of day

Dates are rarely mentioned - 'it was on a Thursday' or 'one Sunday', or a saint's day or other feast of the Church.

Times of day are usually indicated in terms of sunrise or sunset, sometimes cockcrow, sometimes dinner or supper time. 'Terce', 'none' and 'vespers' are also used; these were respectively the third, fifth and sixth hours of prayer, but the actual time would depend on the season of year and length of daylight available. It is easiest to think of them as 'morning', 'afternoon,' and 'evening'.

Rock crystal

Very precious and expensive, this was used to decorate helmets and sometimes the boss or rim of a shield. There are frequent references to crystals, and to gold ornaments as well, being cut off in battle.

Siege weapons

These include different kinds of stone-throwers - catapults, mangonels and trebuchets - which hurled projectiles and were worked either by levers and ropes or by torsion; battering rams; and movable castles, 'cats' and 'dogs' of varying sizes and a *mustela*, a 'weasel'. These gave sappers or other troops protection against fire from the ramparts they were attacking. Movable boiled-leather shelters are also mentioned.

Subheadings

Subheadings in bold type throughout the following text are provided by the translator to help readers follow a story that was never meant to be read, but to be listened to and watched.

Square brackets show where phrases have been supplied to fill a lacuna, and dotted lines indicate a gap in the text.

Footnotes

In an attempt to keep these short, notes have not usually been supplied for place names - please see maps and plans. Individuals are only given a note when first mentioned; after that, see the Index and refer to the first entry.

References to the Martin-Chabot edition of the text, abbreviated M.-C., do not only mean 'this information is drawn from Martin-Chabot', they also mean that a fuller discussion of the various problems is to be found there.

The manuscripts

There is only one complete manuscript of the *Canso*, no. 25425 fonds français in the Bibliothèque nationale, Paris, beautifully written in a southern hand in about the year 1275. We have no way of knowing how distant from hand in about the year 1275. We have no way of knowing how distant from the original copy this manuscript may be. It is extremely handsome, and contains thirteen admirable line drawings, scenes of warfare, siege, and so on, which never received the paint for which they were intended. The artist has been careful to display shields and horse-armour so as to allow the illuminator plenty of scope for blazoning the armorial bearings of the contestants.

We also have two manuscript copies, one sixteenth and the other early seventeenth century, of extracts from the *Canso* based on other manuscripts now lost. One of these gives an alternative reading for the first laisse, which Martin-Chabot prefers to the version in no. 25425 and uses for his edition; this is the reading used here.

Besides these there are two prose versions of the *Canso*, one probably fifteenth century, existing in three manuscripts and published by Molinier in vol. 8 of the *Histoire de Languedoc* of Dom Vaissete, the other early sixteenth century, incomplete and unpublished. See Martin-Chabot, vol. i, pp. xvii-xxviii, for full descriptions and discussion of all the above.

Bibliography

Editions of the text

Fauriel, Claude (1837), *Histoire de la Croisade contre les hérétiques albigeois*, Paris.

Gougaud, Henri (1984), *La Chanson de la croisade albigeoise*, édition bilingue: occitan-français, Berg International, Paris; with facsimile of the manuscript; also available without facsimile as a *Livre de Poche*.

Martin-Chabot, Eugène, ed. and tr. (1973-89), *La Chanson de la croisade albigeoise*, 3 vols, CHFMA, ed. Les Belles Lettres, Paris, (abbreviated as M.-C.).

Meyer, Paul, ed. and tr. (1875-79), *La Chanson de la croisade contre les Albigeois*, 2 vols, SHF, Paris.

Other sources

Guillaume de Puylaurens: *Chronique*, available in: *Recueil des historiens de la France*, ed. Dom Brial, t. xix, pp. 193-225; and in: *Troisièmes mélanges d'histoire du moyen âge*, ed. A. Luchaire, (1904), fasc. 18 de la Bibliothèque de la Faculté des lettres de Paris, pp. 119-175, Paris.
Also - *Chronica magistri Guillelmi de Podio Laurentii*, ed. and trans. J. Duvernoy, parallel Latin and French texts (Paris, 1976).

Peter of Les Vaux de Cernay: *Hystoria albigensis* in *Recueil des historiens de France* ed. Dom Brial, t. xix, pp.1-113; also ed. P. Guébin and E. Lyon, SHF, 1926-30, Paris; translated into French, P. Guébin and H. Maisonneuve, Paris, 1951; and forthcoming in English as *The History of the Albigensian Crusade*, tr. and ed. W.A. and M.D. Sibly, Boydell & Brewer, Woodbridge.

10

Modern works

Costen, Michael (forthcoming), *History of the Albigensian Crusade*, Manchester University Press, Manchester.

Hamilton, Bernard (1974), *The Albigensian Crusade*, Historical Association pamphlet G.85.

Paterson, Linda (1987), 'La *Chanson de la croisade albigeoise*: mythes chevaleresques et réalités militaires' in *Actes du Colloque d'Amiens*, 18-22 mars.

Paterson, Linda (1993), *The World of the Troubadours*, Cambridge University Press.

Ricketts, P.T. (1982), 'The *Canso of the Albigensian Crusade*: literature and patriotism' in *Proceedings of the 2nd conference on Medieval Language and Literature*, University of Birmingham, 28-30 March.

Sumption, Jonathan (1978), *The Albigensian Crusade*, Faber & Faber, London.

Wakefield, W.L. (1974), *Heresy, Crusade and Inquisition in Southern France, 1100-1250*, Allen & Unwin, London.

Acknowledgements

Grateful thanks are due and are most sincerely paid to many kind helpers, especially to Dick Barlow for typesetting and maps, to Clive Burnham of Cerberus Printers, Kirkby Stephen, to Graham Paxman for blazoning and drawing the coats of arms on page 65, and to Malcolm Barber, Daniel Barlow, Michael Costen, Simon Gaunt, Bernard Hamilton, Christopher Holdsworth and Pauline Matarasso. Caroline Cornish of the Scolar Press has been infinitely patient. I must also record my gratitude to Eugène Martin-Chabot, most recent translator and editor of the *Chanson de la croisade albigeoise*, for the thoroughness and clarity of his edition. Where I have occasionally ventured to disagree with his interpretation, it has been with diffidence.

The Song of William of Tudela

William's prologue

Laisse 1

In the name of the Father and of the Son and of the Holy Spirit!

Listen to Master William's song! William is a clerk in holy orders and was educated at Tudela in Navarre. From there he went to Montauban where he remained eleven years, but in the twelfth year he went away because he could foresee the tragedy which lay ahead. He had long studied geomancy[1] and was skilled in this art, so that he knew that fire and devastation would lay the whole region waste, that the rich citizens would lose all the wealth they had stored up, and the knights would flee, sad and defeated, into exile in other lands, all because of the insane belief[2] held in that country. For this reason, as you have heard, he left Montauban and went to join Count Baldwin[3] - may Jesus guard and guide him! - at Bruniquel, where the count was delighted to welcome him. Baldwin later had William appointed, unopposed, to a canonry at Bourg St Antonin, which he had garrisoned.[4] Master Tecin and Geoffrey of Poitiers[5] both did all they could to help Master William in this matter.

And then William composed and wrote this book. Once he began it, he thought of nothing else till it was done and indeed scarcely gave himself time for sleep.

The book is well made and full of good writing. Listen to it all of you, great and small, and you will learn both wisdom and eloquence, for the man who wrote it is brimming over with both. If you do not know it yet, you cannot imagine what you are going to hear.

Laisse 2

My lords, this song is modelled on that of Antioch[6] and has the same verse structure and, for those who can use it, the same melody.

Early attempts to fight the Cathar heresy

Of course you all know how this heresy - God send his curse on it! - became

---

1. 'Divination by points, and circles made on the earth', Randle Cotgrave.
2. The Cathar heresy.
3. Count Baldwin, youngest son of Raymond V, count of Toulouse, and his wife Constance, who was sister of Louis VII, king of France. In May 1211 Baldwin took himself and Bruniquel over to the crusading side, opposing his brother Raymond VI (laisses 73-77). Hanged on Raymond's orders, February 1214. See also laisse 75, n. 3.
4. Bourg St Antonin (now S-Antonin-de-Rouerge, Tarn-et-Garonne) was captured by Simon de Montfort in May 1212 and held on his behalf by Count Baldwin; see laisses 113 and 114.
5. Tecin or Tédise, canon of Genoa, sent with others by Innocent III in 1209 to combat the Cathar heresy; bishop of Agde in 1215. See also laisse 149. Geoffrey of Poitiers is mentioned in laisse 38 as having educated young Raymond of Toulouse.
6. A fragment of a late twelfth-century *Song of Antioch* written in Occitan is still extant M.-C. i, p. xv and L. Paterson *World of the Troubadours*, p. 20, n. 27.

so strong that it gained control of the whole of the Albigeois, of the Carcassès and most of the Lauragais. All the way from Béziers to Bordeaux many, or indeed, most people believed in or supported it.[1] When the lord pope[2] and the other clergy saw this lunacy spreading so much faster than before and tightening its grip every day, each of them in his own jurisdiction sent out preachers. The Cistercian order led the campaign and time and again it sent out its own men. Next, the bishop of Osma[3] arranged a meeting between himself and other legates with these Bulgars[4] at Carcassonne. This was very well attended, and the king of Aragon[5] and his nobles were present. Once the king had heard the speakers and discovered how heretical they were, he withdrew, and sent a letter about this to Rome in Lombardy.[6]

God grant me his blessing, what shall I say? They think more of a rotten apple than of sermons, and went on just the same for about five years. These lost fools refused to repent, so that many were killed, many people perished, and still more will die before the fighting ends. It cannot be otherwise.

Laisse 3
Not far from Lerida is a Cistercian abbey called Poblet.[7] Its abbot[8] was a wise and excellent man, who was promoted to higher and still higher posts. From Poblet he went to be abbot of Grandselve, and then, being so dear to God, he was immediately chosen as abbot of Cîteaux. This most holy man, and others too, went up and down the heretics' country, preaching to them and begging them to repent. But the more he begged them, the more they laughed at him and scorned him for a fool. Wretched misbelievers, this was the legate they were mocking, the pope's own representative, with power to destroy them![9]

Laisse 4
Led by Brother Arnold, abbot of Cîteaux, friend of God, the preachers travelled on foot and on horseback among the wicked and misbelieving heretics, arguing with them and vigorously challenging their errors, but these fools paid no attention and despised everything they said.

---

1. The strict Cathar regime was rigorous and only the fully professed, the 'perfect', followed it. More numerous were the 'believers' or supporters, many of whom postponed full commitment until at the point of death.
2. Innocent III, pope 1198-1216.
3. Diego of Acebes, bishop of Osma in Old Castile, Spain, 1201-07.
4. Bulgars: the heresy was thought to have come to western Christendom from Bulgaria. William seems to have confused two conferences; M.-C., i, p. 10.
5. Peter II, 1174-1213, king of Aragon and overlord of lands on both sides of the Pyrenees.
6. 'Lombardy' was a term often used to mean the whole of Italy.
7. Poblet near Lerida in Catalonia, Spain: a Cistercian abbey founded in 1149 from Fontfroide near Narbonne.
8. Arnold Amaury, abbot of Poblet 1196-98, of Grandselve (Tarn-et-Garonne) 1198-1200, then of Cîteaux in Burgundy, and thus head of the Cistercian order. Archbishop of Narbonne 12 March 1212.
9. The bull granting him powers 'to destroy, disperse and root up' for the restoration of the faith is dated May 1204.

Murder of Peter of Castelnau, 14 January 1208

At this time Peter of Castelnau[1] was travelling out of Provence on his pacing mule. He reached the Rhône[2] at St Gilles, and there he excommunicated the count of Toulouse[3] for supporting the mercenaries who were ravaging the countryside. Thereupon an evil-hearted squire, hoping to win the count's approval, stepped like a traitor behind the legate, drove his sharp sword into his spine and killed him. The man fled at once on his fast horse to his home town of Beaucaire, where he had kinsmen.[4]

Yet the legate raised his hands to heaven before he died and in the sight of all those present asked God to forgive this wicked man. This was while he was receiving communion at about cockcrow. Then he died, just as the day was dawning. His soul went to God the Father and they buried him at St Gilles with many a *Kyrie eleison* sung and many candles burning.

A crusade is decided on

Laisse 5
You can be sure the pope was not pleased when he heard of his legate's death. He grasped his chin in anger and called on St James of Compostela and on St Peter of Rome who lies in the chapel there. He spoke his anathema and then dashed out the candle. Brother Arnold of Cîteaux was present, and so too were Master Milo,[5] that fine Latinist, and the twelve cardinals all in a circle. There it was they made the decision that led to so much sorrow, that left so many men dead with their guts spilled out and so many great ladies and pretty girls naked and cold, stripped of gown and cloak. From beyond Montpellier as far as Bordeaux, any that rebelled were to be utterly destroyed. This was told me by Master Pons of Mela,[6] who was present on behalf of the king who holds Tudela, lord of Pamplona and Estella, the best knight who ever sat a horse.[7] (Miramelis, commander of the heathen, felt his strength! Castile and Aragon were there too; side by side their kings rode and fought.[8] I intend to make a good new song about this, and shall write it out on fair parchment.)

Laisse 6
The abbot of Cîteaux, however, sat with his head bent. Then he rose and, standing by a marble column, said to the pope:

---

1. A monk of Fontfroide; papal legate at Toulouse in 1203.
2. The Rhône was the boundary between the Empire and Provence. Beaucaire and St Gilles on its west bank were at the limit of Raymond's lordship.
3. Raymond VI, count of Toulouse and St Gilles, duke of Narbonne and marquis of Provence from 1194, died 1222.
4. The murderer's identity is not known.
5. Milo, papal notary, sent as legate to Languedoc in March 1209. Died in the winter of 1209/10.
6. Not identified.
7. Sancho VIII, king of Navarre, 1194-1234.
8. This refers to the battle of Las Navas de Tolosa in Andalusia on 16 July 1212 when the kings of Castile, Navarre and Aragon defeated the emir of Morocco. He was called Commander of the Faithful, in Arabic 'emir al moumenin', here corrupted to 'Miramelis'.

'By St Martin, my lord, this talking is a waste of time! Come, have your letters written in good Latin, and then I can set off. Send them to France, to the Limousin, to Poitou, the Auvergne and Périgord; have the indulgence proclaimed here too and all over the world as far as Constantinople. Proclaim that any man who does not take the cross shall drink no wine, shall not eat off a cloth morning or night, shall wear neither linen nor hemp and when he dies shall lie unburied like a dog.' He fell silent, and his advice seemed right to all who were there.

Laisse 7

Everyone greatly respected the abbot of Cîteaux (who later became archbishop of Narbonne, the best who ever wore mitre there), and when he had spoken, no one said a word. Then the pope, looking thoroughly unhappy, spoke as follows:

'Go to Carcassonne, brother, and to great Toulouse on the Garonne and lead the armies against the ungodly. Cleanse the troops from their sins in the name of Christ, and in my name preach to them and exhort them to drive the heretics out from amongst the virtuous.' After that, at about the hour of none, the abbot left the town and spurred hard on his way, accompanied by the archbishop of Tarragona, by the bishops of Lerida, of Barcelona and of Maguelonne near Montpellier and, from beyond the Spanish passes, those of Pamplona, Burgos and Tarazona. All these rode with the abbot of Cîteaux.

The crusade is preached

Laisse 8

As soon as they had taken leave, the abbot mounted and rode to Cîteaux, where all the white monks who wore mitres had gathered for the chapter-general on the feast of the Holy Cross in summer,[1] as is their custom. In the presence of the whole assembly he sang mass and after that he preached to them and showed every one of them his letter and explained that they were to go here and there about the world, over the whole length and breadth of holy Christendom.

Recruits flock in

Then, once they knew that their sins would be forgiven, men took the cross in France and all over the kingdom. Never in my life have I seen such a gathering as that one they made against the heretics and clog-wearers![2] The duke of Burgundy[3] took the cross there and so did the count of Nevers[4] and many great men. What they must have cost, those gold embroidered crosses and bands of silk which they displayed on the right breast! Nor shall I try to tell you how they were armed, equipped and mounted, nor about the iron-clad horses and their emblazoned trappings, for God has made never a clerk or a scholar clever enough to tell you the half of it, nor to list all the abbots

---

1. 14 September.
2. 'Clog-wearers', *ensabatatz*, a nickname given to followers of Peter Waldo of Lyon, seekers of poverty who wore sandals or clogs; also called Waldenses or Vaudois.
3. Odo III, duke of Burgundy, born 1166, died 1218.
4. Hervé de Donzy, count of Nevers in right of his wife Mahaut.

and the priests gathered there in the host that lay on the plains outside Béziers.

Count Raymond appeals to his nephew

Laisse 9
I do not suppose the count of Toulouse, the other barons and the viscount of Béziers[1] were pleased when they heard that the French were taking the cross; indeed, as the song says, they were very concerned. Count Raymond appeared at a meeting of the clergy held at that time up country at Aubenas,[2] where he knelt down and made an act of contrition before the lord abbot[3] and asked for his forgiveness. But the abbot said he would not give it him, that he could not do so until the pope and the cardinals at Rome had first granted him some release. I see no need to make a long story of it - the count rode fast to his nephew the viscount and begged him not to attack him; let them stand together in defence and avert their own and their country's destruction. But instead of Yes the viscount answered No. They parted on bad terms and the count rode away in anger to Provence, to Arles and Avignon.[4]

William's second prologue

My lords, listen to my song, for now the pace quickens. Master William began it in the year of Our Lord Jesus Christ 1210 in the month of May when the trees put forth their leaves, while he was living at Montauban. Indeed, if he had had the luck of many a foolish minstrel or wretched knave, he would not now be suffering for want of some good, honest man who would give him a horse or a Breton palfrey to carry him pacing across the plain, or clothes of silk, precious embroideries or rich brocades! But daily we see the world turning to perdition, and wealthy men who ought to be virtuous are evil and refuse to give away so much as a button. For my part, I don't ask them for the value of the filthiest bit of ash lying on their hearths, and may God who made the heavens and the firmament confound them all, God and his blessed Mother!

Count Raymond takes steps to avoid attack

Laisse 10
The count of Toulouse, lord of Beaucaire, saw that his nephew the viscount was against him, saw too all his enemies poised to attack, and knew that the crusaders would invade all and any part of his lands without hesitation. He sent

---

1. Raymond Roger Trencavel, son of Roger II and of Count Raymond's sister Adelaide, viscount of Béziers, Carcassonne, Razès and Albi. See laisses 37 and 40 for his death in 1209.
2. William is the only authority to mention this meeting at Aubenas in the Alpes de Haute-Provence.
3. Of Cîteaux.
4. That is, Count Raymond rode back to the lower Rhône valley.

into Gascony therefore, to his comrade the archbishop of Auch,[1] being sure he would not refuse to travel on his behalf, and to the abbot of Condom,[2] a man of noble birth, to Raymond of Rabastens,[3] a generous giver, and to the prior of the Hospital,[4] a good physician. All these were to go to Rome and then to the emperor.[5] They would speak to the pope, for they were eloquent men, and would make some arrangement.

Winter 1209, Raymond and the pope reconciled

Laisse 11
These envoys rode off to Rome as fast as they could. Why make a long story of it? They said enough and they made gifts enough to reconcile the lord pope and the count of Toulouse. This is how it was settled: Raymond was to make seven of his strongest castles over to the lord pope as a guarantee of future obedience. The pope sent a most worthy clerk called Milo[6] who was to give the count his orders (this Milo died at St Gilles before the end of the year).

When the viscount of Béziers heard that Count Raymond had indeed made his peace, he bitterly repented and would have been glad to make terms too if he could. But Milo despised him and refused his request. So the viscount summoned his forces from his whole fief, horse and foot, every able-bodied man, and waited inside Carcassonne for the crusading armies to arrive. How wretched were those who had stayed at Béziers! I doubt if as many as fifty or a hundred of them escaped death.

The crusade masses against Béziers

Laisse 12
My lords, you have heard how this host was first assembled. The abbot of Cîteaux rode with it,[7] accompanied by so many archbishops and learned men that when they proceeded to some council meeting in the encampment, their lines were longer than the whole army of Milan gathered into one place. Near the clergy rode the brave duke of Burgundy, his banner displayed, bringing his entire host, also the count of Nevers, banner flying, the count of St Pol[8] at the head of a strong force, Count Peter of Auxerre[9] with all his men, Count William of the Genevois,[10] a rich land, Sir Adhémar of

---

1. Bernard of Montaut, archbishop of Auch. Asked by the pope to resign, 1211; deposed, 1214.
2. Montazin of Galard, abbot of Condom.
3. Raymond of Rabastens, former bishop of Toulouse, deposed by the pope 1205.
4. Peter Barravi, prior of the Hospitallers at Toulouse.
5. Otto IV c.1182-1218, son of Henry the Lion duke of Saxony and of Matilda, daughter of Henry II of England, brought up at the court of his uncle Richard I.
6. The same Milo mentioned in laisse 5.
7. As papal legate the abbot was in supreme command of the crusading forces.
8. Gaucher of Châtillon, count of St Pol.
9. Peter of Courtenay, count of Auxerre, a cousin of Raymond VI, being like him a grandson of Louis VI king of France.
10. 'William', probably Humbert, William's son; Genevois, a county straddling what is now the boundary between Switzerland and France.

Poitiers,[1] neighbour and enemy of the count of Forez, bringing the men from his lands, and Peter Bermond from Anduze.[2] If I spoke from now till nightfall or till tomorrow's dawn, I could not tell you the names of those who came to join the crusade from Provence itself, besides all the others who flocked to it, for no one could reckon the numbers, not to mention the countless horsemen brought by the French.

Laisse 13
God be my witness, it was an enormous force. It contained twenty thousand knights all fully armed and more than two hundred thousand villeins and peasants, not counting clergy and citizens.[3] They came from the whole length and breadth of the Auvergne, from Burgundy, from France, from the Limousin, from the whole world - north and south Germans, Poitevins, Gascons, men from the Rouergue and Saintonge. God made never a clerk who could write them all down, however hard he tried, not in two months or three. Provence was there in full and so was Vienne; from the Lombardy passes all the way to Rodez every man came flocking because the pardon offered to crusaders was so generous. They rode in close array with banners raised, not expecting to meet any opposition in the whole Carcassès, and intending to take Toulouse (but it had made its peace[4]) and Carcassonne, they said, and the Albigeois. All their armour, victuals and other supplies were loaded onto boats and sent by water.[5] Count Raymond hurried out to meet them, for he had promised faithfully to ride with them.

Parenthesis: A crusade from the Agenais

Another crusading army arrived from the Agenais.[6] It was not so large as the French force and had been travelling for a month. With it rode Count Guy,[7] a courteous Auvergnat, the viscount of Turenne,[8] very active in raising this force, the bishops of Limoges and of Bazas, the good archbishop of Bordeaux,[9] the bishops of Cahors[10] and Agen, Bertrand of Cardaillac,[11]

---

1. As a vassal of Raymond VI, Adhémar, count of Valentinois and Diois, was a reluctant crusader; see laisse 154 for his armed support of Raymond in 1216. Nothing is known about his relationship with the count of Forez.
2. Peter Bermond, lord of Sauve (Gard); husband of Raymond VI's daughter Constance, and as such tried to get the pope to grant the county of Toulouse to him instead of to his brother-in-law young Raymond; died 1215.
3. Figures such as these are meant simply to convey the idea of huge numbers, not to indicate a precise figure. Wakefield suggests that the crusade numbered some 5,000 horsemen and 10,000 to 15,000 others (p. 112, *Heresy, Crusade and Inquisition*).
4. In December 1203 the legates Peter of Castelnau and Ralph accepted the sworn promise of the inhabitants of Toulouse to be true to the Catholic faith.
5. Down the Rhône and then west along the waterways of lower Languedoc, and along the River Orb to Béziers.
6. This expedition is not mentioned in other sources.
7. Guy II, count of Clermont and the Auvergne; made his will 27 May 1209, being 'about to depart to fight the heretics'. 'Courteous' is a stock epithet in epic poetry for men from the Auvergne.
8. Raymond III, viscount of Turenne 1191-1212.
9. William, archbishop of Bordeaux.
10. William of Cardaillac, bishop of Cahors, died 1234; uncle of the Bertrand mentioned below.
11. Bertrand II, lord of Cardaillac in Quercy.

the lord of Gourdon[1] and Ratier of Castelnau[2] with all the men of Quercy. This army took Puylaroque, which was not defended, laid waste Gontaud and sacked Tonneins. But they failed to take Casseneuil because it is a strong place and was well defended by its garrison, who were Gascons, expert javelin-men and very light of foot.

Laisse 14

They laid siege to Casseneuil, which was defended by many archers and many good knights under Seguin of Balenx,[3] and would have taken the place if Count Guy had not prevented it. He had much property there, and so he quarrelled with the archbishop on this score.[4] I do not know how they came to withdraw or upon what terms.

Heretics burned

This host condemned many heretics to be burned and had many fair women thrown into the flames, for they refused to recant however much they were begged to do so. And the bishop of Le Puy arrived from Chassiers; he received large sums of money from Caussade and from the Bourg. From St Antonin where he first arrived, he went to the army besieging Casseneuil, for he thought they were few in number and wanted to join them.

The inhabitants of Villemur suffered a sad blow, for a lad told them that the army was about to move and had already struck camp at Casseneuil. Hearing this rumour, they set fire to their own stronghold on the Monday evening and burned it down and then fled away by moonlight.[5]

The main crusade

I shall tell you no more about that army but shall return to the other, now at Montpellier. Count Raymond is guiding them and indeed they need his help. Each day he rides ahead and shows them where they can camp in the lands belonging to Raymond Roger his nephew, his sister's son, who is making constant war on him.

Laisse 15

Day and night Raymond Roger the viscount of Béziers worked to defend his lands, for he was a man of great courage. Nowhere in the wide world is there a better knight or one more generous and open-handed, more courteous or better bred. He was Count Raymond's nephew, his own sister's son. And he was certainly Catholic; I call to witness many a clerk and many a canon in their cloisters. But he was very young[6] and was therefore friendly with

---

1. The lord of Gourdon was also called Bertrand.
2. Ratier, lord of Castelnau-de-Montratier, a follower of the Gourdons.
3. Seguin of Balenx from the Agenais.
4. Guy count of Auvergne; the archbishop probably of Bordeaux; nothing is known about this dispute.
5. Villemur (Haute-Garonne) on the Tarn is about 100 km from Casseneuil. Full moon was on Sunday 21 June 1209.
6. Raymond Roger Trencavel, nine when he succeeded his father, only 24 when he died. See laisse 9, n. 1.

everyone, and his vassals were not at all afraid or in awe of him but laughed and joked with him as they would with any comrade. And all his knights and other vavassors maintained the heretics in their towers and castles, and so they caused their own ruin and their shameful deaths. The viscount himself died in great anguish, a sad and sorry loss, because of this grievous error. I never saw him, though, except once, when Count Raymond married the lady Eleanor, the best and fairest queen[1] in Christian or heathen lands or anywhere in the whole wide world. All the good I can say of her, all the praise I can give her, must always fall short of her worth and excellence.

The siege and fall of Béziers

I return to my subject. When the viscount of Béziers heard the report and knew that the army had passed Montpellier, he mounted his thousand-shilling horse[2] and rode into Béziers one morning at dawn before it was fully light.

Laisse 16
Old and young, great and small, the citizens heard of his arrival and hurried at once to meet him. He told them to defend themselves with all their strength and said that they would very soon receive good support.

'I must leave for Carcassonne,' he said, 'they have been waiting for me there too long.' That said, he rode out of the town. The Jews of Béziers followed him, and the other inhabitants were left in great distress and anxiety. The bishop[3] of the town, an excellent man, rode into Béziers, dismounted and gathered all the people together at the high church, a place full of powerful relics. They sat down and he told them about the crusaders and how they had set off, and said that rather than be defeated and killed or imprisoned, their goods and clothing taken from them, they should surrender the town; if they gave it up like this, it would at once be restored to them. If they refused, they would be stripped of all they had and put to the sword.

Laisse 17
The bishop told them all this and begged them to make an agreement with the clergy and the crusaders rather than be slaughtered. But the majority of the townspeople said they would rather be drowned in the salt sea than take his advice, that the crusaders should not get so much as a pennyworth of their possessions from them or in any way change their rule over the town. They were sure the host could not hold together, it would disintegrate in less than a fortnight, for it stretched out a full league long and could barely be contained on the roads and pathways. Their city was so strongly placed, they said, and its walls defended it so well that even after a month's siege it could not be stormed. As Solomon said to the wise queen of the south, a fool's notions often fall short.[4]

---

1. Raymond's fourth wife. She was the sister of the king of Aragon, Peter II, so that William gives her the title of queen.
2. His 'thousand-shilling horse' translates the one word *milsoldor*, see Introduction p. 8.
3. Rainaud of Montpeyroux, old and respected, who had gone out to meet the crusading forces.
4. *D'aisso que fols pessa falh trop a la vegea.* Proverbs XVI: 22 has 'doctrina stultorum fatuitas'.

When the bishop saw that they were determined to fight and thought no more of his advice than of a peeled apple, he got on his mule and rode away to the army, which was still on the march. Those who went with him saved their lives, those who stayed behind paid for it dearly. He reported as soon as he could to the abbot of Cîteaux and the other lords, who all listened attentively. Fools, they considered them, and madmen, for they knew very well that suffering, pain and death awaited them.

Laisse 18

On the feast of St Mary Magdalen[1] the abbot of Cîteaux brought his huge army to Béziers and encamped it on the sandy plains around the city. Great, I am sure, was the terror inside the walls, for never in the host of Menelaus, from whom Paris stole Helena, were so many tents set up on the plains below Mycenae nor so many splendid pavilions erected by night in the open air as the French pitched now, for with the exception of the count of Brienne[2] there was not one baron of France who did not do his forty days' duty there.

An evil gift the men of Béziers received when they were told to stand firm and give battle day in day out! Listen to what they did, these ignorant peasants, stupider than whales:[3] they kept charging at the host, waving white flags made of cheap cloth and shouting aloud, as if they thought they could terrify them as birds are scared off a field of oats with shouts and yells and cloths flapping in the morning when the day dawns clear.

The crusaders' kitchen boys take a hand

Laisse 19

When the chief of the servant lads saw them attacking the French forces with shouts and yells and saw them throw one of the French crusaders off a bridge and cut him to pieces, he called all his lads together and shouted out: 'Come on, let's attack!' As soon as he spoke, each one got himself a club - they had nothing else, I suppose - and there were more than fifteen thousand of them, with not a pair of shoes between them. In their shirts and trousers they began to go round the town taking the walls apart stone by stone, they jumped down into the ditches and set to work with picks, and others went to batter and smash down the gates. Seeing all this, the inhabitants took fright, and now the crusading knights were shouting, 'To arms! To arms!' What a crush you would have seen there as these lads struggled to get into the town! They forced the defenders off the ramparts and the men, women and children of Béziers fled into the church and rang the church bells. It was their only refuge.

Laisse 20

The townspeople saw the crusaders drawing near, saw the chief of the servants leading the attack and his lads jumping down into all the moats, breaking down the ramparts and opening the gates, they saw the great mass of the French host making ready for battle and they knew in their hearts that

---

1. 22 July 1209. The town fell the same day.
2. John of Brienne had just been offered the crown of the kingdom of Jerusalem.
3. *La balena*, the whale, is the rhyme word; there is no reason to suppose medieval whales were a byword for stupidity.

they could not hold. Hurriedly they took refuge in the high church. The priests put on vestments for a mass of the dead and had the church bells rung as for a funeral. And in the end the servant lads could not be kept out but forced their way into the town. There they took what houses they liked, and could have taken ten each if they had wanted to. They were in a frenzy, quite unafraid of death, killing everyone they could find and winning enormous wealth. Rich for life they'll be, if they can keep it! But very soon they'll be forced to let it go, for the French knights are going to claim it even though it was the lads that won it.

A tactical decision

Laisse 21
The lords from France and Paris, laymen and clergy, princes[1] and marquises, all agreed that at every castle the army approached, a garrison that refused to surrender should be slaughtered wholesale, once the castle had been taken by storm. They would then meet with no resistance anywhere, as men would be so terrified at what had already happened. That is how they took Montréal and Fanjeaux and all that country - otherwise, I promise you, they could never have stormed them. That is why they massacred them at Béziers, killing them all. It was the worst they could do to them. And they killed everyone who fled into the church; no cross or altar or crucifix could save them. And these raving beggarly lads, they killed the clergy too, and the women and the children. I doubt if one person came out alive.[2] God, if it be his will, receive their souls in paradise! So terrible a slaughter has not been known or consented to, I think, since the time of the Saracens.[3]

The servant lads had settled into the houses they had taken, all of them full of riches and treasure, but when the French discovered this they went nearly mad with rage and drove the lads out with clubs, like dogs, and stabled their pack and saddle horses in the buildings, for it's certainly might that mows the meadows.[4]

Béziers set on fire

Laisse 22
The chief and his servant lads expected to enjoy the wealth they had taken and be rich for evermore. When the barons took it away from them, these filthy stinking wretches all shouted out, 'Burn it, burn it!' and fetched huge flaming brands as if for a funeral pyre and set the town alight. Panic spread and the town blazed from end to end. (Even so did Ralph of Cambrai burn a rich city near Douai and afterwards his mother the lady Alice rebuked him so

---

1. The word 'princes' translates *princeps*, used here and elsewhere to mean great nobles.
2. The legates' report to the pope says that 'almost 20,000' died.
3. A reference to Moslem massacres in the eighth century and later. Moslem forces from Spain overran the south of France; defeated by Charles Martel at Poitiers in 732, they were forced back into Provence. Access by sea from Spain was easy, the Moslems were firmly established in Provence at La Garde-Freinet (Var), and the whole area remained subject to devastating incursions.
4. There is an untranslatable pun here: *car la forsa l prat paihs*, where *forsa* means both 'violence' and 'shears'.

strongly that he made as if to hit her in the face.[1]) When they felt the scorching heat, everyone drew back and the houses and all the palaces were burned, and with them many helmets and padded jerkins and jackets made in Chartres, in Blaye or Edessa and many fine things that had to be abandoned. And the church too, built by Master Gervase,[2] that was completely destroyed; the heat cracked it down the middle and it fell in two parts.

Laisse 23
My lords, it was tremendous, the booty the French and the Normans captured at Béziers, and would have made them rich all their lives long but for the chief of the servants and his wretched lads who burned the town, burned the women and children, old men and young, and the clerks vested and singing mass there inside the church.

The crusaders move on to attack Carcassonne

Three days they stayed in the green meadows and on the fourth day the knights and sergeants set off and rode across the plains with their banners borne high and blowing in the wind. On a Tuesday evening they came to Carcassonne just as the bells were ringing for vespers. Great was the grief there for the deaths at Béziers.

The viscount stood on the roundwalk and looked in amazement at the crusading host. He called his knights and sergeants, men who could fight and handle weapons, and spoke to them:

'To horse, my lords!' he said. 'We'll ride out there, four hundred of us with the best and fastest horses, and before it's dark, before the sun has set, we shall defeat them.'

Laisse 24
'My lords,' said the viscount, 'get ready, put on your armour, mount! We'll charge all together, we'll make a united attack.'

'By God,' said Peter Roger of Cabaret,[3] 'I advise you not to go out there. I think you'll do enough if you can defend your town. Those French, tomorrow after they've eaten they'll move up and come close to your ditches, they'll try to cut your access to the water you all drink. There'll be plenty of fighting then.' All the most sensible men there agreed with this advice.

Armed knights rode on guard duty all round the town, which is very strongly placed, so strongly indeed that the emperor Charles, that great crowned king, held it besieged, they say, more than seven years and could never take it, winter or summer, until when he went away the towers bowed down to him, and so he returned and took it. That is what happened, if the story does not lie, for in no other way could he have taken it.[4]

---

1. This refers to the epic poem *Raoul de Cambrai*, probably to an earlier version than the one we have (ed. Meyer & Longnon, 1882).
2. Nothing is known of this builder.
3. Peter Roger shared the lordship of Cabaret with his brother Jordan.
4. The legends of Charlemagne include the story of his recapture of Carcassonne from the Saracens.

The crusaders capture the town but not the castle

Laisse 25

The viscount of Béziers set a strong guard all night and next morning[1] rose at dawn. The French ate their meal and then throughout the host they put on their armour. The men of Carcassonne too prepared for battle. Many were the blows struck that day, and on both sides many lay dead or bleeding. The crusaders took heavy casualties and very many of the defenders were killed or wounded. But the attackers fought so hard that they succeeded in burning the whole town as far as the citadel and pressed on so strongly that they encircled them and cut them off from their water supply, the River Aude. They set up mangonels and catapults and battered the length and breadth of the ramparts day and night.

Listen to the wonderful work of God! The defenders had crossbowmen stationed high up on the towers, and when they shot at the host, not even half their quarrels reached it, but dropped down instead into the ditches. And I have heard it said for certain and know it to be true that no ravens or vultures or other carrion-eating birds flew above the host that whole summer. Victuals were so plentiful, too, that bread was sold at thirty loaves for a penny. People got salt from the salt pans and brought it there, which allowed them to recoup their losses, for what they lost on bread they made up on salt. But you can be sure no one recovered his costs, all of them suffered loss.

The king of Aragon intervenes

Laisse 26

It was in August that the host sat down around Carcassonne. Very soon King Peter of Aragon arrived there, bringing with him a hundred knights at his own expense. The crusaders were at their meal, eating roast meat, and when they saw the king and his knights coming they by no means hung back: princes and prelates, they all went forward to meet him. He greeted them politely, and with equal courtesy they replied:

'You are very welcome.'

Laisse 27

In a meadow beside the river near a leafy wood stood the rich tent of the count of Toulouse, and here my lord the king and his men from Catalonia and Aragon dismounted. When they had eaten and drunk, he mounted his palfrey, a bay with a fine mane, and rode into the town without shield or weapons. Three men rode with him, the rest stayed behind. When the viscount saw him, he and all his men ran forward to meet him in great joy, for they thought he was going to help them, as they were his vassals[2] and his friends, very dear to him. Dear to him they were, but he had not come to bring support. He had no power to help them, there was nothing he could do for them except pray, or so he said. The viscount explained what had happened and told him about the slaughter at Béziers and how the crusaders had devastated his lands.

The king listened attentively and then said,

---

1.   3 August.
2.   As count of Barcelona, the king of Aragon was overlord of Carcassonne and Razès.

'In Jesus' name, baron, you cannot blame me for that, since I told you, I ordered you to drive out the heretics, as there are so many people in this town who support this insane belief.'

Laisse 28
'Viscount,' continued the king, 'I am very unhappy for you, because it's nothing but a few fools and their folly that have brought you into such danger and distress. All I can suggest is an agreement, if we can get it, with the French lords, for I am sure, and God himself knows, that no further battle with lance and shield offers you any hope at all, their numbers are so huge. I doubt very much whether you could hold out to the end. You are counting on the strength of your town, but you have got it crammed with people, with women and children; otherwise, yes, I think you could see some hope in that. I am very sorry indeed for you, deeply distressed; for the love I bear you and for our old friendship's sake, there is nothing I will not do to help you, barring great dishonour.' The viscount saw well enough that he and his barons urgently needed an agreement with the crusading force.

Laisse 29
'My lord,' said the viscount to King Peter, 'you may do as you wish with the town and everything in it, for we all belong to you and before that we belonged to the king your father, who loved us dearly.'[1]

At these words the king remounted his palfrey and rode back to the host. He spoke to the Frenchmen and to the abbot of Cîteaux, who was sent for, as nothing could be settled without him. The king told them what he and the viscount had said to each other and spoke as forcefully as he could on behalf of the young man and his followers. But for all he said, for all he urged on them, this was the best he could get: that for his sake the crusaders would allow a dozen men, that is, the viscount and eleven others of his choice, to leave the town, with whatever they had on them. Everything else must be surrendered to the host.

'That,' said the king between his teeth, 'will happen when donkeys fly.' Angry and distressed, he went back into the citadel and told the viscount and his men what had been said. When he heard the terms offered, the viscount said he would rather let his men be skinned alive, would take his own life; never in all his days would he accept these terms nor abandon even the worst of all his vassals. He asked the king to go away and said he would defend himself inside Carcassonne to the utmost of his power. Grieving at the way it had turned out, the king mounted his horse.

King Peter returns to Spain

Laisse 30
King Peter of Aragon went away very sad, unhappy at having failed to save them. Angry and sorrowful, he rode back to Aragon.

---

1. Raymond Roger's father Roger did homage to Peter's father Alfonso II (1162-96) in 1179.

The attack on Carcassonne castle

The crusaders prepared to fill up the ditches and had branches cut and cats built both large and small.[1] The commanders of the host went armed all the time and looked for a place where they could take the defenders by surprise. The bishop, the priors, monks and abbots cried out: 'To the pardon, the pardon! Why do you delay?'

The viscount and his men took their places on the walls, crossbowmen loosed their feathered bolts and many on both sides died. If the place had not been so full of people, refugees who had crowded into it from all around, no one could have taken it by siege or by assault, not in a whole year, for the towers were high and the walls crenellated. But they were cut off from their water supply, and the wells were dry because it was the height of summer and very hot. They suffered from the stench of men who had fallen ill and of the livestock brought in from all around, then slaughtered and skinned,[2] from the crying and shrieking of the women and little children that packed the place, from the flies that tormented them all in the heat - never in all their days had they known such suffering.

Raymond Roger Trencavel asks for terms

Less than a week after King Peter had gone, one of the crusading commanders suggested a parley. And the viscount, having been given a safe-conduct, went out with a few of his men to meet them.

Laisse 31
The viscount of Béziers went out for the parley, taking with him about a hundred of his knights, and the crusading commander had only thirty.

'My lord,' this man said to the viscount, 'I am your kinsman.[3] May God the Father Almighty help and protect me just as much as I sincerely hope you will reach agreement with us, and as I hope too that you and your people will prosper! I certainly advise you to hold out if you are expecting relief to arrive soon. But you must be well aware that nothing of the kind will happen. Make some sort of agreement with the pope and the crusading lords, for I assure you that if they take you by assault you will get the same treatment as they got at Béziers. Save your bodies, at least, from torment and death! Money you can get again, if you live long enough.' The viscount listened and replied,

'My lord, at your command and at that of King Philip, lord of France, I would immediately settle everything properly with him, if I could go safely into the host.'

'Then I will take you there in safety and bring you back here to your own people, I give you my faithful word.'

Laisse 32
Out to the parley went the viscount of Béziers with his hundred knights, and the commander from the host with his thirty.

'My lord,' said this commander, 'I am your own kin. May God the Father so help me, as I truly wish you to reach this agreement, wish for the

---

1. *Gatas e gatz*, wheeled shelters which protected the assailants.
2. Fresh hides were used to protect wooden defences against fire.
3. His identity is not known.

well-being of your people and yourself!' Talking like this, they reached the tent of the count of Nevers where the discussions were being held. Knights and sergeants were watching him on all sides, so a mass priest reported, when he deliberately and of his own free will made himself a hostage. To my mind he acted like a lunatic, putting himself into custody.

Laisse 33
The viscount of Béziers stood in the tent of the count of Nevers together with his companions, nine of the most distinguished of his household, and the French and the Burgundians watched him closely.

15 August 1209, the fall of Carcassonne

.... Out they came, citizens, knights, noblewomen and girls, each running as in a race, till there was no one left in the town, no sergeants or boys, no women, no youngsters, no men, great or small. Quite unprotected, they rushed out pell-mell in their shirts and breeches, nothing else; not even the value of a button were they allowed to take with them. This way and that they scattered, some to Toulouse, some to Aragon, others to Spain, and the crusading army entered freely into the citadel and occupied the hall, the towers and the keep. They piled all their fine booty up into a single heap, and shared out the many mules and horses as they thought best.

Heralds went to and fro among the troops shouting: 'Come to the pardon! The abbot of Cîteaux is going to address you.' So then they all ran to him and gathered round. The abbot climbed up onto a marble plinth.

'My lords,' he said, 'now you can see what miracles the king of heaven does for you, since nothing can stand against you. In the name of God I forbid you to keep any of the town's wealth for yourselves, not so much as the value of a bit of charcoal, for if you did, we would instantly excommunicate and curse you. We shall give it all to some powerful lord who with God's grace will hold and keep this country so that the wicked heretics can never retake it.' All present agreed to the conclusion the abbot laid before them.

Laisse 34
Carcassonne was taken as you have heard and all the inhabitants of that district fled. The crusaders garrisoned Montréal and Fanjeaux; not one local man remained there, great or small. A brave mercenary commander called Peter of Aragon got himself a great deal of money there, so it was said.

Simon de Montfort appointed to command the crusade

Never think that the abbot of Cîteaux neglected his duty! He sang them a mass of the Holy Spirit and preached on the birth of Christ; then he said that he wanted a good lord to be chosen now to rule the land the crusaders had conquered. He called on the count of Nevers to accept this task, but the count absolutely refused to stay in that country on any terms, and so did the count of St Pol who was chosen next. They both said they had plenty of land in the kingdom of France where their fathers were born, however long their lives might be, and they did not wish to take another man's inheritance. There was no one present who would not feel himself utterly disgraced if he accepted the fief.

Laisse 35

One member of that council was a rich and valiant baron, a tough fighting man, wise and experienced, a good horseman, generous, honourable and pleasant, kind, frank and courteous, a man with a good understanding. He had served much overseas, at Zara, against the Turks and elsewhere and was lord of Montfort and its fief and also earl of Winchester, if the record is correct.[1] They decided unanimously to ask this man to take over the entire viscountcy and all the other lands belonging to heretics.

'My lord,' said the abbot to him, 'in the name of God Almighty, accept the fief they offer you, for God and the pope will defend you and so after them will we ourselves, so will we all; we will give you our help and support all your life long.'

'I will do it,' said Count Simon, 'on this condition: that the princes gathered here swear to me upon oath that if I am in trouble they will all come to my help when I send for them.'

'We will do so,' they all said, 'we give you our faithful word.' At this, Simon at once and boldly accepted the fief, the land and the country.

Some of Count Simon's men

Laisse 36

Once settled in the fief and county of Carcassonne, the count de Montfort became anxious, for very few of his friends decided to stay with him; most of them preferred to go back to the neighbourhood of Paris. The mountains are wild and the passes dangerous and none of them wanted to be killed in that country. However, some nine or ten of the greatest lords did stay:[2] Simon, known as de Cissey; Sir Robert of Picquigny, a Norman I believe;

---

1. Simon de Montfort, lord of Montfort and Epernon, inherited the earldom of Leicester (not 'Winchester') through his mother, Amicia of Beaumont and Leicester, but had access to nothing more than the bare title, since King John sequestrated the property as belonging to a vassal of the king of France. Although Montfort was only a lordship, not an earldom, Simon became known as the count de Montfort from this titular possession of the earldom of Leicester. He had accompanied the Fourth Crusade to Zara, but as this belonged to the Christian king of Hungary, he left the crusade and went to fight in Syria.
2. Those who can be identified are:
   Simon or Perrin de Cissey, one of a family of Norman knights.   —PERRIN !
   Robert of Picquigny from the Vexin; one of the barons who in 1215 took oath to implement Magna Carta.
   William of Contres, from Burgundy, near Nevers.
   Guy, a younger son of the Lévis family, whose fiefs marched with those of the de Montforts. As marshal of the crusading army, he was in charge of the horses.
   Robert was from Picardy.
   Lambert came from Burgundy; was known as Lambert of Limoux after receiving this fief from Simon de Montfort; see laisse 37. Simon also appointed him seneschal of Beaucaire.
   Pons of Beaumont died murdered as warden of Lagrave; see laisses 108 and 109.
   Rouaud, viscount of Donges, from Brittany.
   Roger des Essarts or de l'Essart from Normandy.
   Hugh de Lacy, second son of Hugh de Lacy, lord of Meath, Ireland; rebelled against King John; was banished and joined the crusade. Returned to England 1222. See M.-C., i, 88 ff. for detailed discussion of these individuals.

Sir William of Contres, always striving to increase his fame, so help me St Denis; Sir Guy the Marshal, strong and valiant; Robert of Forceville; Lambert of Crécy; Rainier of Chauderon; Ralph of Agis; Sir Pons of Beaumont; his cousin Sir John; and a great many others whose names I never learned. The viscount of Donges stayed too, with Sir Roger d'Andelys, Sir Roger des Essarts and Sir Hugh de Lacy. If I had been there with them and seen and met them and travelled with them in the land they conquered, this book would be the richer, I promise you, and the song much better.

Count Simon allocates duties

Laisse 37
Having established himself in Carcassonne, Simon de Montfort summoned his comrades in arms. William of Contres, God be good to him! he sent into the Biterrois, for there was no one more valiant or better able to defend a castle or keep good hold of a rich city. Indeed, if Sir William had charge of Portugal or the kingdom of Leon, he would rule them, Christ bless me! better than those stupid fools their kings, whom I count not worth a button. Count Simon sent Lambert of Crécy to Limoux and the other barons some here, some there, to defend the land as he thought best. And he himself, the lion-hearted, remained at Carcassonne, where he held the viscount prisoner. (The viscount died later of dysentery, and wicked scoundrels who know nothing whatever about it and cannot tell yes from no said he was killed at night by treason. Not for anything in the world, by Jesus in heaven! would Count Simon ever have allowed such a thing.)

Laisse 38
All the counts, princes and marquises, as I told you, begged the count de Montfort to accept the fief, and he did so on the understanding that they would come to his help if summoned. He required each of them to promise this on oath.

Young Raymond is brought to meet the crusaders

The count of Toulouse sent for his son[1] because the crusading lords, Raymond's friends from Paris and that neighbourhood, wanted to see the boy. Raymond of Ricaut[2] brought him on a Thursday. The child was good-looking and very well brought up, for Geoffrey of Poitiers had taken great care of him. The duke[3] could not fail to approve of him, as did his cousin, the count of St Pol. Then, fearing the approach of winter, the crusaders rode to Montpellier and so on home to Troyes and Paris.

The crusade challenges Toulouse, whose citizens appeal to Rome

Laisse 39
The great host broke up, for it could hold together no longer, but before it did so, messengers were sent to Toulouse to see if they were ready to come to

---

1. Young Raymond, born July 1197, now twelve.
2. One of Count Raymond's most trusted advisers, his warden at Toulouse in 1202, seneschal in 1210.
3. The duke must have been Odo III of Burgundy

terms. Many good knights went on this embassy. The Toulousains replied that they would do whatever the pope of Rome thought best, and that they wanted to go and see him. That was absolutely all the envoys were able to achieve, and so they came back along the high road and returned with the host direct to Montpellier.

The count of Toulouse prepared to go to Rome, for I believe he wanted to see the pope as soon as he could, intending to be there before January. But he sent his envoys ahead of him: Raymond of Rabastens, only just back from Rome, and the abbot of St Audard, who was ill rewarded, for he was held prisoner almost a whole year.[1] A worthier abbot no man ever had at his command. These went to inform the pope that Count Raymond was coming; he might be sure he would not fail.

Count Raymond's travels

Laisse 40
The valiant count of Toulouse was preparing for the long journey he intended to make. First he would go to France to talk to his cousin,[2] then to the emperor, if he could find him, and then to the pope. He wanted to try all three of them. The abbot of Cîteaux said there was no need for this, that if Raymond would trust him he need not go to such trouble or expense, he could achieve just as much here with him, the abbot, as he could by going to see those others; but Count Raymond insisted on going.

Death of Raymond Roger Trencavel

Now I want to talk about the count de Montfort. He held the viscount prisoner and had him well guarded and lavishly supplied with everything he needed. But no one can change the future: the viscount fell ill of dysentery, I believe, and so he had to die. But first he wanted to receive communion and the bishop of Carcassonne had the rite decently performed. Then afterwards at nightfall the viscount died. The count de Montfort behaved like a man of honour and had his body plainly displayed to the people of his fief so that they could all go and mourn him and pay their respects. What crying and weeping you would have seen there! Then he had the body buried, and many followed after in the cortège. May God, if he will listen to prayer, take care of his soul, for this was a great tragedy.

Count Simon's problems

Laisse 41
When the crusaders had gone back to their own lands, the count de Montfort was left in great difficulty and almost without companions after their departure. He now reached a settlement with the count of Foix,[3] who voluntarily gave him his youngest son as a hostage. This agreement did not last

---

1. Raymond Azémar. Count Raymond's treatment of him is one of the complaints lodged by the council of Lavaur in 1213.
2. Philip Augustus king of France 1180-1223. He and Raymond were both grandsons of Louis VI.
3. Raymond Roger, count of Foix, died March 1223. His youngest son's name was Aimery.

long, for they soon broke all its terms and then made vigorous war on each other.[1]

Gerald of Pépieux[2] behaved badly towards Count Simon, for he had made his peace with him and come to an agreement, but then they parted over an unhappy occurrence. It is true that a Frenchman killed Gerald's uncle, but the count de Montfort was extremely angry at this and had the culprit thrown into a pit and buried alive. Never had any man been so punished for such an offence. As the culprit was a Frenchman of France and very highly connected, Sir Gerald ought to have found this revenge sufficient. His uncle's murder led him to break with the count, who had heaped honours upon him and taken him much into his confidence. Yet Sir Gerald uttered no defiance, took no leave of Count Simon, but went and burned down a rich castle[3] belonging to him. If he had been found there, I think he would have paid for it dearly.

Bouchard[4] was holding Saissac, which had been given to him. He and fifty Frenchmen went out in arms one day and encountered the men of Cabaret.[5] There were at least ninety of these, horse, foot and fourteen archers, and they encircled the French and attacked and pressed them hard. But our Frenchmen kept close-ranked and in good array and were not alarmed by their threats and shouting, so that many were killed on both sides. In the end, sadly, it was Bouchard's men who suffered defeat, and he himself was captured and taken away. As for those who died, they are forgotten. May God receive their souls in his glorious heaven when the world comes to its end.

Laisse 42
The count de Montfort was very angry at the capture of Bouchard and his companions. All through that winter he lost ground, until the season of Lent arrived, leaves grew green again and the crusade returned as usual for a fresh campaign.[6]

Count Raymond in Rome and France; returns to Toulouse

The count went to Rome, as the song says, and so did the consuls[7] of Toulouse, who laid out a great deal of money there. They went to France first and found Philip the mighty king very cheerful; but later he was displeased, being angry with them because of the emperor Otto.[8] The

---

1. The breakdown came in the autumn of 1209.
2. Gerald was a knight of the viscountcy of Béziers; Pépieux is in the Minervois.
3. The castle of Puisserguier.
4. Bouchard, lord of Marly 1204-26, a Montmorency and cousin of Alice, countess de Montfort. His brother Matthew, his cousin and his mother Matilda of Garlande also joined the crusade.
5. Saissac was strongly placed on a rocky spur in the Montagne Noire between Castelnaudary and Carcassonne. Cabaret (20 km east of Saissac), Termes and Minerve were the last three castles in the viscountcies of Carcassonne and Béziers still holding out against the crusaders.
6. Spring 1210.
7. The consuls or *capitoliers* of Toulouse formed the Capitol, its governing body. We do not know how many of them went to Rome on this occasion.
8. Raymond saw Otto in January or February 1210 in Italy on his way back from Rome. Philip Augustus was certainly not pleased.

countess of Champagne,[1] a worthy and courteous lady, received them kindly, as did many of the other nobles. So too did the valiant duke of Burgundy who gave them many gifts, and the count of Nevers who was very friendly towards them and entertained them handsomely.

Laisse 43

The pope of Rome and all the cardinals gave Count Raymond the welcome due to a lord of such high birth. The pope presented him with a princely cloak and a ring of fine gold, the jewel in which alone was worth fifty marks of silver, and a horse as well. Thereupon the two of them became cordial friends. He showed him the Veronica[2] belonging to the holy father, and when Raymond touched the face on it, which seems like that of a man of flesh and blood, the pope absolved him of all the sins he had committed until that moment, for the two men were then in close accord.[3]

Laisse 44

When the count of Toulouse had done all he intended, he took leave of the pope and set off at once, travelling fast out of Lombardy by long stages for fear of contracting disease there. In France they stopped one day in Paris and saw the king, who made his displeasure very clear.

The count came away and he and his retinue entered Toulouse in the usual manner, amid great rejoicing.

A further meeting

Count Raymond then met the count de Montfort for discussions, near an abbey, in the presence of the abbot of Cîteaux and the other clergy. And I would have expected them to make peace and agree never to fight each other again all their lives long, so much loving-kindness did they display. Certainly I would never in a thousand years have expected the abbot to enter Toulouse, whoever had told me so. But they made over to him the castle on the Narbonne road;[4] the abbot and Bishop Fouquet[5] were in full military command.

---

1. Blanche of Navarre, regent of the county during the minority of Theobald IV.
2. St Veronica is said to have wiped the sweat from Jesus' face as he carried his cross to Calvary, and the cloth she used received a miraculous imprint of the divine face. Such a cloth was much revered in Rome from the eighth century onwards.
3. William exaggerates. Innocent absolved the inhabitants of Toulouse, but only granted Raymond the right to defend himself before a council to be called in France.
4. The Narbonnais castle, built on the remains of a Roman stronghold, was the fortress of the counts of Toulouse. It derived its name from its situation, commanding the road to Narbonne.
5. Fouquet, Folc or Folquet, born at Marseille, a famous poet, entered the Cistercian monastery of Thoronet in 1201, became its abbot, and in 1205 bishop of Toulouse. Helen Waddell tells us that after he entered religion he repented of his early life and that always, even at the table of the king of France, if he heard one of his own songs sung, he would refuse all food and drink but bread and water. She also quotes Dante's vision of Folco praising God in Paradise, aware of past sin but too full of joy to grieve for it (Waddell, *Wandering Scholars*, p. 198, n. 3).

The abbot of Cîteaux commands in Toulouse

Laisse 45
Into Toulouse came the abbot of Cîteaux, to the astonishment of everybody, great and small, old and young, of the very children. In the presence of the whole people the count made the castle over to them - as fine a castle, I think, as any ever seen in flat country. Many a charter they drew up, many briefs and letters, which the abbot sent all over the world as far as Mount Etna. The king of Aragon rode from Muret to meet the lord abbot and they talked in a meadow at Portet,[1] but reached no conclusion worth a trashy buckle-ring.

Preaching falls on deaf ears

Laisse 46
Fouquet of Marseille, bishop of Toulouse, a man of incomparable goodness, took counsel with the abbot of Cîteaux. Both of them preached assiduously to audiences who remained wrapped in slumber, and they spoke against money-lending and usury. They travelled all over the Agenais, even riding as far as St Bazeille. Not one word of their exhortations did those people listen to, but said scornfully, 'There's that bee buzzing round again!', so that I myself, God help me, cannot wonder that they are robbed, pillaged and suffer violent punishment.

Disputes inside Toulouse

Laisse 47
In Toulouse the citizens of the fraternity and those of the town[2] were in constant conflict, and in the end achieved nothing worth an acorn or a rotten apple. Those who believed in or supported the heresy said that the bishop, the abbot and the clergy were deliberately creating this disagreement so that the Toulousains in their folly would destroy each other, for if men hold together all the crusaders in the world can do them no harm. That is what they said to the count and his companions, those wicked fools who believed the heresy. They will yet see clearly, may God bless me! what counsel they have been given by those whom God must surely curse. It will lead to the death of many and the destruction of the land, laid waste and ravaged by foreigners, for the French of France and the men of Lombardy and the whole world hate them worse than Saracens and have gathered to attack them.

June and July 1210, Count Simon takes Minerve

Laisse 48
Now in summertime, my lords, when winter was past and fine days and hot weather had returned, the count de Montfort prepared his expedition against

---

1. Portet lies between Muret and Toulouse.
2. Of the city and of the suburbs respectively. Many of the former, persuaded by the bishop, had taken the cross and supported the invaders, whereas the suburbs stood by Count Raymond.

Minerve, which lies towards the coast.[1] He laid siege to the place as he had planned, and set up his catapults, making Bad Neighbour the queen and lady of all his siege engines. He smashed openings in the high walls and in the stone-built hall, mortared with sand and lime; many a good penny they had cost and many a *masmudina*.[2] If the king of Morocco and his Saracens had sat down all around the place, by St Catherine, they could have done no damage worth an Anjou halfpenny, but against the host of Christ, the judge of all, no high rocks, no steepness may avail, no mountain fortress hold out.

Laisse 49

Minerve castle is not in a plain but stands, God be my witness, on a high spur of rock.[3] There is no stronger fortress this side of the Spanish passes, except Cabaret and Termes at the head of Cerdagne. William, lord of Minerve, had shut himself into the castle with his whole troop and was taking his ease there.[4] But our Frenchmen and men from Champagne, from Maine, Anjou and Brittany, from Lorraine, Frisia and Germany drove them all out by force before the grain ripened. And there they burned many heretics, frantic men of an evil kind and crazy women who shrieked among the flames.[5] Not the value of a chestnut was left to them. Afterwards their bodies were thrown out and mud shovelled over them so that no stench from these foul things should annoy our foreign forces.

Countess Alice joins her husband

Laisse 50

With Minerve taken, the count de Montfort went from there to Pennautier up in the Carcassès and sent for the countess[6] to join him. She came as soon as she had his message. No wiser woman, so God and the faith help me, has anyone ever met in the length and breadth of the world. She remained three days with the host, which was very large.

The siege of Termes planned

Early on a Thursday morning the count joined the barons and princes in a palace, and it was decided to to lay siege to Termes up in the Termenès. This is a wonderful castle, and before it falls many souls will quit their bodies, dying unconfessed, and the siege will cost many a mark and many a penny of Tours. Horses and palfreys will be won, and much other wealth, much fine armour, by men on either side to whom it is predestined.

---

1. Nearer the coast than St Antonin where William was writing, Minerve is 50 km from the sea.
2. Gold coins, *dinar masmoudy*, issued by Arab rulers in Spain.3. Minerve stands on a high limestone bluff, deeply undercut by the Rivers Brian and Cesse which meet there. It fell to Simon's siege engines after more than a month.
4. Literally, he rested and took baths, *sojorna e se banha*.
5. More than 140 heretics refused to recant and died in the fire. Peter of Les Vaux de Cernay, fiercely anti-Cathar, says they were so obstinate in their wickedness that there was no need to throw them into the blaze, they flung themselves in; and that Bouchard's mother Matilda pulled three women off the pyre and reconciled them to the church. Peter of Les Vaux de Cernay, i, p. 161.
6. Alice, daughter of Matthew of Montmorency, constable of France, and his second wife Alice of Savoy, widow of Louis VI and mother of Louis VII.

Laisse 51

The count de Montfort entered the palace with the countess and all his lords, and they took their seats on a carpet of silk. Robert of Mauvoisin[1] and Sir Guy the Marshal had been summoned and were there side by side, and so was Sir William of Contres, for in the whole viscountcy there was no more powerful or more valiant lord. He was born, I am told, in Burgundy, two leagues from Nevers. These recommended that siege should be laid at once to the castle of Termes, and many other good men supported this proposal.

William of Contres to command in Carcassonne

The council broke up after a short meeting; then, after a brief interval they had dinner and returned for another session. The count de Montfort was very anxious to choose the right man to defend Carcassonne, but in the end he was advised to appoint either Sir Lambert of Crécy, a powerful and respected baron, or Sir Rainier of Chauderon. Both these were chosen, but neither of them would stay in that country, not for a kingdom, so hostile did they perceive it to be. But then they begged William of Contres to take on the task, and he, having considered it, agreed to do so. The count de Montfort, though, was very angry at this, and would not have left him in Carcassonne if he had had anyone else to put there, for in the whole land there was no wiser man nor a better or more reliable knight, more courteous, more valiant or more loyal, so God grant me his blessing!

Laisse 52

Having listened and reflected, Sir William of Contres said:

'In the name of Jesus Christ and St Mary, I will stay here since each of you asks me to do so.' But the count de Montfort would not have left him there if he had had any alternative, yet in the end since no one else would stay, he reluctantly agreed.

The men of the host, the knights and the countess all wanted Sir William appointed. And for companions the count de Montfort gave him Crespi of Rochefort,[2] a very courteous man, and Sir Simon the Saxon,[3] may Jesus bless him, his brother Sir Guy,[4] whose very face shows his courage, and many other nobles of his host from Burgundy, France and Normandy. Then they separated and the count set off with his great lords to lay siege to Termes. Sir William of Contres parted from him the same day in the meadows by Pennautier and reached Carcassonne before moonrise and before it was fully dark.

Siege engines attacked

Laisse 53

William of Contres left Pennautier, rode hard for Carcassonne and arrived there just as the townspeople were getting up from supper and about to go to bed. The castle servants ran to help him unarm; they lit the fire in the

---

1. An important noble from the north of France. Took part in the Fourth Crusade, was one of the first to join in the war against the Cathars; died 1214.
2. He took his name from Rochefort-en-Yvelines, a dependency of the Montforts.
3. Died at Pujol 1213; see laisse 133.
4. Guy de Montfort was not present; this Sir Guy was a brother of Simon the Saxon.

fireplace up in the great hall, prepared plenty of beef, pork and other food for them to eat, then made up the beds in the place where they were to sleep, for they would all have to get up at dawn next day in order to guard the mangonels and other engines which they were taking to Termes in carts for the attack on the castle. This was at Count Simon's command; he had ordered them most urgently to send the siege engines and to guard the city; any other needs must take second place. The engines were to be closely guarded for those three days and when they arrived he would have them set up. Sir William of Contres immediately had them dragged out of the town onto the ground beside the River Aude and loaded promptly onto horse-drawn carts.

Laisse 54

A spy left the host and went quickly to Cabaret, where he immediately told them that the count had sent wretched and useless men to transport the siege engines and that their escort would not number more than a hundred, horse and foot. When they heard that, they were delighted. They rode out of Cabaret by moonlight, captained by Peter Roger, if the account is correct, and by William Cat,[1] Raymond Mir[2] and all their kinsmen. More than three hundred of them there were, each outriding his neighbour and galloping full tilt for Carcassonne.

Brave Sir William of Contres had the carts and siege engines under careful guard. When these guards saw the knights spurring towards them they shouted out, 'To arms! To arms! Shame on any who turn away!' Sir William heard these shouts, and quietly told his knights to hurry to arms, and that quickly; if glorious Jesus, the Father Almighty and the blessed mother Mary willed it, he would fight these men, and soon. Why make a long story of it? Sir Peter Roger and his men did not flinch, they dismounted, smashed the mangonels in the sight of all the bystanders, and used straw to set them alight. The fire blazed up, and if there had been a breath of wind all the engines would have burned at once, but God did not want this.

Laisse 55

William of Contres heard the voices and instantly shouted, 'To arms, knights!' He had at least eighty sergeants with him, not counting the other knights, and they had the gates opened in blessed Mary's name and attacked Peter Roger's men there in the meadow. These saw them coming and did not despise them but rode boldy forward to meet their charge. Ah God, what good lances were shattered that day, what mighty blows struck on helmets from Pavia! Sir William of Contres spurred his Hungarian warhorse and charged raging and angry, may God bless me, into the thickest of the fight. He rode into the River Aude and there in the water thrust through the mêlée. He encountered one of Mir's men and struck him so hard on his flowered shield that his hauberk was no more use to him than a rotten apple; down into the water he went, as all could see. Next he overtook a wretch in flight and struck him from the side with his bright sword; and he struck down another man at this time. Nor did Crespi of Rochefort or Simon hang back: no one they hit ever needed a road to walk on again.

---

1. A knight from Montréal in the Carcassès. Like others, he had abandoned his castle and joined the resistance in Cabaret.
2. Peter Mir, one of a noble family from Fanjeaux; M.-C., i, p. 127.

They pressed home this attack for some time, and in the end Sir Peter Roger and all his men had by far the worst of it. Not one of them but cursed him for the way it had turned out. Defeated and fewer in number they rode away. Sir William of Contres gathered his men and went back into Carcassonne. They were all delighted at having saved the siege engines and the whole troop rejoiced at their victory.

August-November 1210, siege and fall of Termes

Laisse 56
Count Simon de Montfort laid his siege before and all round Termes, and then he heard this news. You can imagine how pleased he was with Sir William of Contres and his companions for saving the siege engines, and more pleased still at their defeat of the baron called Peter Roger - God do him no good! For I believe the count would not be so delighted to be given all the gold of Mâcon as he was when they told him of the great victory Sir William of Contres had won. Ah God, how well the news was announced by the noble young man Sir William sent to escort those weapons! That task too, he did well, I can truthfully say, bringing them safely all the way to the siege before Termes.

Here there were many barons, many tents of rich silk and fine pavilions, many silk tunics and rich brocades, mailshirts too and many a fine banner, many an ashen haft, ensigns and pennons, many a good knight and fine young men of noble race - Germans, Bavarians, Saxons, Frisians, men from Maine, Anjou, Normandy and Brittany, Lombards and Longobards,[1] Gascons and Provençals. The lord archbishop of Bordeaux was there and so was Sir Amanieu d'Albret[2] and men from Langon. All those who came did their forty days' duty, so that as some arrived, others left. But Raymond, lord of Termes,[3] counted none of them worth a button, for no one ever saw a stronger castle than his. There they kept Pentecost, Easter and Ascension and half the winter, as the song says.

No one ever saw so numerous a garrison as there was in that castle, men from Aragon, Catalonia and Roussillon. Many were the armed encounters and shattered saddle-bows, many the knights and strong Brabanters killed, many the ensigns and fine banners forcibly borne off into the keep against the crusaders' will. As for the mangonels and catapults, the defenders did not think them worth a button. Meat they had in plenty, both fresh meat and salt pork, water and wine to drink and an abundance of bread. If the Lord God had not dealt them a blow, as he did later when he sent them dysentery, they would never have been defeated.

Laisse 57
My lords, will you hear how Termes was taken and how Christ Jesus there displayed his mighty power?

Nine months[4] the army sat around that stronghold until its water supply dried up. They had wine for another two or three months, but I do not think

---

1. Lombards came from northern Italy, Longobards from the south.
2. Amanieu V, lord of Albret (Labrit, Landes) c.1209-40.
3. Raymond of Termes was old but strong and 'feared neither God nor man'; M.-C., i, p. 135.
4. No: from late July to 22 November 1210

anyone can live without water. Then, God and the faith help me, there was a heavy downpour of rain which caused a great flood, and this led to their defeat. They put quantities of this rainwater into butts and barrels and used it to knead and cook with. So violent a dysentery seized them that the sufferers could not tell where they were. They all agreed to flee away rather than die like this, unconfessed. They put the ladies of the castle up into the keep, and then when it was dark night and no one could see what was happening, they went out, taking with them no possessions, nothing, I believe, except money. At that point Raymond of Termes told them to wait because he was going back into the castle, and while they waited some Frenchmen met him on his way in and they captured him and took him to the count de Montfort. The others, Catalans and Aragonese, fled to escape being killed. But the count de Montfort behaved very well and took nothing from the ladies, not even the value of a penny coin or a Le Puy farthing.

Laisse 58
When it was known throughout the land that Termes had fallen, all the strongest castles were abandoned, and Le Bézu[1] was taken, without any need for sieges. The men of these garrisons who left the castles never supposed that the crusaders would get that far. God who is full of mercy worked a great miracle there, for he gave finer winter weather than anyone has known in summer. I return to my subject, which I have left too long.

Conference at St Gilles

After the count of Toulouse was told of the fall of Termes, he went to a great assembly at St Gilles.[2] This had been called by the clergy, by the abbot of Cîteaux and the other crusaders (for Milo was dead and buried). Count Raymond brought with him my lord Guy Cap de Porc,[3] the best lawyer in all Christendom, who is also a distinguished knight of the highest rank and so learned that compared with his, no one's knowledge is worth a dice. This man supports Count Raymond, but he is so well informed that his opponents would put their own eyes out before they would let him speak. The abbot of Cîteaux rose to his feet.

'My lords,' he said to them, 'you must know that the count of Toulouse has done me great honour and has yielded me his fief, for which I am very grateful to him, and I beg you to treat him well.'

Then they unfolded the letters which had been sent to the count of Toulouse from Rome. Why should I make a long story of it? These letters made such demands that when the reading was done, Count Raymond said he could never pay them all, not with the whole of his county. He set foot in his stirrup and in distress and anger rode back to Toulouse and his own land as fast as he could go.

Further meetings

Laisse 59
Then Count Raymond attended another such meeting at Narbonne on

---

1. A castle between Coustaussa and Puivert.
2. This meeting began on 10 July 1210.
3. Guy Cap de Porc, a senior official in the chancellery of the counts of Toulouse; served Simon de Montfort once the latter took possession of the county of Toulouse.

St Vincent's day.[1] King Peter of Aragon was present, as were many important people. They achieved nothing, not the worth of a rose-hip.

Demands presented to Count Raymond

Then there was another meeting, this time I think at Arles.[2] At this one they wrote down a list of all their conclusions and gave it to the count, who was waiting for them outside in the wind and bitter cold, with the king of Aragon. In the sight of all those present the abbot of Cîteaux, accompanied by Master Tecin, the best and most learned clerk in the world, and by the bishop of Uzès[3] and a hundred other clerks, handed him the list. Accepting it, the count at once quietly summoned his scribe, and when he had heard it read carefully from beginning to end, he called in anger to the king of Aragon.

'Come here, my lord king,' he said with a smile. 'Listen to this document and the strange orders the legates say I must obey.' The king had it read out again and when he had heard it, he said in a quiet voice,

'Almighty God in heaven, this must be changed!'

Grasping the document, to which he made no answer, and in such anxiety that he took no leave, Count Raymond rode away as fast as he could to Toulouse, and then on to Montauban, to Moissac and Agen, all in the one journey.

Laisse 60

The valiant count of Toulouse returned to the Toulousain and entered Toulouse, then Montauban, Moissac and Agen, with this list in his hand. In all these places he had it read out, so that everyone, knights, citizens and priests who sang mass, should know what it contained.

This is what the document said and how it began: that the count and those who were with him must keep the peace; they must dismiss the mercenaries that same night or next morning; must restore their rights to the clergy, who should be supreme in everything they might require; the count must expel all faithless Jews from his jurisdiction; within a year's time he must hand over to the abbot and his advisers all the heretical believers they would point out, for them do as they pleased with at their absolute discretion. The count and his followers were not to eat meat more than twice,[4] nor in future should they wear clothes made of rich fabrics but only coarse brown capes, which would last better. They must dismantle their castles and strongholds. No knight must reside in a town but out in the country among villeins; they must never exact unjust tolls on the roads but only those established by ancient custom; they must pay four Toulousain pence a year to peace-keepers, who would be appointed. All usurers must renounce usury and must at once return any interest they had taken. If the count de Montfort or any crusaders should in future ride honestly against them, and should take anything of theirs, they must on no account defend themselves. They must abide in all things by the law of the king of France. Count Raymond must cross the sea and go to the River Jordan and stay there as long as the monks should require, or the

---

1. 22 January.
2. Possibly Montpellier.
3. Raymond, bishop of Uzès.
4. More than twice a week, probably.

cardinals in Rome or those whom they should appoint. Then he was to join the Order of the Temple or of St John. When he had done all this, they would return his castles to him. If he did not, they would drive him right out and make him destitute.

Reactions to the list of demands

Laisse 61
When the vassals of the fief, the knights and citizens, heard this read to them, they said they would all rather be dead or imprisoned than endure those conditions or do what was required, that it would reduce them all to the status of serfs, villeins and rustics. The citizens of Moissac and Agen said they would sooner take boat for Bordeaux than have Frenchmen or Barrois[1] for their lords; or if the count wished, they would go away with him into some other land and live there, wherever he preferred. Hearing this, the count thanked them warmly.

Then he had letters written and sent out to all his friends, up to the Albigeois, on this side to Béarn and to the count of Comminges,[2] also to the count of Foix and beyond to the Carcassès. He also begged Sir Savari of Mauléon[3] to stand by him, and in reply Sir Savari promised his ready and willing help, whether anyone else liked it or not.

Spring 1211, a fresh crusade arrives

Laisse 62
At the beginning of Lent when the cold weather has gone and the warmth of Easter is approaching, the crusading army began to move, summoned to action by our preachers. The bishop of Toulouse - God grant him honour! - was received in the town as lord, with a great procession as if for an emperor. He absolved them from the interdict, so that I thought then that they would have made peace for all time and been glad to do so, but later I saw how furiously they threw themselves into battle. Bishop Fouquet went away to France and preached there daily, and the princes, counts, barons and knights of those parts took the cross.

Release of Bouchard and surrender of Cabaret

Laisse 63
Count Peter of Auxerre, Robert of Courtenay[4] and the precentor[5] of Paris, as the book says, brought a very strong force from the Paris region and entered Carcassonne. Hear what a miracle Jesus did there, as the book tells you -

The men in Cabaret were very alarmed at the arrival of this contingent, and one morning very early Peter Roger, lord of Cabaret, went to see his prisoner

---

1. Vassals of the count of Bar in the Meuse valley, and from Lorraine and the Rhineland in the Empire.
2. Bernard IV (1181-1225), a grandson of Alfonso Jordan, count of Toulouse, and thus cousin to Raymond VI.
3. Savari of Mauléon, warrior and poet from Poitou. Below in laisse 123 he uses harsh measures to obtain due payment for his services from Raymond VI.
4. Count Peter's brother.
5. William of Nemours, brother of the bishop of Paris, possibly archdeacon as well as precentor; became bishop of Meaux in 1213.

Sir Bouchard in the room where he lay in irons.

'Bouchard,' he said, 'I know you have a noble heart, you are a true and valiant man and would never do anything that should not be done. I don't know whether I shall meet with thanks and compassion if I set you free, but I am going to take the risk.'

'I have never done or commanded anything dishonourable.'

'Well then,' said Peter Roger, 'you are no longer a prisoner, and here and now I make over to you my castle and myself.' He sent for a smith and had Bouchard released from his irons, had him given a comfortable bath and his hair cut, and besides this he gave him very handsome clothes and a bay palfrey, for he was not joking but in good earnest. You can imagine Bouchard's delight. Never had he known such happiness since the day his mother gave him birth.

Laisse 64

My lords, just as I have been telling you, the lord of Cabaret omitted nothing: he summoned a smith and had Sir Bouchard freed from his irons and nobly clad in rich robes; he gave him a pacing palfrey to ride, the handsomest ever seen; and when he was properly dressed he gave him three young noblemen on horseback for an escort and himself rode with him out of the castle. Before they went, he invested him with the castle and with himself and did him un-conditional homage. Sir Bouchard promised him on oath that he for his part would never betray Peter Roger's trust, and that when his case was finally settled no one should think him a fool or laugh at him for releasing Sir Bouchard. Nor did Bouchard break his word, for he kept his promise faithfully.

Laisse 65

You need not ask whether the count de Montfort and his lords were glad when they heard that Bouchard was free and would soon be with them. They all went at once to welcome him. When they had met and kissed, they begged him to say whether or not he had given hostages, and he said no, indeed he had not.

'On the contrary, I am absolutely free and we have command of the castle. Listen, and I'll tell you how it happened: my lord Peter Roger has given me the lordship of his whole castle which he was holding against us, and has established friendship and a close alliance with me. And I, God grant me his blessing! have promised him that he shall be the better for this all his life long, and I will give him twice as much as he now possesses.'

'In that case,' said the count de Montfort, 'it would be very wrong if our company were not to be good to him. Not one of you must hold him at arm's length.'

'Ah God,' said they all, 'blessed Mary! What a noble deed he has done, what an act of courtesy! There's not a man in France, I'm sure there never will be, who could have done this.'

Laisse 66

Sir Bouchard celebrated his release all that night till dawn, and at first light the majority of the force entered Cabaret. There the terms of the agreement were announced and discussed. Bouchard spoke first, in the hearing of them all, and the agreement was fully accepted by all parties on both sides. Count Simon's banner was raised on top of the tower.

That is how Cabaret was taken, and how our crusaders manned its castle.

See what a miracle it was, for if all the people ever born in the world surrounded that fortress, the defenders would think them worth less than a peeled apple, it is so strong. But against the host of Christ no castle, no citadel can stand, however strong its battlements. Only a fool opposes the crusaders, a fool who may rejoice at first but in the end must be defeated.

March-May 1211: Siege and fall of Lavaur

Laisse 67
As soon as Cabaret had surrendered, the count de Montfort and the crusaders moved on and marched towards Lavaur down in the Toulousain. For a month and five weeks[1] they besieged it and attacked it vigorously with siege engines and catapults. If they had been able to defend themselves or if Count Raymond had come quickly to their help, it would not have fallen as soon as it did, God be my witness. Food was dear, both its cost and its transport, and this angered the people of Toulouse, who prevented supplies and convoys of weapons reaching the crusaders. But as the proverb says, they did not notice until too late that they had closed the stable door after the horse had gone, and the crusaders kept up a vigorous attack on Lavaur and its defenders.

Laisse 68
Lavaur is a very strong town; no one in any kingdom has ever seen a stronger in flat country, or one with better ramparts or deeper ditches.[2] There were many knights inside, all well armed, including Sir Aimery,[3] brother of Lady Girauda, who was lady of Lavaur. Sir Aimery joined her there after he had left the count de Montfort without a word of farewell. He had lost Montréal, Laurac and all his other lands to the crusaders; they had reduced his fief by two hundred knights, and he was angry. There was not a richer knight in all the Toulousain nor the rest of the county, nor a more generous spender or of higher rank. Alas the day he met the heretics and clog-wearers! Never so far as I know has so great a lord been hanged in all Christendom, nor with so many knights hanged at his side. More than eighty of them, there were, so a clerk told me. As for the townspeople, they collected as many as four hundred of these in a meadow and burned them. Beside this, they threw Lady Girauda into a well and heaped stones on top of her, which was a shame and a sorrow, for no one in this world, you may take my word for it, ever left her presence without having eaten. This was done on Holy Cross day in May, in summer time.[4]

The crusaders brought the cat close against the walls beside the ditch and dug so deep that the garrison surrendered, for they were taken and forced. Then there was so great a killing that I believe it will be talked of till the end of the world. My lords, it is right that they should be punished and suffer so terribly, for as I myself have both seen and heard, they refuse to obey the clerks

---

1. William exaggerates the length of the siege, but it certainly lasted a full month: M.-C., i, p. 162.
2. It stood above the River Agout, which formed part of its defences.
3. Aimery, lord of Montréal and Laurac, handed these fiefs over to Simon de Montfort after the fall of Minerve; but not being adequately compensated, left the crusaders and joined his widowed sister Girauda at her castle of Lavaur.
4. 3 May 1211.

and crusaders, they will not do as they are commanded. Yet in the end they will have to do so, when they are stripped of all they possess, as these did at Lavaur, and they will find no grace in this world or with God.

German crusaders killed near Montgey

Laisse 69

The count of Foix and his companions took the field at the same time that Lavaur was under siege. A number of Count Raymond's men rode with him, and squires and boys as well.

.... the Germans came spurring fast, five thousand of them at least, so the song says. When they reached Montgey they put on their armour and moved forward in close array, as if in a procession. But the lion-hearted count of Foix and his companions did not stop to talk but attacked from every side. They met with fierce resistance, for the Germans and Frisians fought hard and long, close by a small wood, but were at last miserably defeated. There the German knights died, unshriven most of them, for the villeins and filthy wretches of that district went and clubbed them to death with sticks and stones. That is why Montgey was destroyed.[1] The Lord God of glory forgive me my sins - if those villeins who killed and robbed the crusaders had been hanged as thieves, I would have been delighted.

Laisse 70

As I told you, the moment the villeins of that fief saw the count of Foix they all went to his help, and a pretty penny they made out of it. But they paid a high price before the army went away. One young nobleman escaped the slaughter, and he made his way to the crusaders and told them what had happened. When the French heard it, they almost went out of their minds. More than fourteen thousand of them ran to horse, and as long as the light lasted they rode in hot pursuit. But the brave count of Foix did not loiter; each man rode full tilt and that night they slept at Montgiscard. The plunder they had taken would keep them handsomely for weeks, for months, for a year. Their pursuers had to give up at nightfall; angry and sorrowful, they turned back, and slept at Lanta. When the other knights heard of this episode, they were appalled.

The deaths at Lavaur

Laisse 71

Count Peter of Auxerre and the counts of Courtenay and de Montfort saw that the count of Foix had got well away and there was nothing they could do, so returned to the main army at Lavaur. They had taken this place, as the book says. There they burned at least four hundred evil heretics, heaping them all onto one great funeral pyre. Sir Aimery was hanged, along with many other knights - four score they hanged there like thieves on the gibbets, some here, some there. Lady Girauda was taken, and she shrieked and screamed and shouted. They held her across a well and dropped her into it, I know this for certain, and threw stones on top of her. This caused great dismay. But the other noblewomen were all set free by a kind and courteous Frenchman,

---

1. By Simon de Montfort towards the end of May 1211.

who behaved most honourably. Many a bay and sorrel warhorse they took at Lavaur, good iron armour, ample supplies of corn and wine, and cloth and rich clothing, which pleased them all immensely.

Crusading finance

Laisse 72
All this enormous booty the count de Montfort owed to a rich merchant called Raymond of Salvanhac,[1] a wealthy native and citizen of Cahors. It was he who had financed the crusade, lending money to the count. Then in payment he received cloth, wine and corn; all the booty from Lavaur was handed over to him. Once they had taken this town, the crusaders subdued the surrounding country as far as Montferrand within a year.

Count Baldwin surrenders Montferrand

Inside Montferrand was brave Count Baldwin, valiant as Roland or Oliver. If he had enough land, as many other princes do, he would win plenty more before his day is done. His brother Count Raymond had stationed him in the castle of Montferrand, and if the place had been as strong as its name implies,[2] never in all their days would the French or Germans have taken it. Fourteen knights and a number of other men, how many exactly I do not know, are with Count Baldwin as he waits now for the proud French who are coming to besiege him.

Laisse 73
Count Baldwin is shut inside the castle. With him are a very valiant knight called Peter,[3] also the viscount of Monclar[4] and red-haired Pons of Toulouse;[5] fourth, Sir Hugh of Le Breil,[6] a very courageous man; fifth, Sancho Espada,[7] an excellent knight; and Raymond of Périgord, who is very much afraid, for he is one of the mercenaries and expects to die with them.[8] Outside among the besiegers is the count of Alos.[9] If all-powerful Jesus does not pay attention to them, they will all be dead or taken before sunset, for the castle is weak, unprovided, and has no defence.

Laisse 74
The crusading commanders now ordered all their men to go together and fill up the ditches. They did so, and you would have seen not a hundred but more than ten thousand men at work. They set up the catapults out there in the ravine and the knights and sergeants began their attack.

---

1. He had been funding the crusaders for almost a year; received the fiefs of Pézenas and Tourves during the siege of Minerve.
2. Iron Mountain.
3. Not identified.
4. Monclar-de-Quercy, a dependency of the county of Toulouse.
5. Either the Pons de Tolosa who died at Muret or another of the same name and nickname who presided over a judicial enquiry at Montauban in November 1214.
6. Probably from the neighbourhood of Moissac.
7. 'Sancho the Sword', became prior of the Knights of St John in Toulouse, 1225.
8. The crusade was directed against highway bandits as much as against heretics. As a captain of mercenaries, Raymond could only expect death.
9. Not identified. Perhaps the same as the count of Chalon, mentioned overleaf.

But brave Count Baldwin and his knights put up a stubborn defence. They threw blazing fire onto the brushwood in the ditch and burned it up; but the attackers immediately flung in just as much more. It was a great miracle almighty Jesus did for them in preventing their capture in this first attack.

The count de Montfort and many others were well disposed towards Count Baldwin. They heard good reports of him and were sorry for him, though they would not have given a walnut for the rest. Now the count of Chalon[1] behaved very well and sent out a crusader, who shouted loudly,

'My lord Count Baldwin, come out in safety, for my lord the count[2] is waiting here outside for you. All the barons want an agreement with you.'

I don't know why I should make a long story of it: when he heard these words, Count Baldwin went out. He was well aware that he had almost no defence left. Once it was settled, he surrendered the castle to them, with all the victuals, bread, wine and corn it contained. He and his men all came out with their arms and armour and swore on the holy Gospel that they would never in all their lives make war on crusaders or support the wicked race of misbelievers. The army at once left Montferrand and went back to the place it came from.

Other castles fall to the crusaders

Laisse 75
The army moved back to the area it had left and took Rabastens, Gaillac and Montégut as well as La Garda and Puycelci, places which all surrendered out of fear. Then the men of St Antonin arrived without shields or weapons and very sensibly made an agreement with the crusaders. Laguépie and St Marcel submitted. Now the crusaders have thoroughly subdued the whole of the Albigeois, and its bishop - a good and worthy man, so help me God - has come to a thoroughly satisfactory arrangement with them.

Bruniquel changes allegiance

But Count Baldwin, whom I mentioned to you, protected Bruniquel[3] and forbade its inhabitants to set fire to it, as they wanted to do for fear of the crusaders who were riding to attack them, and as Count Raymond would have been glad to do, if the townsmen in their grief and anxiety had listened to his advice.

Laisse 76
Valiant Count Raymond was in Bruniquel. Everyone inside the castle wanted to escape from it, but Count Baldwin told them privately to hand it over

---

1. John, count of Chalon-sur-Saône.
2. Simon de Montfort.
3. Baldwin was viscount of Bruniquel; his brother Raymond as count of Toulouse was its overlord. As we saw in laisse 74, Baldwin is in the process of going over to the crusaders' side. He had been born and brought up in France, where his mother Constance had gone to live after separating from her husband Raymond V in 1165, and he claimed that Raymond had denied him his proper share of his paternal inheritance. Guillaume de Puylaurens says that when Baldwin originally arrived from the north to join Raymond, Raymond refused to accept him as his brother and sent him back to France to obtain proofs of identity; quoted Meyer, *Chanson*, ii, p. xxxv.

to him, that he would protect them, but did not want to be under his brother's control. At this the knights and sergeants asked Raymond,

'My lord, is it your will that Baldwin should be our protector?'

'I shall do as you wish in this matter,' Raymond answered. In the sight of all present, he released them then and there from their oaths, and they made their agreement with Count Baldwin. Rich and poor, they all swore allegiance to him for the castle.[1] Afterwards Baldwin went to the crusaders, who were well disposed towards him, and asked them to give him their assurances. They said they would do so, on condition that he should hold by them; anything he should conquer with them should be entirely his own. All this they granted him without dissent, as long as he should help them.

Laisse 77

Having settled matters with the count de Montfort, good Count Baldwin rode to Toulouse to talk to his brother. Raymond had never much liked him or been willing to give him a brother's share or do him honour in his court. None the less Baldwin two or three times asked Raymond to promise on holy relics that he would stay with the crusaders. There was nothing more Baldwin could do. Not wanting to remain there any longer, he took leave of Raymond, and for the sake of his oath he rejoined the crusading army. Baldwin would never have wanted to make violent war on Raymond, if the latter had not so very wrongly had his castle of Bruniquel sacked.[2]

The crusade approaches Toulouse

The count of Bar[3] now arrived and the count de Montfort went to meet him. They stopped at Montgiscard and then returned to the army and sat down to supper. The count of Bar intended to besiege great Toulouse and they were all going to ride there together. On a Thursday morning[4] they broke camp and those who knew the way set off in front to guide them. As the army began to cross the ford across the River Hers, a messenger brought this news to Toulouse and Count Raymond and his men hurried to arms, as did the count of Comminges who had come to their support, the count of Foix and the mercenaries from Navarre. Five hundred knights there were, all arming, and countless foot-soldiers. If you had been in the town and seen all the activity, men putting on quilted jackets, lacing helmets, and fastening iron horse-armour and emblazoned trappings onto their mounts, you would have said that four armies together could not stand against them. Indeed, if they had had any courage or if God had helped them, I doubt if the crusaders could have borne the shock of their attack in the field.

Laisse 78

There was an unusual encounter near the bridge at Montaudran[5] after the army crossed the ford on its way to the town. Indeed, it was a full battle, for I am sure you would have seen more than a hundred and eighty dead on the two sides. In the gardens outside Toulouse there was neither count nor king[6] but

---

1. Transfer of homage from Raymond to Baldwin.
2. After Baldwin had obtained possession of it as described in laisse 76.
3. Theobald I, count of Bar and Luxembourg.
4. 16 June 1211.
5. Four km from Toulouse.
6. A set expression common in epic verse; there were no kings involved.

rode and struck so hard that you would think I was romancing if I described it to you. Some thirty-three villeins of the district died at the edge of a meadow near the barbican. Count Raymond's son Bertrand[1] was taken, I believe. He paid them a thousand shillings and all his armour; they got his horse, his arms and equipment and everything else he possessed.

The first siege of Toulouse

Laisse 79

Fierce and wonderful was that army, my lords, a proud and terrible host. They forced the river crossing and headed for Toulouse. No fear, no hindrance can stop them laying siege to the city on its strongest side. There are greater numbers inside the place, if only they were as strong! It is the flower and rose of cities all, but its men are not as brave as the crusaders, so the story says, and so it proves to be.

The crusaders attack

Laisse 80

The brave count of Bar opened the attack, together with the count of Chalon and their whole power. They brought up great boiled-leather shelters to protect them from quarrels and forced their way on towards the ditches, into which they swiftly flung large quantities of brushwood. Seeing this, the defenders hurried in great anxiety to meet their assault and fought so hard that more than a hundred were killed on the two sides and at least five hundred wounded. So bitter was the engagement that the count of Comminges, to my knowledge, lost a good knight there, Raymond At of Castillon,[2] mourned by many.

Now the crusaders drew off, taking nothing with them, for I promise you the good Toulousains[3] captured three of the big leather shelters, they did indeed. Knights and sergeants returned to their quarters and the men of Toulouse also withdrew. Patrols kept watch that night till dawn. The crusaders cut down all the vines, corn and trees they could find, everything that grew, and piled it into a heap near a gully. With that, they thought, they would surely be able to fill up the ditches as they intended.

Laisse 81

The crusaders, who are wise and valiant men, were afraid of attack from Toulouse, and all day long the nobles went fully armed. Each one protected his own quarters as best he could, this being their usual practice.

Sir Hugh of Alfaro[4] was inside the town. He was seneschal of the Agenais, a man of great courage and a very valiant knight. His brother, Sir Peter Arcès, was with him, and so were the pick of their family, all excellent knights,

---

1. A younger and probably illegitimate son of Raymond VI.
2. A cousin of the count of Comminges.
3. 'Toulousains' translates *Afozenc*, meaning subjects of the house of Alfonso, count of Toulouse, 1117-48, grandfather of Raymond VI. See M.-C., i, p. 193.
4. Originally from Navarre, husband of Guillemette, an illegitimate daughter of Raymond VI. We know nothing of his brother Peter, mentioned below. See M.-C., i, p. 195 for the appearance of their family name, well disguised, in medieval 'Pharaoh Street', Toulouse.

proud and fierce. These men armed themselves privately in their own quarters, but the count of Toulouse almost went out of his mind with rage. Because they were willing to take the risk of making a sortie, he thought they wanted to lose him his inheritance, and he forbade them to go out.

Laisse 82

The men in Toulouse would not endure this. Count or no count, they opened the gates and made a two-pronged attack on the besiegers. This was on a Wednesday morning, so I was told, just before terce, immediately after the crusaders had had their dinner. But the count de Montfort never took off his armour, nor did most of them lay aside their hauberks; and they ran to horse at once. What blows you would have seen struck on both sides, what spears ringing on helmets, what shields shattering - you would have said the world was coming to its end!

The Toulousains caused much grief by killing Sir Eustace of Cayeux.[1] He had ridden too far ahead, and died as he was trying to turn and get back to his own men.

Laisse 83

Very great was this encounter, Christ protect me! when the men of Toulouse and Navarre charged into the crusading host. You would have heard the Germans shouting aloud, all of them yelling, 'A Bar, a Bar!'[2] Sir Eustace of Cayeux was crossing a small bridge when he took a blow from an ash-hafted lance with a pennon patterned vair, a blow so heavy he could not get up again. The priest could not reach him in time to give him the last rites, there was no confession or penance. But it was only two days since he had done penance, so that I am sure Jesus Christ would forgive him. When the French saw him struck down, they all rode to his help, but the wretched mercenaries began to retreat when they saw the crusaders pressing forward. Well did they know in their hearts they could not stand against them. How light was their plunder, how easy to carry off! All they had done was kill a great lord for whom many would weep, a rich and powerful man. His vassals had his body taken to his own fief, where they would give him honourable burial.

29 June 1211, the siege of Toulouse abandoned

One morning early at daybreak the crusaders began to strike their tents. They had spent a fortnight cutting down the vines, but now they decided to move. Food was too dear, they could not get supplies: one loaf cost at least two shillings and made only a small meal. They had nothing to eat but beans, apart from any fruit they could find on the fruit trees. The whole army set off to go and attack the count of Foix and moved up to Auterive to cross the bridge.[3] They would spend the whole summer making war on him in his own lands; on this they were determined.

---

1. Probably from Ponthieu, Somme.
2. The count of Bar had brought a large number of German troops to the siege of Toulouse.
3. Over the Ariège.

Campaign against Raymond Roger, count of Foix

Laisse 84

The count de Montfort and most of the crusaders marched at daybreak to attack the count of Foix. At this point the count of Alos withdrew, as he had remained with the crusade a long time. He very much wanted to make an agreement with Toulouse, but could not, because of the French princes and lesser nobles, and because of the bishops, clergy and preachers, who spoke about the heretics and their insane error. (At least ninety-four of these fools and traitors were found concealed in a tower at Cassés, hidden away there by their friends the Roquevilles, in spite of their overlord.[1] I was told this by my lord Isarn, prior of the whole of Vielmorès[2] and that fief.)

After a long stay in the district of Foix doing all the damage it could, devastating foodstuffs, corn and arable crops, the army left that area when the hot weather came to an end, and the count de Montfort rode to Rocamadour.

The abbot of Cîteaux was staying in the cloister at Cahors, and was afraid to leave it. I doubt if he would have come out of it till Easter if the count had not gone to fetch him.

Laisse 85

The crusaders left, as I told you, and the count de Montfort began his journey,[3] going as he had promised to Rocamadour. The abbot of Cîteaux stayed, I believe, in Cahors with nobles of that district, and he begged and commanded them to pledge their faith to the count de Montfort, so that he should hold the fief. And he had letters written out on parchment which he sent into Provence to all his friends there. When the count moved on, the abbot joined him, and valiant Count Baldwin travelled with him too. They slept at St Antonin (which they later laid waste) and then went on to Gaillac.

Laisse 86

Returning, the count de Montfort slept at St Antonin, went by way of Gaillac to Lavaur, and then to Carcassonne, beyond Laurac. The abbot went to Albi and so up to Saissac. They were very apprehensive about Count Raymond, who was summoning his host from Toulouse, Agen and Moissac, from his whole fief and every district he possessed. He also sent a hundred thousand crowns in payment to Sir Savari,[4] who was bringing all his cavalry to join him from their quarters at Bergerac.

---

1. The Roquevilles, a noble family suspected of heresy, held the lordship of Les Cassés as well as other fiefs. See M.-C., i, p. 201. Their overlord was Count Raymond of Toulouse.
2. Isarn, not identified. The archdeaconry of Vielmorès was part of the diocese of Toulouse.
3. To take possession of the county of Cahors, whose bishop had done homage to him on 20 June 1211.
4. Savari of Mauléon, seneschal of Poitou for King John, who may have sent him to help Raymond VI, husband of John's sister Joan.

Count Raymond prepares an offensive

Laisse 87
When Count Raymond heard that the count de Montfort had dismissed his forces,[1] he summoned his host from every corner of his fief and sent to tell all his supporters to prepare at once.

Many great lords assembled: the count of Comminges, lord of St Gaudens, the count of Foix and many other barons all met on a certain day. The seneschal of Agen,[2] who has charge of Penne, and all the mercenaries set off, as did the men of Montauban, whom indeed I do not forget, and, may God bless me, of Castelsarrasin.

On a Sunday morning as day was breaking they heard that Sir Savari was on his way to join them. How delighted they all were - and how little did they know what the outcome would be!

Ah glorious God the Father, ah Mary, blessed Lady, did anyone ever see an army so strong or so well equipped as that of Toulouse, or cavalry like theirs? Here is the whole host of Milan, you would have said, here are the hosts of Rome and Lombardy and of Pavia too, when it was mustered out there on the plain.

Count Raymond takes the field

Laisse 88
Very great and marvellous, my lords, was the host of the count of Toulouse and of the city. Toulouse was there and Moissac, Montauban and Castelsarrasin, with Isla Jordan and the whole Agenais, not a man stayed behind. All the men of Comminges rode with them and the men of Foix, also Savari of Mauléon, welcomed with joy, as well as Gascons from Gascony and men from Puigcerda.[3] More than two hundred thousand they are, as they stand arrayed in the field. Villeins urge on the beasts pulling carts laden with bread, wine and other supplies; buffaloes and heavy oxen haul the catapults. 'Traitor!' most of them cry, 'son of a whore!' and threaten Count Simon and his men; there in Carcassonne they will besiege him by force, they will take him and skin him alive. Montréal and Fanjeaux shall fall to them, they say; they will ride in strength to Montpellier and as they come back they'll conquer Lavaur and the whole Albigeois.

Laisse 89
Great was the Toulousain army, God be my witness, when the French knights rode away from the Carcassès. In it were mercenaries from Navarre and from the Aspe valley,[4] more than a thousand mounted men and fifty and three; Gascons, men from Quercy and from Agen; banners raised, they rode for the Lauragais, not expecting to meet a living soul between there and the Biterrois.

---

1. Their forty days' duty done, the last German contingents had left for home from Rocamadour.
2. Hugh of Alfaro.
3. Vassals of the count of Foix from the most distant part of the Cerdagne.
4. Between Oloron and the Somport pass.

Count Simon gathers his troops

But the count de Montfort instantly summoned every Frenchman he could reach. He sent for the viscount of Donges, for my lord Bouchard who was in Lavaur, and for all the rest, near and far; for Martin Algai,[1] too, and to Narbonne for Sir Aimery;[2] they must all come. And come they did; no one dared disobey when Count Simon spoke.

Count Simon calls a conference

Laisse 90

The count de Montfort summoned his barons. On a certain day he was at Carcassonne, as the song says, and all around him were at least three hundred companions, all good fighting men and brave as lions.

'My lords,' he said to them, 'hear what I have to say. The count of Toulouse has summoned his vassals from all his own and his allies' fiefs. They number more than two hundred thousand, so the young man reports who was sent to me by the warden of Limoux. They are gathering at Montferrand and near Avignonet and they intend to besiege me - so brave they are! - wherever they can find me, upstream or down, here or there. I require your counsel: what do you advise me to do?'

Laisse 91

When the count de Montfort had spoken, Sir Hugh de Lacy stood up.

'My lord,' he said, 'since you ask counsel, let all who wish speak freely. Trust me, there is only one thing to do. If you shut yourself up in Carcassonne and they go after you, they will lay siege and keep you there, trapped. Go to Fanjeaux and it will be just the same. Wherever you go, they will track you down, and you will be defeated and disgraced till the end of the world. Believe me, you should go to the weakest castle you possess, wait for them to come up and then, once you have reinforcements, attack, and I am certain you will defeat them.'

'Excellent!' said the count. 'This is good advice. Whatever happens, you shall not be the worse for it, for I can see you have advised me well.' None of those present disagreed; on the contrary, there was a unanimous shout,

'My lord, he gives good counsel, we ask you to accept it.' Then they separated and went to their own quarters or their inn and so to bed till morning.

Count Simon in Castelnaudary

Laisse 92

Next day the count de Montfort and all his company were up at first light. Lances raised, they rode for Castelnaudary, and there they waited for the enemy.

---

1. A famous Spanish mercenary, brutal and brave; employed by Richard I; seneschal of Gascony and Périgord for King John; became lord of Biron by marriage; fought for Simon de Montfort but later for Raymond VI; taken by the crusaders at Biron and executed as a traitor (laisse 115). This Martin may be the same man as the Martinet le Hardi and Martin of Olite of laisses 108 and 109.
2. Aimery, viscount of Narbonne, did not obey this summons.

On a Tuesday morning after dinner the Toulousain army reached some fields only half a league away and encamped in the meadows by Castelnaudary. What shouting and hubbub rose from that mass of foreigners - a meeting, you would have thought, of heaven and earth! And God above, how many tents were pitched there that day, each crowned with its golden ball and its eagle cast in metal! They set the trebuchet up on a roadway, but neither on road nor path could they find stones which would not shatter on impact. They brought three from a long league away and with one they smashed a tower and with another a great hall. The third stone shattered, or it would have cost the townspeople dear.

Laisse 93

The count de Montfort, as I told you, had settled in Castelnaudary as all could see. Sir Bouchard and a number of others were at Lavaur, with the son of its castellan, a good and valiant man. There were at least a hundred knights, brave fighters all of them. Martin Algai was present with only twenty men; they rode straight to the count de Montfort at Castelnaudary, and so did the bishop of Cahors. Together they left Castres and rode towards Carcassonne, from which heavy loads of wine and corn were being brought to the count de Montfort, as well as baked bread, and oats, supplies for those inside the castle.

Now the count of Foix and his whole company sallied out along a dip leading from the Toulousain camp. All the mercenaries rode with him as well, vying with each other to join him. I doubt if a single knight of that army was left behind, or any of the good brave sergeants, except Savari and his Normans who stayed in comfort with Count Raymond.

Up rode Bouchard in good array and each party had a plain view of the other. The count of Foix arrayed his men, four hundred of them and more if the record does not lie. Bouchard had fewer men, I believe, in their helms and hauberks, whereas Foix and his allies numbered a good two thousand and had fast horses, hauberks or quilted jackets, strong shining helmets or good iron headpieces, sharp spears, strong ashen hafts and crushing maces.

Battle of St Martin Lalande

Now hear the clash of battle as the two forces meet, louder than any since Roland's time or since Charlemagne conquered Agolant and won Galiana, daughter of King Braimant, in spite of the courteous emir Galafre of the land of Spain.[1]

Laisse 94

Across the plain towards Castelnaudary ride Frenchmen from Paris and knights from Champagne. But the count of Foix blocks their way, he and his whole company and their Spanish mercenaries. They think Bouchard and his French not worth a chestnut and tell each other,

'Keep hard at it, don't rest till we have killed these foreigners, then they'll take fright in France and Germany, in Poitou and Anjou and throughout Brittany and up there in Provence, up to the Spanish passes, they'll all learn their mistake!'

---

1. This refers to a legendary adventure of Charlemagne; M.-C., i, p. 219, n. 4.

Laisse 95

As my lord Bouchard and his companions were moving towards Castelnaudary, a white falcon flew out on their left and crossed above them, flying strongly towards the right. At this Martin Algai said,

'By St John, my lord, however the day goes, we shall win. You and yours will hold the battlefield, but there'll be heavy losses first.'

'Good luck to us!' said Bouchard. 'I don't care a glove for that. As long as we keep the field, we shall win glory, dead or alive - the more dead, the greater the glory. And all who die like this will be saved. If we have losses, so will they, they will lose the best of their men.'

Laisse 96

The count of Foix rides with his troop towards St Martin de Lasbordes, for that is its name.[1] They carry their lances upright on the front saddlebows and as they ride across the fair wide plain they shout, 'Toulouse!' Crossbowmen loose bolts and arrows, and from the noise and uproar you would say the very sky was falling. They lower their lances, charge, and great is the encounter. 'Toulouse!' cry the Toulousains and 'Comminges!' the Gascons; others shout, 'Foix!' and 'Montfort!' and 'Soissons!' Gerald of Pépieux, riding with the count of Foix, one of the best of his knights, drives his sharp spurs into his charger's sides and encounters one of Bouchard's companions, a Breton, full in his way beside a wood. Through shield, through arm-guard and hauberk and deep into the rear saddlebow he struck, and his pennon was red with blood. That one fell dead unshriven. The French saw it with fury; angry as lions and like true knights they raced to the rescue.

Laisse 97

Like true warriors the French spurred on the hillside as hard as they could ride. My lord Bouchard bore a silk pennon with a painted lion[2] and sat a horse worth - I tell you the truth! - more than a hundred pounds. There on the road to Montréal they charged the mercenaries in one united attack and with their sharp swords did them great harm, leaving dead a hundred men who will never see Christmas again or be troubled by Lent or carnival. In that encounter an arrow struck the son of the castellan of Lavaur on the nasal and through the eyehole of his helmet. There and then he fell dead in front of the seneschal.[3]

Laisse 98

My lord Bouchard spurred, as I have told you, along the roadway and he and the French charged together into the thick of the oncoming host. Loudly they all shouted, 'Montfort!' and above the rest his voice cried, 'Holy Mary, blessed Lady!' Towards him at full gallop rode the count of Foix with all his lords. What broken shields you would have seen, what shattered lances strewn on the meadow, thick underfoot! How many fine horses, too, ran free with no one to hold them! Martin Algai, whatever anyone tells you, fled from this encounter with all his men, until the fight was won; and then he said

---

1. St-Martin-Lalande near Lasbordes, 6 km east of Castelnaudary.
2. The Montfort lion; Bouchard's own emblem was an eagle.
3. Presumably Hugh of Alfaro, seneschal of the Agenais.

he was returning from pursuit of the mercenaries. Thus each covered up his own villainous behaviour. (The bishop of Cahors and the unarmed men fled a full league away towards Fanjeaux; but that the bishop's companions should do this does not surprise me).

All the goods being transported were taken by these Toulousains, God curse them; but all they did was damage their own cause, for they pillaged right to the end of the battlefield and then fled, each immediately making off with his loot. (The good pacing mule belonging to Sir Nicholas,[1] the mercenaries took both it and his lad that day, but he himself escaped with the other clergy. I am very glad he did, may God bless me, for Master Nicholas is my dear friend and comrade.)

Laisse 99
The French spur on softly at a walk, all helmets closed. Don't think they will flee or turn back; they are not stingy, they'll give plenty of fine blows, well struck. The place is broad and fair, the fields level. Thin men and fat, French and Toulousain, on both sides they die, as Master Nicholas described it to me. The Toulousain army watches in terror, for it is beaten.

Count Simon sallies from Castelnaudary

Laisse 100
The count de Montfort, who was in Castelnaudary while those others were fighting so hard, ordered his own men who had come with him to hurry to arms and told them that their comrades who had gone out and my lord Bouchard had lost the supply convoy. He was well aware that their defeat would lose him both land and castle, he would be held there and blockaded and would never leave it except in defeat. As soon as he could he rode out, fully armed with lance and shield. Foot-soldiers remained inside the castle and would defend it until he and his men returned.

Defeat of the count of Foix

Laisse 101
The count de Montfort and the men from the castle rode to battle with banners flying. The men inside it shut the gates securely; if need be, they would put up a strong defence. When Foix and his allies saw them coming, they were dismayed; most of them knew that this meant defeat. That is what their mercenaries achieved by looting the battlefield. 'Montfort!' cried our French lords and, 'Holy Mary help us!'

Laisse 102
Eager to strike hard, his drawn sword in his hand, the count de Montfort spurred into battle along the trodden way, his men at full gallop behind him. All he could find he killed and took and slew. The wretched mercenaries and misbelievers were so terrified at the sight that they could do nothing to help themselves. Only the count of Foix fought back, and his shield was split and his sword notched from all the blows he had struck. His son Roger Bernard broke through the throng and so did the knight Sir Porada[2] who wielded a

---

1. Not certainly identified, perhaps the 'magister Nicholaus, phisicus et sacerdos' of a charter of 1217; M.-C., i, p. 227, n. 3.
2. A dispossessed knight from the Carcassès.

heavy mace; and Sir Isarn of Puylaurens[1] was in the thick of the fight. There they were, they and the other dispossessed knights, plucking the stork[2] and dealing out mortal blows. If the others had done as much, the battle would not have been so quickly lost nor Foix and his men defeated; that is my own opinion.

Laisse 103

The struggle lasted long enough, my lords. On both sides, friends of yours or enemies, many died, I promise you. The castellan of Lavaur lost three finer sons there than any count or king possessed.

There was panic in the Toulousain army in the meadows below Castelnaudary; every man was anxious to retreat. Savari shouted aloud,

'Stay calm, my lords, don't move! No one take down or fold his tent, or you are all dead men!'

'Ah, Lord God of glory, by your most holy law,' said each man to himself, 'keep us from shame, do not let us be disgraced!'

Laisse 104

When the count of Toulouse learned that the count of Foix and his men had been defeated, they were all sure they had been betrayed. They wrung their hands and said to each other: 'Holy Mary, blessed Lady! who ever heard of such a thing? We outnumbered them ten to one, I promise you.' Raymond of Ricaud was so terrified that he fled away to Montferrand in the sight of them all; then after a while, hearing that the count de Montfort had not attacked them, he came back again. But he never disarmed or undressed or went to bed that night or closed his eyes or slept, in good truth, that day or next.

Laisse 105

My lords, now listen, and may God bless you! and hear what the count de Montfort did next. Battle over and victory won, both he and Sir Bouchard cried aloud,

'Forward, my lords, attack! Their army's beaten!' Then all together they launched a strong assault on the tents and pavilions of the forces of Toulouse. These would have had no use for all the gold of Pavia if it had not been for the ditches they had dug. The crusaders' horsemen could not get through, they felt they were as good as dead, and told each other it would be madness not to withdraw, they had done enough already.

Before disarming, our French troops went by moonlight to ransack the battlefield. No one can describe the immense wealth they gained there; it will make them rich all their lives long.

Laisse 106

The count de Montfort went back into Castelnaudary, rejoicing at his success. In the morning at first light, when the French had gone, the Toulousain commanders ordered their men to arm, and they very quietly folded their tents and clothing and loaded the carts. They left the trebuchet

---

1. Possibly the Sicard, lord of Puylaurens, who shares in the defence of Toulouse (laisse 197), more likely a relative.
2. 'Plucking the stork' translates literally *pelan la grua*, but the meaning of the idiom is lost.

to the wind and rain; I don't think they would have brought it away with them for a hundred thousand marks of silver.

Puylaurens makes peace with Count Simon

The men of Puylaurens were in a state of great dismay, for they had sworn oaths and broken them. Immediately and before any others did so, at least five hundred of them went to Count Simon at Lavaur and made their peace. They had also been the first to renegue, so obedient were they to that insane belief.

Laisse 107
The count of Toulouse, son of Lady Constance, went away and took his troops with him. The French made no pursuit whatever, I am certain of this, for they had already hit them hard enough with lance and sword.

Revolts in the Albigeois and Quercy

The inhabitants of Rabastens, entirely trusting in these wicked heretics and their mad ideas, now renegued, for they were sure the crusaders would never reach them, and indeed, thought they had been defeated. So thought all those in the district who shared the hopes of the men I have just been telling you about.

Laisse 108[1]
As you have heard, the men of Toulouse went away angry, grieving and anxious. Wherever they went, they announced that the French had been defeated and that the count de Montfort had fled by night. They told such lies that Rabastens surrendered to them and so did Gaillac. And Count Baldwin, Jesus guard and guide him! was at Montégut with Martinet the bold.[2]

Sudden news came to them from Gaillac that the warden[3] of Lagrave had been murdered, that they should go there before the castle could be garrisoned, and that the citizens of Gaillac had been party to this killing. Baldwin and the others saddled up and rode fast for Lagrave as soon as it was light.

Laisse 109
Sir Doat Alaman[4] and the men of Gaillac saw Baldwin's banners blowing in

---

1. This and the next laisse are very succinct. The course of events seems to have been as follows: local men in Lagrave and Gaillac revolted against the crusaders, killing the French commander in Lagrave. Baldwin of Toulouse, Raymond's brother but supporting the crusaders, rode off towards Lagrave to deal with this. Inside Gaillac, Sir Doat Alaman and the other locals saw Baldwin's banner and mistook it for that of Raymond. But they then also saw the crusading banner of Martin of Olite, bringing his troops up the Tarn by boat, and understood the situation. 'Our men', presumably Baldwin's crusaders, were glad to see Martin's arrival. Martin and Baldwin together recaptured Lagrave, installed a garrison in its castle and returned to Montégut.
2. Martin of Olite, a mercenary commander from Navarre; perhaps the same as Martin Algai in laisse 89.
3. Pons of Beaumont, the French knight who commanded the crusading garrison in Lagrave.
4. Lord of two fiefs in the Albigeois.

the wind, and they were all delighted, for they could see the Raymond cross[1] shining as it blew and thought Count Raymond was arriving at the head of his men. But soon they realized that it was Baldwin's cross and they were sad and sorry. And then the banner of Sir Martin of Olite was seen floating up the Tarn, the opposite way to the Agout, towards Lagrave. How glad our men were to see it! They garrisoned the castle. Why tell you any more? Pons of Beaumont, the warden, died at cockcrow. The crusaders returned to Montégut one evening at sunset, and Count Baldwin went on at once to Bruniquel. He had lost Salvagnac, where there is good wheat, at which he was very angry.

Towns taken and retaken

Laisse 110
The Toulousain forces very soon returned[2] and valiant Count Raymond moved with his whole force to Rabastens; then they went up as far as Gaillac. He had regained it all: La Garda and Puycelci, a place he loved, St Marcel and Laguépie, he rode to each of these. Then the count besieged and took Parisot; the inhabitants of St Antonin returned to him; and before the month was out Montégut surrendered. Except for Bruniquel, he recovered them all. They were told, and by my belief in God above, they really thought that the count de Montfort had been driven off the battlefield and had fled to his native land, and that never in all their lives would they see any crusaders again, as most of them had been killed.

But before the year was half done, it was all very different, for the count de Montfort brought in Frenchmen. In Touelles, which surrendered to him, he killed every wretch he could find there. Next he crossed to this side of the Tarn, not by a ford but by the bridge at Albi. In two days he took Cahuzac and then sent to Bruniquel for Count Baldwin, who was glad to bring his cavalry to join him there.

Laisse 111
They stayed a week at Cahuzac because there was plenty of food in the town. This was at the feast called Epiphany, in the bitterest depth of winter. They laid siege to St Marcel and acted very stupidly, not achieving anything there worth a rotten apple, nothing but expense, may God bless me! Count Raymond held Montauban, and if he had wanted to, could easily have destroyed them, but he and his men were so much afraid of Sir Alan of Roucy[3] and Sir Peter of Livron,[4] Jesus bless them, that they made no attempt at an attack.

---

1. *La crotz ramondenca* (gules a cross clechée voided and pommetée or), the cross of the counts of Toulouse. See illustration on page 65.
2. From Castelnaudary, see laisse 106.
3. From Roucy (Aisne), vassal of the king of France and of the count of Champagne; a famous jouster.
4. A French vassal of the count of Nevers.

March 1212, reinforcements arrive for the crusade

On Easter eve[1] the bulk of the cavalry moved before dawn and withdrew to Albi because food was short and they could get no supplies; it remained there over six weeks. Then great companies of crusaders arrived from Germany and Lombardy, as well as men from the Auvergne and from Slavonia. One after another these forces set off. A league and half away Raymond's men saw them coming and did not wait for them to get any nearer.

Count Simon recovers the Albigeois

Laisse 112
The crusading host was enormous, as you heard me say. All over the country men fled; they had to abandon Montferrand and Les Cassés. All of them, I believe, went to great Toulouse; no one who could get away stayed in the area. The crusaders began to assemble up at the bridge of Albi. Neither Rabastens nor Gaillac could stop them settling wherever they pleased and so they fled, for a man must protect himself. The men of St Antonin were brave enough at first, relying on Sir Adhémar Jordan, but in the end no one there had any cause for joy. God bless me, never have I seen so many castles abandoned and captured with so little fighting. The crusaders promptly put their own garrisons into La Garda and Puycelci; you would not have found one man brave enough to sleep there, they all fled away by night.

Laisse 113
There was great noise and uproar in the crusading host; they were dismantling and razing St Marcel, I believe, and then they all quartered themselves in St Antonin. You would hardly have had time to cook an egg before they took the place that night.[2] The citizens lost at least twenty eight killed or drowned; ten managed to escape. Women and men all fled into the church, but every one of them was stripped and left naked. The clergy were robbed too, and the lads and servants caused them much distress.

Laisse 114
St Antonin was taken, as the song says. Sir Adhémar Jordan was led away captive, and so too were Sir Pons the viscount[3] and I don't know how many others. May the Lord God of glory never forgive me my sins, if while they were fighting, the clergy did not at the same time sing the *Sanctus Spiritus* in a great procession, so that you would have heard it half a league away.[4]

What more should I say, or why make a long story of it? One day the count de Montfort, the other barons and the army put spurs to their horses and rode away. They left Count Baldwin and his companions to garrison St Antonin, but first they went to take possession of Montcuq and its keep. The army travelled on and passed Tournon; blessed by God, it entered the

---

1. 24 March 1212.
2. 20 May 1212.
3. Not identified.
4. *Veni Creator Spiritus*. Crusading clergy used the weapon of prayer while troops made their assault.

Agenais. Arnold of Montaigu[1] and the other Gascons were well able to guide them in this region. They took Montcuq, which belonged to Count Raymond, and then did not stop until they reached Penne in the Agenais.

June and July 1212, siege and capture of Penne

They met with no resistance at all, except at Penne, which once belonged to King Richard.[2] They set siege all round it on a Tuesday.[3] There were many Frenchmen in the crusading host, many Normans and Bretons, there were Germans, Lorrainers and Frisians, many lords from the Auvergne and important Burgundians, but the castle was strong and its defenders thought them not worth a button. The crusaders brought up mangonels, catapults and battering rams. Inside Penne were Sir Hugh of Alfaro from near Aragon, Bausan the captain of mercenaries, Sir Bernard Bovon, Gerald of Montfabès[4] who is warden of Montcuq and a crowd of others whose names I do not know.

They set the siege after Ascension and it lasted, as the song says, until September and the time of the vintage.[5]

Laisse 115

It was a very great siege, so Jesus Christ keep me! and the castle was too strong to storm. The crusaders from the Barrois[6] hurled so many stones from their big mangonels that they almost breached the walls. Inside there were many knights, many mercenaries, many from Navarre. Sir Hugh of Alfaro held it for Count Raymond.[7] Certainly, if they had had food and drink, the besiegers would still be outside, unable to get in. But the heat was tremendous and they could not endure it. Thirst tormented them and made them ill; the wells had dried up, which alarmed them; and every day they saw the besieging forces growing larger and never less.

When they saw Count Guy[8] arrive, together with Sir Foucaud of Berzy riding a dappled grey and his brother Sir John[9] clad in ermine and miniver, the precentor of Paris[10] who preaches so well and many more barons than I can tell you, and on their side they could find no succour - then, however reluctantly, they were compelled to surrender the castle.

The count de Montfort had it well repaired and enclosed on all sides with mortar and lime. I shall not describe the encounters that took place there, for

---

1. Lord of Montaigu-de-Quercy, 6 km south of Tournon. In laisse 116 he is made castellan of Biron.
2. Penne and the whole of the Agenais had come to the counts of Toulouse as the dowry of Joan, sister of Richard I, when she became Raymond VI's third wife in 1196. She died in 1199.
3. More probably on a Sunday, 3 June.
4. The three knights last mentioned are not identified.
5. From early June to late July, according to Peter of Les Vaux de Cernay.
6. Germans from the Rhineland.
7. He had expelled the civilians, burned the town, and was holding the castle with 400 men.
8. Guy de Montfort, Simon's brother.
9. Foucaud and his brother John came from Berzy-le-Sec (Aisne). Guillaume de Puylaurens describes them as valiant, harsh and cruel; M.-C., i, p. 259.
10. Probably William of Nemours, archdeacon of Paris; see laisse 63, n. 5.

the song is a long one and I do not want to linger; I have broken my thread and will take it up again.

Once the castle had fallen, they did not want to stay there any longer than was necessary, so they had the tents and pavilions struck and loaded onto carts and then went away towards the sea,[1] to Biron. This belonged to Martin Algai and was the base from which he rode out to raid. Périgord and Saintonge had come to our crusade to complain about this.

A mercenary captain executed

Laisse 116
Count and crusaders rode along the highway, the oriflamme borne aloft, to the castle of Biron which they took at once. They put Martin Algai to a shameful death, dragged out by a horse, that is the proven truth, and then hanged in the meadow in the sight of all. They then entrusted the castle and the whole district to Sir Arnold of Montaigu. Next morning they went back towards Moissac, travelling at a good three leagues a day, the troops well arrayed and making all possible speed. Count Simon sent for my lady the countess, a brave and intelligent woman, and she joined them at Catus, bringing fifteen thousand good fighting men with her. They stopped overnight at Catus, which had surrendered to Count Baldwin and our crusaders.

The army gathered at Penne in the Agenais. Next morning at dinner time it reached Montcuq; the following day it was at Moissac after the bells rang for terce.[2] A strong body of mercenaries had arrived the night before and was now inside the town.

Moissac invested

Laisse 117
The citizens of Moissac watched the crusaders encamp around them beside the Tarn, and it is no wonder they were dismayed. If it were not for the mercenaries, they would have been glad to make an agreement.[3] They knew very well that in the long run they could not hold out. They could have escaped through the vines - what is a vintage not yet harvested when compared with life? - and three of them did so, I assure you, and never lost a pennyworth by it. But no one can change what is to come.

Castelsarrasin makes terms

The inhabitants of Castelsarrasin[4] managed to save themselves like the worthy, loyal and upright men they are, against whom there is never a word spoken. They understood that if Count Raymond recovered his fief and made

---

1. *Pres de la mar* may come in for the sake of the rhyme. The crusaders travelled north-west into Périgord, and could have reached the Atlantic if they had continued a good deal further.
2. At about 9 a.m., 14 August 1212.
3. The citizens of Moissac had sent to Toulouse for mercenaries to help defend them; M.-C., i, p. 263 n. 2.
4. 8 km from Moissac.

an agreement with the pope, or if the king of Aragon succeeded in overcoming the crusaders, defeating them in battle and driving them off the field, then he would recover them too at the same time. That being so, they had no intention of getting themselves slaughtered. They followed the example you heard me mention, that of the citizens of Agen who had already surrendered.

'Of two evils,' said Bernard of Esgal,[1] 'one must always choose the less. If you are going along a path and see your companion fall into the mud, or if you are crossing a ford, don't lead the way but keep in the middle, so that if you see anyone drowning, you can go back at once.' For that reason, so help me God, the men of Castelsarrasin must not be blamed, as their garrison on whom they ought to have relied, Gerald of Pépieux and all his knights, had gone out of the castle and away along the Garonne; he said he would stay there neither for gold nor coin.

Now the crusading army is about to slaughter and maltreat the men of Moissac and capture their town.

August 1212, the siege of Moissac

Laisse 118
Was it misfortune or justice that the citizens of Moissac refused to make any kind of peace at the time Penne was taken? I do not know. Never in all their days did they think their town could fall, and the Toulousains who had entered it kept exhorting them and stirring them up to resistance.

The archbishop of Reims[2] sat robed in miniver on a brown cushion inside his tent. The count de Montfort was there, with the precentor of St Denis,[3] and so was the countess, who sat in front of them. Many other barons sat beside them, including Sir William of Contres, beloved of God, Sir Peter of Livron who prays much in church, and Sir Lambert of Limoux. He was wearing a shirt of Phrygian silk because of the heat. These all recommended that Moissac should be besieged and they sent for the army.

Laisse 119
At the beginning of September, when August was over, they laid vigorous siege to Moissac on all sides. Count Baldwin spent freely there; many a goose did he eat and many a roast capon, so his warden and the provost told me. Siege engines and cats were set up. There was wine for sale in plenty and no shortage of other supplies.

Laisse 120
Conflicts during this siege were frequent and fierce. The mercenaries inside Moissac harried the crusaders, who very often killed many of these wretches. Count Baldwin, Christ Jesus keep me, lost a young nobleman killed: neither hauberk nor vental could save him, for a quarrel drove through his guts as into a sack of straw.

The count de Montfort now ordered his men to go and fetch timber for his many carpenters to dress. He and all his companions rode with them fully armed, in case of attack.

---

1. Not identified.
2. Aubry, archbishop of Reims.
3. The abbey of St Denis, burial place of the kings of France, stood just north of Paris.

Laisse 121

Count Simon and the other barons had catapults set up, a cat built and a battering ram made. This hammered day and night against the town wall. Inside Moissac the town's defenders raged and sorrowed. One day they all took arms quietly, secretly, and then spurred out in a furious sally, carrying firebrands and intending to burn the cat. 'To arms!' shouted the French and Burgundians, and out from their quarters came Poitevins and Gascons, with Flemings and Lorrainers, Normans and Bretons. Many were the hauberks and good quilted jackets they put on, many the silk and brocaded surcoats. And the count de Montfort came spurring across the levels, his lion displayed on coat-armour and shield. Close by a copse they killed his warhorse under him and he would have been taken then and there but for William of Contres, the Lord God be good to him, and his comrade my lord Moreau.[1] This is an excellent knight, valiant and courteous, daring, handsome and good. Fast to the rescue rode Peter of Livron and Sir Foucaud of Berzy, together with Count Guy de Montfort. They charged all together and with such impetus that they brought the count off in spite of his attackers. He suffered a slight wound at the back [of his foot]. The archbishop's nephew was captured by four lads, who killed him instantly.[2]

Laisse 122

My lords, that was a great and wonderful encounter. When the French, Bretons and Normans came up, the mercenaries at once fled back into the town. The archbishop mourned his dead nephew.

Encounter near Montauban[3]

Next morning before the bells rang for terce,[4] a number of crusaders were riding from the direction of Cahors. The men of Montauban, who were watching the roads, sallied out and attacked them from front and rear. News of this came quickly to the siege and Count Baldwin and all his companions hurried to arms. Armand of Mondenard,[5] who has a good fast horse, and the sons of Hugh of Le Breil, valiant men all of them, pursued and surrounded these men, and captured eight good horses. One was an iron-grey, and went to a crossbowman.

Laisse 123

Brave Count Baldwin and all his knights returned to their quarters the same evening. At Moissac the catapults battered the walls all day long, breaking them down and opening breaches, so that it is not surprising the defenders took fright, for they could expect no help from anyone. It was a full month since the count of Toulouse had gone to see Savari at Bordeaux and he never got a pennyworth of good out of doing so, except that he recovered his son and paid a large sum over to Savari.[6]

---

1. Not identified.
2. The archbishop of Reims. His nephew's name is not known.
3. This attack on the crusaders is not mentioned elsewhere.
4. Terce, about 9 a.m.
5. Mondenard is in Quercy about 15 km north of Moissac.
6. Savari had failed to obtain payment for his services from Count Raymond, so had taken young Raymond prisoner and held him hostage until the count paid up.

The walls of Moissac are breached

I return to my subject and do not intend to leave it. Let me tell you briefly of a miracle that Jesus the righteous did for the crusaders: a great section of the wall now fell into the moat and opened a way in.

No need to ask you if the citizens were terrified when they saw this, and the mercenaries too. They tried to make an agreement with the count de Montfort, but he swore by all the saints of the Holy Land that he would not let one of them escape alive unless they handed over the mercenaries who had caused them so much trouble. I don't know what more I could tell you if I talked all day, except that they loved their own selves better than wife or brother, cousin or kinsman.

8 September 1212, surrender of Moissac

Laisse 124
One fine morning Moissac surrendered to the crusaders and the mercenaries were made prisoner and taken away. By St Martin, I believe they killed more than three hundred of them, and took possession of their armour, horses and packhorses. The citizens paid over a hundred marks of pure gold in ransom. All their neighbours in the district were terrified. My lord William of Contres received Castelsarrasin, Count Baldwin was given Montech and Sir Peter of Cissey had Verdun on the Garonne. Then the crusaders set off for Montauban.

Roger Bernard holds Montauban

Laisse 125
The son of the count of Foix rode from the Puigcerda region with a hundred knights and entered Montauban. This is a very strong place; no one has ever seen a town in flat country so well defended or with such deep ditches. The great men of the crusade, those who controlled it, saw that summer was ending and winter drawing on and that Montauban's defenders were no more afraid of them than of an acorn. Furthermore the abbot of Pamiers and one of his chaplains kept telling them all day long that they would lose Pamiers, that its garrison would surrender unless it had immediate relief, for the men of Saverdun had cut off all their supplies of wine and bread, and their vines had gone unharvested, I believe, for more than a year.

The crusaders subdue Gascony and Béarn

For this reason they all moved in that direction, setting off next day and travelling by long stages. They went by way of Auterive, where the Germans from the Carcassès joined them, with many a rich pennon and many an oriflamme.

Laisse 126
At the sight of these banners the men of Saverdun came down out of the castle and fled at full gallop; and with them rode the count of Foix, who had gone there expecting to be safe. I need not tell you all this at great length: throughout the whole of Gascony the crusaders entered wherever they wished: St Gaudens and Muret, castle and keep, Samatan and Isla Jordan,

right across to Oloron, they conquered everywhere, and in the fief of Gaston of Béarn too, for except when they entered Foix they met with no resistance.

Winter 1212-13

Then when it seemed good to them they went home to their own countries, having completed their forty days' duty and won their pardons. That winter they rested. Count Simon guarded his fief well, he and his brother Sir Guy. Then he called an assembly to which many barons came, with many bishops and other worthy men. All the castellans of his fief attended in response to his summons.

Conference at Pamiers, 1 December 1212

Laisse 127
Many clergy attended the meeting at Pamiers, many great bishops and mighty lords. You must know that they laid down the customs and usages to be prac-tised in these wide lands and had them drawn up in charters and sealed letters.[1] After that they returned to their own lands.

Exploits of William of Contres earlier in 1212

Cheerful and contented, the wise and valiant Sir William of Contres left the count de Montfort and arrived in the meadows near Muret on the feast of St Denis.[2] Peter of Cissey rode with him, as did Bernard Jordan,[3] who was born in La Isla. Bernard remained in his own town while the others went on after a halt at La Isla and reached Verdun, where they dined.

Next day the mercenaries[4] took to the roads and swept right up to the moat of Castelsarrasin, capturing many sheep and much other plunder. They were reck-oned to number more than a thousand, all mounted. The alarm no sooner ran through the country than Sir William of Contres at once put on his armour, as did my lord Moreau who rode at his side, and Sir Peter of Cissey, who was soon ready. Once arrayed, they were no more than sixty, but few as they were they put the plunderers to flight and hunted them all the way to Montauban, drowning many in the Tarn. Nightfall deprived the crusaders of their prey; their horses, too, were exhausted. They untied the captives and set them free, and recovered the plunder.

Laisse 128.
William of Contres did battle with the robbers, he recovered all the plunder and took booty from them as well. Back they rode then, he and his whole

---

1. The statutes of Pamiers dealt with much more than William thinks it necessary to record: feudal relationships between local inhabitants, the Church, French barons and Simon de Montfort; ecclesiastical independence, the repression of heresy; weights and measures, tolls; matters of marriage and inheritance, especially the right of primogeniture. They were intended to establish the customs of Paris and the Ile de France instead of southern written law. See M.-C., i, p. 281, n. 3.
2. 9 October 1212.
3. Husband of Indie, sister of Raymond VI. Co-operates with the crusaders in 1215 and 1217, but as soon as Simon is dead, hands over his town of La Isla to young Raymond, and in 1219 comes to defend Toulouse against Louis of France.
4. Supporting Count Raymond.

company, rejoicing at the goods they had won. Lances raised, they came to Castelsarrasin, and did not reach their quarters till after midnight or eat until almost morning. I am sure they slept until the bells rang for terce.

On another occasion the mercenaries took the field and overran the whole of the Agenais. Their troop could hardly move for the weight of stolen goods. Sir William of Contres was not pleased at this and led his whole company out to the attack. Many were the blows struck with lance and sword, many the broken hafts strewn on the reddened ground, many the wretches you would have seen lying there open-mouthed, bloody and dead. Not one pennyworth of plunder did Sir William let the robbers keep. He and the resolute men he had brought here from Burgundy and France utterly defeated them all.

Laisse 129

William of Contres, as I told you, defeated all the mercenaries, recovered their plunder and captured their horses and pack animals. They ravaged the country around Castelsarrasin on another occasion, but I promise you they never got away with anything belonging to him, not so much as would cost two coins from Poitou; on the contrary, they were beaten and flung themselves into the Tarn. Sir William's horse was struck by five or six darts, and Sir William fell to the ground in the sight of all his friends. Valiant man that he was, he leaped to his feet, grasped his sword and shouted his warcry, 'St Denis!' the Paris cry. My lord Moreau spurred his fine costly charger and
all the others rode up to help him. In the mêlée and confusion they were not sure they could save him or prevent his capture. 'God help us!' they shouted and 'St Denis!' Then you would have seen many a squire of his company killed and his warden severely injured. But Sir William mounted a spirited horse, charged the mercenaries and thrust them back, right into the waters of the Tarn; and then he began to laugh about his fall.

Laisse 130

My lords, God did many great miracles for Sir William of Contres, a man who took so much trouble that everyone who saw him liked him at once. Certainly no better man ever came here on crusade from Burgundy, nor ever will, unless a still richer and greater lord arrives.

King Peter of Aragon prepares for war

I return to my subject. King Peter of Aragon gave one of his sisters to the count of Toulouse, and afterwards married another to his son, in spite of the men on this side.[1] Now he went to war, and said that he would bring at least a thousand knights, all paid by him, and if he could only find the crusaders, would face them in battle. And we, if we live long enough, shall see who wins and we will set down what we recall, we will continue to record the events we remember as long as we have matter to write and until the fighting is done.

---

1. Eleanor of Aragon married Raymond VI in 1204; (William was there; laisse 15). The marriage of Raymond (VII) and Sancha of Aragon was agreed in 1205. 'The men on this side', presumably of the Pyrenees, are the crusaders, angered by this marriage.

Laisse 131

Many a blow will be struck and many a lance broken before the fighting is done or peace returns, many a new banner will lie on the meadow, souls be driven from their bodies and noble widows left desolate.

Peter, king of Aragon, rode out with his household; he summoned his men from his entire kingom and gathered a great and noble company. He announced to them all that he intended to go to Toulouse to fight against the crusade because it was wasting and destroying the whole country. Furthermore, he said, the count of Toulouse had appealed to their compassion to prevent his land being burned and laid waste, for he had done no harm or wrong to any living soul.

'And as he is my brother-in-law, my sister's husband, and I have married my other sister to his son, I will go and help them against these accursed men who are trying to disinherit them.'

End of the section written by William of Tudela

6 The cross of the counts of Toulouse and the Montfort lion

The Song continued by William's successor

Peter is still speaking

Laisse 132

'The clergy and the French are trying to disinherit my brother-in-law the count and drive him out of his fief. No one can point to any crime or any sin he has committed; they are simply trying to eject him for reasons of their own. And I ask my friends, I ask those who would do me honour, to concentrate now on preparing arms and equipment, for in a month's time I intend to cross the passes together with all those of my companies who are willing to join me.' And they replied,

'This must indeed be done, my lord. Never can we oppose any wish of yours!' Then they separated and went to make their preparations; each man did all he could, bargaining and raising loans, to get armour and equipment together. And the king commanded them all to have the pack-beasts and carts loaded up, for it would soon be summer, they would find the fields and meadows growing green again and the vines and trees putting out fresh leaves day by day.

July 1213, Count Raymond captures Pujol

While the king of Aragon was busy with his preparations, the count of Toulouse considered going to recapture Pujol, and spoke about this to the Capitol.[1] Its members all replied:

'Yes, certainly, let us do that.' Immediately they had it proclaimed throughout the town that everyone should go out along the road by the mills, and they mustered in the Montaudran meadows.

'My lords,' said Count Raymond, 'I have called you here because I have been having careful watch kept on my enemies. They want to destroy us, they will harass us so that we cannot get this year's harvest in. And look how near you they are: they are this side of Lanta.'[2]

'My lord,' said the people, 'let us go and surround them, for with God's help you will have plenty of companions. We are all armed, we shall be able to cut them to pieces. And the valiant count of Foix, God save and keep him, and the count of Comminges, they can join you, and the Catalans too, who have come here to help you. We are all well equipped; let us move fast before those drunkards can find out and get away.'

Laisse 133

The French soldiers have entered Pujol and the great count of Toulouse has surrounded them. With him are the count of Foix, his valiant son Roger Bernard, the count of Comminges, nobly equipped, and the Catalans brought by King Peter, as well as the men of Toulouse who came with all speed, knights, citizens and commoners. First a wise lawyer[3] spoke, a member of the Capitol and an eloquent man:

---

1. The 24 consuls or *capitoliers* who dealt with the administrative and judicial affairs of Toulouse.
2. Lanta is 6 km west of Pujol; the crusaders were 13 km from Toulouse.
3. Master Bernard, mentioned by name in laisses 191 and 204.

'My lord, great count and marquis,[1] if it please you, listen; and you too, all you others gathered here:- We have brought up the catapults and other siege weapons so as to fight hard against the enemy, for I trust in God we shall defeat them quickly, as we are in the right and they are in the wrong. They are destroying our inheritance before our very eyes. I tell you this, my lords, and you may know it for truth: we have seen letters and sealed missives sent us by dear friends of ours: if we do not defeat those men before tomorrow evening, they will receive help and strong reinforcements, well equipped knights and armed sergeants, and they will do us great dishonour and a double injury if we go away without cutting them to pieces. We have plenty of crossbows, plenty of feathered quarrels. Let us fill up the ditches, and let us make sure our deeds are equal to our words! Now let us all go together to get branches and sheaves of corn, let us fetch enough to fill the ditches. For inside that castle are the flower of all the crusaders and if we can take them, we shall bring down the pride of Sir Simon de Montfort who has sworn such oaths against us. Now let us show why we are gathered here, let us go and fetch filling for the ditches!'

Laisse 134
At once the whole host went to get the filling; not one knight, citizen or sergeant but instantly shouldered a load. Into the ditches they tossed it and filled them up to the foot of the walls so that then they could sap the stonework with massive picks. But the French fought back, they flung down blazing fire and a torrent of rocks and great dressed stones and after that boiling water which fell on their armour. When they felt that, the attackers drew back, shaking themselves, and said to each other,
    'It's worse than the itch, this hot water of theirs!' And the archers shot so close that none of the French dared be seen, or else he would be hit in the jaw or teeth. The siege engines, too, kept working and to such effect that no one could pause on the roundwalk without falling, tumbling, covered with blood or mortally wounded; they had no shelter, neither galleries nor battlements were any good to them. Then the knights of Toulouse shouted aloud,
    'At them now, citizens, they're yielding!' Therepon they took the town and all its streets. Every Frenchman there, rich or poor, they seized without mercy and put to the sword; a few they hanged. Sixty of their knights died there, great, valiant and courteous men, as well as squires and sergeants.
    Now a messenger arrived, an experienced man, and in a low voice told the Capitol privately, that Sir Guy de Montfort was coming, furious and spurring hard, that he had reached Avignonet, was riding fast and would attack them if he found them still there. Then very cheerfully they sounded the trumpets for retreat, 'for we are well revenged on our enemies.' Back they all went to Toulouse, rejoicing at their success.

Laisse 135
They rejoiced at their success, all the men of Toulouse and their friends. When Sir Guy de Montfort heard that the Frenchmen were dead he was grieved to the heart; he could not hold back his tears, but wept and mourned and bitterly lamented his shame and disgrace.

---

1. Raymond VI count of Toulouse was also marquis of Provence, and, see below, duke of Narbonne.

September 1213, Peter II at Muret

Now let us leave them, for I want to tell you about the good king of Aragon who has ridden his thousand-shilling horse to Muret; he has planted his banner before it and laid siege to the place. Many great vassals has he brought from their fiefs; the flower of Catalonia and gallant fighters from Aragon ride with him; nothing, they think, can stand against them, no warrior oppose them. And the king sent to Toulouse to tell his sister's husband to bring his allies and join him at once; let Raymond come with his army and every fighting man, for he was ready to restore his fief to him, and theirs too to the count of Comminges and his kinsmen. Then he will ride in strength to Béziers; not one crusader will he leave in castle or tower between Montpellier and Rocamadour, all shall die in pain and sorrow. Hearing this, Raymond did not delay a moment but went straight to the Capitol.

Count Raymond joins King Peter before Muret

Laisse 136
To the Capitol went Raymond, count, duke and marquis; he told them that the king had arrived, had brought troops and laid siege to Muret; outside it stood tents closely arrayed; he had the French trapped; 'and we are to bring catapults and all the Turkish bows,[1] and when Muret has fallen we shall go into the Carcassès and, God willing, recover the fief.' And they replied,

'Excellent, my lord count, if it can finish as well as it began. But the French are hard men and dangerous, they are resolute, lion-hearted, and very angry at their loss at Pujol where we killed and wounded so many of them. We must be sure we make no mistakes.'

Then the count's trumpeters blew: the whole host must go at once, fully armed, to the king of Aragon at Muret. Out across the bridges went knights, citizens and the town's militia, and very soon they reached Muret - where they would leave so many weapons, so much fine armour and so many courteous men! This was a tragedy, so help me God, one that diminished the whole world.

Laisse 137
It diminished the whole world, be sure of that, for it destroyed and drove out *paratge*,[2] it disgraced and shamed all Christendom. Now listen, my lords, and hear how it happened.

The good king of Aragon was at Muret, well prepared, and so was the count of St Gilles[3] with all his lords. The citizens and militia of Toulouse set up the catapults, attacked Muret on every side and forced their way into the new town.[4] They pressed the Frenchmen so hard that these all retreated into the castle and took refuge in the keep.

---

1. A short curly-shaped bow of great strength, rare in the west, perhaps introduced from Spain; L. Paterson, *World of the Troubadours*, p. 52.
2. *Paratge* stood for nobility, rightness, honour - see Introduction p. 7.
3. Count of St Gilles, another of Raymond's titles.
4. On Tuesday 10 September 1213.

Then a messenger reported to the king: 'My lord king of Aragon, the men of Toulouse have taken the town, if you will allow it; they have torn down houses and demolished buildings and driven the Frenchmen up into the keep.' When the king heard that, he was not at all pleased. He went at once to the consuls of Toulouse and told them on his authority to leave the men of Muret alone.

'For we should be fools to capture them now. I have had sealed letters telling me that Sir Simon de Montfort will be here in arms tomorrow. Once he is inside there, and my cousin Nunyo[1] has arrived, we'll surround and assault the town and take them all, every Frenchman and crusader. They will never recover, and *paratge* will shine resplendent. But if we capture the garrison now, Simon will get away across the other counties, and if we go after him, we shall have all the work to do twice. Far better if we agree to let them all come in, and then it will be us who hold the dice and we shan't let them go until the game is played out. I want you to tell them this.'

Laisse 138
The young gentlemen went at once to tell the commune's council to pull the militia out of Muret and to forbid any further damage to barricades or defences; they must leave the besieged men alone and go each man to his own tent; these were orders from the good king with the heart of an emperor, because Sir Simon would be there before evening and he wanted to capture him there and nowhere else. And when the men heard this, they all came out and went to the tents, each to his own fireside, and there, great men and small, they ate and drank.

After they had eaten they saw the count de Montfort and his standard advancing over a hillside with many other Frenchmen, all mounted, and their swords and helmets made a glittering crystal of the riverbank. Never, I tell you by St Martial, were so many good men seen in so small a force. Through the marketplace into Muret they rode, and went like true lords to their quarters, where they were well supplied with bread, wine and meat.

Aragon, Toulouse and the other lords confer

Next morning when it was light the good king of Aragon and all his captains met out of doors in a meadow to hold council. The counts of Toulouse and Foïx were there and the count of Comminges, true-hearted and loyal, as were many other lords, with Sir Hugh the seneschal, the citizens of Toulouse and all its craftsmen. The king spoke first.

Laisse 139
The king spoke first, for he knew very well how to do so.

'My lords,' he said to them, 'hear what I want to tell you: Simon is here and he cannot escape. You must realise this: we shall give battle before evening. Be ready, each one of you, to lead your men and to give and take hard blows. If they had ten times the numbers, we should make them turn and run!' Then the count of Toulouse spoke:

---

1. Nunyo was the son of Peter's uncle Sancho, count of Roussillon, Cerdagne and Conflent. He was probably bringing troops from these counties, but did not arrive in time for the battle.

'My lord king of Aragon, if you will listen to me, I would like to tell you my opinion and what is best for us to do. Let us plant barricades round the tents so that no cavalry can get through; then if the French try to attack, first we use crossbows to wound them and then as they swerve aside, we make our charge and rout them all.' At this Michael of Luesia[1] said,

'In no way can I approve of the king of Aragon's ever doing anything so improper. And it is a great pity that you who have lands to live on should have been such cowards as to lose them.'

'My lords,' said Count Raymond, 'all I can say is, be it as you wish, for before nightfall we shall see who is last to quit the field.' Then they cried, 'To arms!' and all went to arm.

They spurred fast towards the gates, herded the French back inside them and flung their lances through the gateway. Attackers and attacked struggled across the threshold, they threw darts and lances and gave great blows; both sides made blood spurt so freely that you would have seen the whole gate dyed scarlet. As the attackers could not manage to get inside, they withdrew to their tents and all sat themselves down to dinner.

Inside Muret, however, Simon de Montfort had orders given in every house: to saddle up and have the horse-covers[2] put on, and they would see if they could take their assailants by surprise. He ordered them all to the Salles gate, and when they were outside it he addressed them:

'Barons of France, my lords, this is all I can say: every one of us came here to risk his life. All last night I lay awake thinking, I did not rest, did not close my eyes, and this is my decision: we must take this path and make straight for their tents, as if to offer battle. And if they come out to attack us, and if we cannot draw them a very long way from their tents, then there's nothing we can do but run all the way to Auvillar.'

'Let us go and try it,' said Count Baldwin.[3] 'And if they come out, be sure and hit hard. Better death with honour than a life of beggary.' Then Bishop Fouquet signed them all with the cross, William of Les Barres[4] took command and divided them into three companies with all the banners in the lead, and they rode straight for the tents.

Count Simon's charge; death of Peter II

Laisse 140

Across the marshes and straight for the tents they rode, banners displayed and pennons flying. Beaten gold glittered on shields and helmets, on swords and hauberks, so that the whole place shone. And when the good king of Aragon saw them, he and a few companions rode fast to confront them. All the men of Toulouse came hurrying up, paying heed to neither count nor king.[5] They had no idea what was happening until the French rode up and converged on the king, once he had been identified. And he shouted, 'I am the king!' but no one heard him and he was struck and so severely wounded that his blood spilled out on the ground and he fell his full length dead.

---

1. From Aragon, a hero of Las Navas de Tolosa; died fighting by Peter's side at Muret.
2. *Las cubertas*, thick protective coverings.
3. Raymond's brother, hanged 1214. See laisses 1 and 75.
4. William des Barres, Simon de Montfort's young half-brother. His father had married the widowed Amicia of Beaumont and Leicester, countess de Montfort.
5. This is a set phrase meaning that they attacked pell-mell, with no discipline.

When the rest saw this, they counted themselves lost and fled away, some here, some there, not one put up any resistance. And the French rode them down and hunted and harried them so fiercely that anyone who escaped alive thought himself the happiest of men. The fighting continued as far as the stream, and the Toulousains who had stayed in the tents were all overcome by panic. Sir Dalmas of Creixell[1] plunged into the river and shouted,

'God help us! Great injury has been done to us, for the good king of Aragon is dead and defeated and so are many other lords, all defeated and killed. No one has ever suffered such a loss!' Then he made his way out of the waters of the Garonne. And the Toulouse militia fled every one of them, great and small, to the river and crossed it - those who could. Many never left it, for the current ran fast and it gripped and drowned them. All their possessions remained in the camp. News of this disaster echoed round the world, for so many men lay dead; great indeed was the loss.

Laisse 141
Great was the loss, the sorrow, the disaster, when the king of Aragon and so many others lay bloody and dead. It dishonoured the whole of Christendom, it dishonoured all humanity. And the men of Toulouse, those that survived and were not still lying there, went home sad and sorrowful into their walled city.

Very cheerful and happy, Sir Simon de Montfort kept the place of battle, from which he gained much armour. He shared out and allocated all the plunder.

Count Raymond leaves the country and Toulouse surrenders

But the count of Toulouse was angry and sorrowful, and in private he told the Capitol to make the best agreement they could. He himself would go to the pope and make his complaint, for Sir Simon de Montfort in brutal cruelty and through evil devices had driven him out of his own fief.

Then he left his fief, and so did his son. The unhappy and defeated Toulousains made an agreement with Simon and swore him their oaths. They also and on proper conditions returned into the Church.

Louis prince of France in Toulouse

Meanwhile the cardinal[2] sent to Paris to tell the son of the king of France[3] to come with all speed, and come he did,[4] lively and cheerful, and together they made their entry into Toulouse, took possession of the town and its buildings and joyfully installed themselves there among its paved streets.

'Let us be patient,' said the men of the town. 'Let us quietly endure God's will, for he can help us, he is our protector.' Then the son of the king of France consented to evil as he, Sir Simon, the cardinal and Sir Fouquet secretly planned together to have the whole town sacked and then set on fire.

---

1. From Creixell near Tarragona in Catalonia, a close associate of the king.
2. Peter of Benevento, sent as papal legate to Languedoc and Provence in January 1214.
3. Louis, aged eighteen, son of Philip Augustus.
4. At the end of May or beginning of June 1215.

Sir Simon, being a harsh and evil man, reflected that it would do him no good to destroy the town; it would be better to have all the gold and silver for himself. They agreed to have the ditches filled in so that no fighting man, however well armed, would be able to put up any defence; all the towers, walls and battlements were to be razed right down to the foundations. Thus it was decided and judgment declared.[1] Sir Simon kept control of all the fiefs of the count of Toulouse and of his supporters; through wicked lies he lost his inheritance. And the king's son went back to France.

Laisse 142

The king's son received a warm welcome from his father and the others, who cherished and made much of him. He had ridden into France on his Arab horse, and now he told his father the king how well Sir Simon de Montfort had succeeded and how rich and powerful he had become. But the king said nothing, he answered never a word.[2] I think they will die for this fief, Sir Simon and his brother Sir Guy, clever as they may be.

Count Raymond and young Raymond in exile

Now let us return to the valiant count who went away a landless man. Harsh have been his trials both by land and sea, yet God and the Holy Spirit brought him safe by miracle to harbour. With but few companions, he and his young son arrived in Rome, where they met with much joy and told each other that God should be their guide. There too were that fine speaker the count of Foix, Sir Arnold of Villemur,[3] a man of good courage, and bold Sir Peter Raymond of Rabastens.[4] And there are many others too, great and resolute men who will uphold their right, if it is refused them, when the full court assembles.

Rome: the Fourth Lateran Council, November 1215

Laisse 143

The court of the lord pope, a truly religious man, was now assembled, and great was the noise that rose from it. This was the council and assembly of the prelates of the Church; cardinals, bishops, abbots and priors were summoned to it, and so were counts and viscounts from many countries.

The count of Toulouse was there with his fine handsome son, who had arrived from England with very few companions. He had passed through many dangerous places as he travelled across France, for noble Sir Arnold Topina[5] brought him there secretly. So he reached the holy city of Rome.

---

1. At Carcassonne, at a meeting of the cardinal, several bishops, Simon de Montfort, Prince Louis and other crusaders. Simon was to hold the lands *in commendam* until the general council summoned by the pope gave its decision.
2. As early as 1208 Philip had written to the pope reserving his rights as feudal overlord in the event of any ecclesiastical expropriation of the count of Toulouse.
3. Two men of this name shared the lordship of Saverdun in 1203. Raymond VI later made one of them his seneschal of Toulouse.
4. One of several co-suzerains of Rabastens, brother of Pelfort, like him an active adherent of Raymond VI; probably related to the deposed bishop of Toulouse mentioned in laisse 10.
5. Not certainly identified; perhaps from Agen.

The pope ordered the boy's absolution, for never was a more charming child born of woman. He was alert, intelligent and well behaved, and of better descent than anyone of these or former days, being sprung from France, from England and from Count Alfonso.[1]

And the count of Foix, that valiant and delightful man, was there as well.

Down on their knees they went before the pope in order to recover the lands of their forefathers. The pope watched the boy and his behaviour, was aware of his lineage and understood the errors of the Church and clergy who opposed him. Grief and anger moved his heart to pity and he sighed and shed tears. In that place, however, neither right, faith nor reason did the counts any good.

But the pope, who is an able and intelligent man, made it clear to the whole court and to all the barons, both in writing and in honest speech, that he did not consider the count of Toulouse guilty of any sin which should cause him to lose his fief or be thought a miscreant, but that he believed him to be Catholic in word and deed. Yet because of the agreement made between the two of them and from dread of the clergy, whom he feared, he took his fief from him and assumed control of it himself, and he wished it to be held by Sir Simon; in trust only, for in no other way should it be given him. Count Raymond was very angry at this, for a man who loses his land suffers deeply.

Now, at the right time and season, the count of Foix stood up before the pope and spoke at length, as he well knew how to do.

Laisse 144

Well he knew how to speak, for he had both sense and knowledge. As he stood on the paved floor and delivered his speech, the whole court listened, watched and paid attention. He was a fine figure of a man, with a fresh complexion. Approaching the pope, he addressed him eloquently:

'My lord and true pope, on whom the whole world depends, you who stand in place of St Peter and wield his authority, in whom all sinners must find a protector, whose duty it is to uphold right, peace and justice, because you are set here for our salvation - my lord, hear what I have to say and restore to me all my rights! For I can defend myself and can truly swear that I have never been a friend to heretics or their supporters. I want no friendship with them nor would my heart allow it, and holy Church has found me obedient. I have come to your court for true justice, I and the mighty count my lord[2] and his son too, who is a fair child, good, intelligent and very young. And since the law does not accuse him, reason does not reproach him, since he has done no wrong to any living soul, I am astonished that any honest man can endure this boy's loss of his inheritance.

The mighty count, who is my overlord and lord of great honours, placed himself and his fief in your mercy, he put Provence, Toulouse and Montauban into your hands.[3] These were then given up to torture and death, to his worst and most cruel enemy, Sir Simon de Montfort, who binds and hangs

---

1. Young Raymond, now 18, was descended from the kings of France through his grandmother Constance, and from those of England through his mother Joan. The name of his great-grandfather, Alfonso Jordan, comes in for the rhyme and represents the house of Toulouse.
2. Raymond VI.
3. At Narbonne in April 1214.

there, who destroys and devastates, a man devoid of pity. It is only since they were placed in your care that they have come to danger and death. And I myself, great lord, at your command surrendered the castle of Foix with its mighty battlements. That castle is so strong it defends itself, and there was bread there, and wine, meat and corn and sweet clear water under the hanging rock and my noble company and much shining armour; I feared no assault. The cardinal[1] knows this and can bear witness. If it is not returned to me in just the same condition as I surrendered it, let no one ever again trust in any fine agreement!'

The cardinal rose and answered well. Drawing near the pope, he said:

'My lord, every word the count says is true. I received the castle and I did indeed entrust it to the abbot of St Thibéry,[2] who in my presence installed a garrison.'

Laisse 145

'The abbot of St Thibéry is a good and able man, the castle is very strong and it is well provisioned. The count has fully obeyed God and yourself.'

At that the bishop of Toulouse sprang up, eager to give his eloquent reply:

'My lords,' he said, 'you have all heard the count of Foix declare that he is free of this heresy and untainted by it. But I tell you that his fief is its major root, that he has cherished, supported and been gracious to them, that his whole county is crammed and seething with heresy, that the peak of Montségur[3] was deliberately fortified so that he could protect them, and he has made them welcome there. And his sister[4] became a heretic when her husband died and she then lived more than three years at Pamiers where she converted many to her evil doctrine. And your pilgrims, who were serving God by driving out the heretics, mercenaries and dispossessed men, he has killed so many of them, slashed and broken and hacked them in two, that their bodies lie thick on the field of Montgey,[5] the French still weep for them, and it is upon you that the dishonour falls! Out there at the gateway rise the moans and cries of blinded men, of the wounded, of men who have lost their limbs or cannot walk unless someone leads them! He who broke those men, maimed and tortured them, does not deserve ever to hold land again!'

Sir Arnold of Villemur jumped up. Everyone watched and listened attentively, for he spoke well and was not in the least afraid.

'My lords, if I had known this complaint would be raised and such a noise made about it in the court of Rome, there would certainly be more men with no eyes or noses!'

'By God,' they said to each other, 'that's a brave fool!'

'My lord,' said the count of Foix, 'my great right, my true loyalty and my honest mind are my defence. Let the law judge me, for then I am safe, as I have

---

1. Peter of Benevento.
2. Berenger, abbot of St Thibéry near Pézenas, Béziers, Hérault. The abbot's nephew, also Berenger, commanded the garrison.
3. Montségur, 'Mount Safe', must have seemed impregnable. Its abrupt peak towers over the surrounding countryside to a height of 1207 metres.
4. Esclarmonde, sister of Raymond Roger count of Foix, widow of Jordan of La Isla Jordan, made her profession as a Cathar 'perfect' at Fanjeaux in 1204.
5. In 1211. See laisses 69 and 70.

never befriended heretics, neither the believers nor the clothed.[1] On the contrary, I offered, gave and made legal donation of myself to Boulbonne,[2] where I was warmly welcomed and where all my ancestors offered themselves and are buried. As for the peak of Montségur, the law there is clear, for I have never for one day been its overlord.[3]

If my sister has done wrong, I ought not to be destroyed for her fault. And her right to remain in the fief was laid down: before he died the count my father declared that if a child of his were suffering in any place, that child should return to the land where it was brought up and should there be given whatever was needed and be made welcome.

And I swear to you by the Lord who was stretched out on the cross that no good pilgrim or traveller to distant Rome making the good journeys ordained by God has been attacked, robbed or killed by me, nor his path invaded by any troops of mine. But those robbers, those traitors and oath-breakers adorned with the cross who have destroyed me, neither I nor mine have laid hold on one of them who has not lost his eyes, his feet, his fingers and his hands! And I rejoice to think of those I have killed and regret the escape of those who got away.

And I tell you that the bishop,[4] who is so violent that in all he does he is a traitor to God and to ourselves, has gained by means of lying songs and beguiling phrases which kill the very soul of any who sing them, by means of those verbal quips he polishes and sharpens, by means too of our own gifts through which he first became an entertainer, and through his evil teaching, this bishop has gained such power, such riches, that no one dares breathe a word to challenge his lies. Yet when he was an abbot and a cowled monk, the light was so darkened in his abbey that there was no goodness or peace there until he was removed. And once he was elected bishop of Toulouse, a fire has raged throughout the land that no water anywhere can quench, for he has destroyed the souls and bodies of more than five hundred people, great and small. In his deeds, his words and his whole conduct, I promise you he is more like Antichrist than a messenger from Rome.'

Laisse 146

'Since Rome's messenger[5] has acknowledged to me that the lord pope is going to return me my inheritance, then let no one think me a fool if I want to recover the castle of Foix, for God knows how carefully I shall keep it! My lord cardinal knows the truth, that I made it over to him readily and in good faith. But a man who keeps for himself what he holds in trust is guilty both in reason and in law.'

'Count,' said the pope, 'you have declared your rights very well, although you make rather little of ours. I will investigate your character and your claim and then, if the claim is valid, you shall recover your castle exactly as you handed it over. If God has inspired your penitence and holy Church receives

---

1. *Ni crezens ni vestitz* - see laisse 2 for the two categories of Cathar, the supporters and the fully committed. The latter, the 'perfecti', were also called *vestitz* because of the dark clothes they wore.
2. The counts of Foix were generous patrons of the Cistercian abbey of Boulbonne near Mazères (Ariège), which was also their burial place.
3. Montségur was a dependency of the viscountcy of Béziers and Carcassonne.
4. Fouquet, a brilliant troubadour before he took the cowl; see laisse 44, n. 5.
5. Peter of Benevento, cardinal and legate.

you as one condemned, you must find mercy. Every sinner whom the Church discovers in danger, every wicked man lost and in chains, she must welcome warmly, provided he repents from a true heart and does her will.'

The pope's decision

Then to the rest he said, 'Hear this decree, for I want everyone to know what I have ordained: Let all my disciples walk in the light, let them bring fire and water, forgiveness and clarity, sweet penitence and true humility, let them bear the cross and the sword with which they will do careful justice, let them bring good peace on earth, maintain chastity, righteousness and true charity; let them do nothing that God has forbidden. Whoever adds to this or preaches anything further, disobeys my words and my intention.'

Raymond of Roquefeuil[1] shouted out,

'My lord, true pope, have pity on the orphan child, young and in exile, son of the honoured viscount whom the crusaders and Sir Simon de Montfort took charge of and then killed.[2] Wrongfully and shamefully he was martyred and *paratge* brought low, brought down by a third, by a half, and yet you have no cardinal or abbot in your court who believes more truly in the Christian faith than he did. As they have killed the father and disinherited the son, do you, my lord, give him his fief and keep your own dignity! And if you refuse to give it him, may God do you the grace to add the weight of his sins to your own soul! If you do not appoint a short day and give him the fief, then I myself claim it, I claim the right and the inheritance from you on the day of judgment when we shall all be judged.'

'Barons,' they said to each other, 'how well he has laid his accusation!'

'Friends,' said the pope, 'this shall certainly be seen to.' Then he and his associates went into his palace, and the counts were left standing on the inscribed marble floor.

'There now,' said Arnold of Comminges,[3] 'haven't we done well? We can all go home, for we have driven the pope indoors.'

Further lobbying

Laisse 147

The pope went from his palace into a garden, to subdue his anger and refresh himself. The prelates of the Church came before him in a body, all arguing with each other and seeking his support. Urgently they blamed the counts, and said,

'My lord, if you return the fief, we are as good as dead. If you give it to Sir Simon, we shall be safe.'

'Excuse me, my lords,' said the pope, 'I am thinking.' He opened a book and

---

1. A vassal of the Trencavels.
2. Raymond of Roquefeuil is appealing on behalf of the Trencavel child born in 1207, son of the viscount of Béziers who was imprisoned by Simon de Montfort and died in 1209 (laisse 37). The boy's inheritance was transferred to Simon in 1211. His cousin the count of Foix later took charge of him.
3. A nephew of the count of Foix, brother of Roger of Comminges.

chanced on a text[1] which showed that the lord of Toulouse could come safe to harbour. 'My lords,' he said, 'this is the problem: how without right or reason can I do so great a wrong to the count, a true Catholic, as to disinherit him unjustly, how can I take away his fief or transfer his rights? I see no justification for such an action. But I do agree to this: that Sir Simon should have all the land which belongs to heretics, except that of widows and orphans. This I confirm to him, from Le Puy to Niort[2] and from the Rhône to the Spanish passes.' Every bishop and prelate there utterly disagreed with the pope's decision.

With these restrictions he granted the fief to the count de Montfort. Later for this same fief they killed Simon at Toulouse, they filled the world with light and set *paratge* free. And I can assure you, Sir Pelfort[3] was better pleased than Bishop Fouquet.

Bishop Fouquet's speech

Laisse 148
Fouquet our bishop stands there before them all and addresses the pope as humbly as he can:

'My lord, true pope, dear Father Innocent, how can you thus covertly disinherit the count de Montfort, a truly obedient son of holy Church, one who supports yourself, who is enduring such wearisome strife and conflict and is driving out heresy, mercenaries and men of war? Yet you take from him the fief, its lands and castles, which he has won by the cross and his own bright sword, you take away Montauban and Toulouse if you separate the lands of heretics from those of true believers and of widows and orphans, and that is not the smaller share. Never have such cruel sophisms or such obscure pronouncements been declared, nor such absolute nonsense! What you have granted Count Simon is in fact a disinheritance, for you favour Count Raymond, you accept him as being Catholic, wise and good, and the counts of Comminges and Foix just the same. And if they therefore are Catholic and you so consider them, you do indeed take back from Simon the fief you had granted, for what you have given him is nothing, does not exist.[4] No, give him the fief complete and entire, make it over unconditonally to him and to his heirs. But if you do not give it him, if he does not hold it in its entirety, may it be swept from end to end by flame and the sword! If you take it away from him because of these Catholics and deny it him for their sake, I who am your bishop swear to you in all truth that not one of them is Catholic, not one keeps his oath.[5] And if after that you condemn Count Simon, you make it very clear that you reject his friendship and have no discretion!'

---

1. Divination by means of *sortes*, forbidden as pagan by St Augustine and others, was none the less much used in medieval times.
2. Niort (Belcaire, Aude) is the rhyme word; the place was a well known Cathar stronghold.
3. Pelfort of Rabastens, brother of Peter Raymond (laisse 142), a defender of Toulouse in 1218 and 1219 (laisses 194 ff.).
4. Fouquet is complaining that in upholding the claims of the widowed and orphaned heirs of heretics, and in declaring the counts of Toulouse, Foix and Comminges to be good Catholics, the pope is taking away from Count Simon with one hand what he has given him with the other.
5. The promise to expel brigands and heretics from his lands.

The archbishop of Auch[1] spoke:

'Great and dear lord, consider the bishop's words, for he is wise and able. It would be unjust and damaging if Sir Simon lost the fief.'

Cardinals, bishops and archbishops, three hundred of them, said to the pope,

'My lord, you are making us all into liars! We have proclaimed and told everyone that Count Raymond lives an evil life and therefore ought not to hold any fief.'

The archdeacon of Lyon defends Count Raymond

The archdeacon of Lyon[2] on the Rhône was seated there. He rose and said to them emphatically:

'My lords, this accusation is displeasing to God, for Count Raymond was the first to take the cross, he has defended the Church and obeyed her commands. If the Church who ought to protect him now makes this accusation, it is she who incurs the guilt, we who are shamed. And you, my lord bishop, you are so harsh and cruel that by your bitter words, which disgrace us all and yourself more than anyone, you are driving more than five hundred thousand people away in sorrow, their bodies bloody and their spirits weeping! And even supposing we had all sworn on holy relics to be enemies of Count Raymond along with all these others who are so fierce against him, all that is needed is for the lord pope to show justice and mercy. Let him do so, and then the count's honoured son, kin to such great houses, will no longer be deprived of his heritage and forbidden redress.'

'My lords,' said the pope, 'it is not right for me to be swayed by your harsh intentions or by your bitter and cruel preaching, delivered in spite of me and without my knowledge, nor by your purposes, for never, I most sincerely assure you, have any words passed my lips to suggest that Count Raymond ought to be condemned. My lords, penitent sinners are welcome in the Church! If ignorant fools accuse the count, if he has ever done anything displeasing to God, he has given himself into my hand with sighs and tears in order to do what we direct and obey our commands.'

Next the archbishop of Narbonne[3] came forward and said, 'My lord, mighty and honoured father, now you abound in wisdom. Give judgment, govern, do not be afraid, do not let fear or money affect you!'

'My lords,' said the pope, 'judgment is made. The count is Catholic and has behaved honestly, but Sir Simon is to hold the fief.'

The pope gives his decision

Laisse 149
'Let Simon hold the fief, if God has promised him it. And let us declare the law, now as at first.' And he spoke and pronounced judgment so that all could hear him: 'Barons, I say that Count Raymond is truly Catholic and if the body is sinful or has erred, yet if the spirit grieves at this and makes moan,

---

1. Garcias de l'Ort, a Benedictine; bishop of Comminges 1210, archbishop of Auch 1211, a zealous enemy of heretics.
2. Although we do not know his name, we do know that he was excommunicated in 1217 and deposed in 1218 'for daring to defend heretics'; M.-C., ii, p. 65, n. 5.
3. This is Arnold Amaury, former abbot of Cîteaux.

if it condemns the body, its guilt must be lifted from it. And I am astonished that you recommend me to assign the fief to the count de Montfort, for I see no reason in law obliging me to do so.' Master Tecin[1] said,

'My lord, the good faith of the count de Montfort who has so successfully driven out heresy and defended the Church ought to ensure that he holds the fief.'

'Master,' said the pope, 'what strongly outweighs that consideration is the fact that he destroys Catholics just as much as heretics. Serious complaints and bitter accusations reach me every month. Good is being brought low and evil exalted.' Men got to their feet by twos and threes all over the court and came forward to ask the pope:

'My lord, great pope, are you aware of the facts? The count de Montfort went to the Carcassès to destroy the wicked and bring in the good, he drove out the heretics, the mercenaries and Vaudois,[2] and brought in Catholics, Normans and Frenchmen. And then with the cross he conquered the whole of Agen and Quercy, the Toulousain and Albigeois, strong Foix and Toulouse and Montauban; all these he put into the hands of the Church and the Church accepted them. For her sake he has given and taken so many blows, spilt so much blood with deadly swords, embarked with vigour on so many actions, that it is neither right nor reasonable to take it away from him now, nor to let it seem possible that this could happen. No, if anyone tried to do so, we would defend him.'

'Barons,' said the pope, 'I cannot but be troubled by the pride and malice now seated among us. It is our duty to govern in good law all that exists, yet we welcome evil men and cause good men to perish. Even if Count Raymond were condemned, which he is not, why should his son lose his inheritance? Remember that Jesus Christ, who is lord and king, said that the son is not guilty of the father's fault.[3] If Christ said that, are we to say that he is? There is no cardinal, no prelate, however skilled his arguments, who can condemn that saying and not be wrong!

Here is another fact you have all forgotten: when the crusaders first entered the Biterrois to destroy the land, and Béziers was taken, the child was so young and so innocent he could not tell good from bad, he would rather have had a little bird or a bow or a snare than a marquisate or dukedom. Which of you then will accuse him, innocent as he is, and cause him to lose fief, rents and revenue? Consider too his lineage, of the best blood that can or does exist. And since this youngster has a courteous heart, since no facts or written evidence accuse him, what voice will sentence him to be lost, and to live on other men's riches? Shall not God, reason and mercy stand by such a one, who ought to be giving alms, not taking them? For a man who depends for his life on another's wealth is better dead or never born at all.'

On all sides the prelates urged the pope:

'My lord, don't be afraid! Let father and son go where fate decrees, but assign the land to Count Simon and let him hold the fief!'

---

1. See laisse 1, n. 5.
2. See laisse 8, n. 2.
3. Part of the epistle for the first Friday in Lent: 'The soul that sinneth, it shall die. The son shall not bear the iniquity of the father, neither shall the father bear the iniquity of the son.' Ezekiel XVIII: 20.

Debate on the status of young Raymond

Laisse 150

'Since I cannot get it back from him,' said the pope, 'let Simon hold and rule the fief. Let him keep it well if he can, so that no one trims any of it away, for I shall allow no public speaking on this subject.' At that the archbishop of York[1] said:

'My lord, great pope, just and true saviour, Sir Simon de Montfort may have sent his brother[2] here to you with Bishop Fouquet as speaker, but the count de Montfort's inheritance will never amount to much, for the king's noble nephew[3] can lawfully trim much of it away. Even if he is unjustly stripped of his father's fief, he must in law and reason keep his mother's, for I have seen the deed in which the notary has written that the dowry is authorised by the court of Rome, and this court has final authority in matrimonial affairs. The child is in no way condemned, he is not lost or a sinner, he is the legitimate son, nobly born, of good family and better lineage than anyone can describe - is he to go wandering through the dangers of the world like some wicked thief? Then indeed would *paratge* be dead and mercy of no effect!'

'No,' said the pope, 'that must not be so. I shall give him as much land as seems right - the Venaissin and the lands formerly dependent on the emperor[4] - and if he truly loves God and his mother the Church and is not proud or false to them, God will give him back Toulouse, Agen and Beaucaire.' The abbot of Beaulieu[5] spoke:

'My lord and giver of light, your son and dear friend the king of England, who became your vassal[6] and sincerely loves you, has told you in a sealed letter and by a spoken message to be mindful of mercy and of the sentence pronounced on Darius.[7] Now send him joyful news that will fill his heart with light'!

'Sir abbot,' said the pope, 'there is nothing I can do. Every one of my prelates speaks against me, so that I keep my own feelings hidden in my heart, for the king's nephew finds here neither friend nor protector. But I have often heard it said that a young man of courage, one who can give generously, can endure suffering and act with energy, will regain his lost home. If the boy is valiant, he will know very well what to do, for the count de Montfort is never going to befriend him, he will not behave like a father to him nor the boy to him like a son.'

---

1. The manuscript reads *larsevesq's dobezin*, which Martin-Chabot emends to *larsevesq's deborvic*, i.e. *d'Eborvic* = 'of York'. Walter Gray, chancellor of England since 1205, was confirmed as archbishop of York at this time. Another possibility is Henry of London, archbishop of Dublin, who is also known to have been present at this council; M.-C., ii, p. 73 n. 4.
2. Guy de Montfort.
3. Young Raymond, son of King John's sister Joan.
4. The marquisate of Provence, lying on the left bank of the Rhône between the Isère and the Durance, had belonged to the empire as part of the former kingdom of Arles.
5. Hugh, abbot of the Cistercian house of Beaulieu, Southampton, was attending the council as one of King John's three envoys.
6. On 15 May 1213 John did liege homage to the pope for England and Ireland.
7. In the twelfth-century *Roman de Thèbes*, the traitor Darius the Red receives forgiveness and his forfeited estates.

For that true prophet Merlin[1] foresaw the stone that was to come and the one who aimed it, so that on all sides rose the shouts and cries: 'May it strike the man of sin!'

Laisse 151
May it strike the man of sin and may God protect the rightful holder of the fief and withdraw his shield from the other!

Foix and Toulouse talk with the pope again

Now the lord pope returned from giving judgment, together with the prelates of the Church who had forced him to confirm the count de Montfort in possession of the fief.[2] The court had risen, its members were taking leave, and the count of Toulouse went to do the same, together with the count of Foix, a man who could both speak and do. They found the pope ready to listen to them. Count Raymond bowed deeply and said:

'My lord, true pope, dear to almighty God, I am astonished that anyone can declare it lawful that I should be disinherited, when I am not guilty of any offence for which you ought to condemn me. I placed myself in your mercy in order to recover my fief and now I am tossed among the waves, I can find no shore, I do not know which way to turn, by land or sea. Nor can I think it was ever supposed that I should go begging my bread through the world! Everyone will rightly be amazed to see the count of Toulouse a prey to all dangers, with no town or burgh of my own to which I can withdraw. When I made Toulouse over to you, I expected to find mercy. If I held it, I should lodge no complaint. Yet it is because I delivered it to you and did not refuse it that I am put in danger and forced to beg your pity. Never did I expect nor ought I to imagine that in the hands of holy Church I should meet such disaster! Your words and my own thoughts made me behave so stupidly that now I do not know where to go or which way to turn. How just is my anger when I think that I who used to give alms must now receive them! And the boy, not capable of doing wrong, you order his fief to be taken from him and want to drive him out! You who should rule by mercy and *paratge* - be mindful of *paratge* and of God! Do not let me be destroyed, for it will be you who are to blame if I have no place where I can survive.'

The pope listened, looking at him with compassion and feelings of self-reproach.

'Count,' he said, 'you must not despair, for I know very well what to do. Give me a little time to consider, and I will make good your right and my own wrong. Though I have disinherited you, God can reinstate you; though you suffer, God can bring you joy; you are defeated, but he can restore you; you walk in darkness, but he can give you light. He has power to take away and to give, so that you must never despair of him in anything. If God

---

1. No such prediction appears in Geoffrey of Monmouth's list of prophecies uttered by the legendary sixth-century Merlin, but later collections attributed to him include the death of a giant besieging Jerusalem or perhaps Narbonne, who is struck by a stone; M.-C., ii, p. 77, n. 7.
2. On November 30 1215 Innocent III declared that Raymond VI had fallen into heresy and his lands must remain under Simon de Montfort's control for the present. He also made Raymond an annual allowance of 400 marks, while he obeyed the Church, and made provision for lands to provide an income for Raymond's wife and son.

allows me to live so that I can reign in justice, I will so maintain and exalt your right that you will have no reason whatever to blame God or myself. And as for those evil men who seek to accuse me, it will not be long before you see me get my revenge. May you leave here in the firm hope that if your claim is valid, God will help and support you! And leave your son here with me, for I want to consider how I can get him an inheritance.'

'My lord,' said Count Raymond, 'to your holy care I commit myself, my son and my whole concern.'

The count of Foix recovers his castle

The pope signed him with the cross as he took leave, and the count of Foix stayed behind to claim his rights. The pope ordered that his castle should be given back to him.[1]

Christmas 1216, Foix and Toulouse leave Rome

Then both father and son were sad, the son because he was remaining in Rome and the father because he was leaving. Count Raymond left Rome at daybreak and reached Viterbo in time for the feast day.[2] The count of Foix joined him there as night was falling and they celebrated the holy day together. Then Count Raymond rode on to watch beside St Mark and do honour to the holy evangelist and his blessed body.[3] From there he went to Genoa, where he waited for his son whom he had left behind in Rome.

Young Raymond leaves Rome

Laisse 152
The boy stayed behind in Rome, not at all willingly, for he could see nothing there to give him any comfort, nothing but his enemies, to whom he could do no harm. But he had the sense to conceal what gave him most pain. Indeed he remained forty days at court in order to look and learn, to listen and find out how the pope would behave towards him. Then Peter Raymond of Rabastens said to him,

'My lord, we can do nothing more in this court. The longer we stay, the more I think we shall suffer.' William Porcellet[4] said,

'My lord, let us go to the lord pope and find out what is to happen to us.'

'I shall be glad to do so,' said the boy. When the pope saw him, he seemed to sigh, took him by the hand and made him sit down. The boy addressed him as follows:

'My lord, true pope, it is time now for me to go, and as I cannot stay any longer and you refuse to tell me anything more, it is for God, yourself and mercy to maintain me. For I do not possess enough land to jump across and as you are my father and the person who should support me, I hope you will show me what road I can take without perishing.'

---

1. Raymond Roger did not get his castle back at once; it was restored to the care of the abbot of St Thibéry. The pope, however, did order Simon and the crusaders not to make war on the count of Foix or on Roger of Comminges.
2. Christmas.
3. At Venice, St Mark's city.
4. Of a well-known family of Arles.

'Son,' said the pope, 'you have spoken very well. If you keep the commandments I shall give you, you cannot fail in this world or in the other. Be sure to love, honour and give thanks to God, obey the commands of the Church and her saints, hear mass, matins and vespers, honour the body of Jesus Christ and make offering, drive out heresy and maintain good peace. Do not attack monastic houses or travellers on the roads nor take other people's goods to increase your own, do not destroy your barons or damage your own people. Allow mercy to defeat and conquer you. But against any who try to disinherit you or bring you down, defend yourself well and maintain your right.'

'My lord,' said the boy, 'how can I help being angry? I cannot be hunter and hunted both at once! Poverty and want are more than I can bear. I have no land and don't know which way to turn, I shall have to live on what other people give me. I don't think I'm saying too much if I tell you that I want to give and take, not receive alms and beg.'

'Do nothing,' said the pope, 'which can anger God, for if you can earn it he will give you plenty of land. I have reserved the Venaissin, Argence and Beaucaire for your needs; this will be enough for you; and the count de Montfort will control the rest until the Church sees whether you can return.'

'My lord,' said the boy, 'how it hurts me to hear that a man from Winchester[1] is to share my land! Christ, if he will, forbid Sir Simon ever to divide a fief with me! Death or the land, that's the choice. Let one of us have the whole fief until it's his time to die. And as I see that it all comes back to fighting, all I ask of you, my lord, is that if I can win the fief, you let me keep it.' The pope looked at him and sighed, then he kissed and blessed him.

'Be careful what you do and remember what I tell you, night is darkest just before dawn. May Jesus Christ let you begin and end well, may great good fortune go with you!'

The young count left Rome and travelled by long stages to Genoa,[2] where his father, I promise you, did not go and attack him when he saw him coming! They did not stay in Genoa but left at once and rode on cheerfully, discussing the future, until they reached Marseille.

Count Raymond and his son in Marseille and Avignon

Laisse 153
Reaching Marseille, they dismounted by the shore and were welcomed with joy and delight. The count took up residence in the castle of Toneu.[3] Then on the fourth day a messenger arrived, greeted the count and said,

'My lord count, tomorrow morning be ready early, for the best men of Avignon are waiting for you on the river bank. More than three hundred will be there to do you homage.' Count Raymond was very pleased to hear this. Next morning he and his son set off and when they had almost reached the meeting place beside the river the count dismounted from his good Arab mule and found the men from Avignon kneeling on strewn branches. They and the count greeted each other with delight.

---

1. Really Leicester.
2. Probably early in February 1216.
3. 'Palatium Tholonei', customs house and stronghold of the viscounts of Marseille.

Arnold Audegier,[1] a good and intelligent man, born of a noble family at Avignon, was the first to speak, for he well knew all their customs:

My lord count of St Gilles, may it please you and your dear son, sprung of a loyal line, to accept a noble pledge: the whole of Avignon places itself in your lordship. Each man here delivers to you his body and his estate, also the keys and the town, the gardens and the approaches. Do not think we speak foolishly, for there is no falsehood, no pride or boastfulness in what we say: one thousand knights, brave and experienced men, and one hundred thousand other valiant men have made oath and pledged by sureties that from now on they will strive to recover all your losses. You shall hold all your rightful lands in Provence, including all rents, quitrents, tolls on goods and on passage, and no one shall use the roads without paying for a safe-conduct. And we shall hold all the crossing places on the Rhône and shall carry death and slaughter across the fief until you have regained Toulouse and your rightful inheritance. And the dispossessed knights shall come out of the greenwood and need no longer fear storms and bad weather. You have no enemy in the world so fierce that he will not suffer shame if he does you wrong or injury.'

'My lord,' said the count, 'in coming to my defence you show both valour and good sense. Your own country and all Christendom will praise you for re-establishing honest men, for restoring *paratge* and joy.'

Next day they rode at once to Marseille, where they did not stay long, and then on to Salon, arriving at nightfall. There they went happily to their quarters.

Advice offered to young Raymond

Laisse 154
Very happily they went to their quarters. Next morning as dew was falling, the clear light of dawn growing brighter and birds beginning to sing, as leaves unfolded and flowerbuds opened, the knights rode two and two across the grassland, talking about their weapons and equipment. But Guy of Cavaillon,[2] riding a bay horse, said to the young count,

'Now is the time when *paratge* urgently requires you to be bad and good.[3] The count de Montfort who destroys men, he and the Church at Rome and the preachers are covering *paratge* with shame, they have cast it down from its high place, and if you do not raise it up, it will be vanish for ever. If worth and *paratge* do not rise again through you, then *paratge* dies, in you the whole world dies. You are the true hope of all *paratge* and the choice is yours: either you show valour or *paratge* dies.'

'Guy,' said the young count, 'I am delighted at what you say and will make you a short answer: if Jesus Christ keeps me and my companions alive and gives me back Toulouse, which I long for, *paratge* shall not suffer poverty or

---

1. There was a distinguished Isnard Audegier, judge, in Avignon, who later was sent on an embassy to the king of France; also a Bermond Audegier, a courageous knight; but there is no recorded Arnold of this name.
2. Knight and poet, he served in the court of Alfonso II, count of Provence; later joined the count of Toulouse; was given important posts by Raymond VII. One of his surviving poems attacks William of Les Baux, prince of Orange, another exhorts the count of Toulouse to go to war and regain his lands.
3. Good to your own, bad towards the enemy.

disgrace, for there's no one anywhere strong enough to destroy me, if it were not for the Church. My right is so clear that however proud and evil my enemies may be, any leopard who attacks me will find he is fighting a lion!'

Joy in Avignon

They rode on talking of arms, of love and gifts until evening fell and Avignon welcomed them. As the noise of their arrival was heard in the town, there was no one, old or young, who did not run out from every street and every house, the fastest runner rejoicing in his good luck, and some cried, 'Toulouse!' and others, 'Joy! for now God is with us!' Greatly encouraged and shedding tears, they all came and knelt before the count and then together said, 'Glorious Jesus Christ, give us strength and power to restore them both to their heritage!' So large were the crowds and the procession that threats and sticks and staves were needed. They went into the church to say their prayers and afterwards sat down to a rich and savoury banquet with many kind of sauces and fish dishes, red and white wines, clove-scented and vermilion, with entertainers, viols, dances and songs.

On Sunday morning the oath and promise were read out. Then they addressed each other in these words:

'True and kind lord, do not hesitate to spend freely, for we shall provide the means and risk our lives until you have won back the fief or we lie dead beside you.'

'My lords,' replied the count, 'rich will be the rewards both God and I will give you.'[1]

The prince of Orange promises support

Count Raymond took counsel with some of his barons; then, valiant and joyful, he rode to Orange. A treaty of love and friendship was made between the count and the prince,[2] and the young count rode at once into the Venaissin to receive and garrison Pernes, Malaucène, Beaumes and many of his vassals' castles.

But soon now came sorrow, evil and strife, for the clergy and bishops were against him, Le Baux[3] made war on him, as did greedy and grasping Raymond Pelet,[4] with Nîmes, Orange and Courthézon,[5] Raimbaud of Lachau,[6] good John of Senuc,[7] Sir Lambert of Montélimar,[8] Sir Lambert of Limoux and many other evil-hearted and treacherous men. But against those were

1. In November 1216 young Raymond granted the knights, citizens and traders of Avignon exemption from all tolls in all his fiefs, including those yet to be recovered.
2. William of Les Baux, prince of Orange and poet, had already taken possession of Count Raymond's lands in Provence; then relinquished them at the pope's command. The agreement mentioned here can only have been brief. William was captured and killed by troops from Avignon in June 1218.
3. 'Le Baux' means the town and its lord, Hugh, brother of the prince of Orange.
4. Lord of Alès, vassal of the count of Toulouse, in July 1217 did homage for his fiefs to Simon de Montfort.
5. Courthézon and Orange belonged to William of Les Baux.
6. Lord of Lachau.
7. Not identified. His epithet 'good' translates bos, the rhyme word.
8. Lord of Montélimar, husband of Tiburge, sister of the prince of Orange.

ranged Marseille and Tarascon, La Isla[1] and Pierrelatte, Sir Guy of Cavaillon, Sir Adhémar of Poitiers and his son William,[2] also the brave and powerful William Artaut of Dia,[3] Sir Bernis of Murel[4] with a strong company, Sir Gerald Adhémar and young Gerald his son,[5] Raymond of Montauban and Sir Dragonet the valiant,[6] Sir Aliazar of Uzès,[7] Sir Albaron[8] and Bertrand Porcellet,[9] Pons who holds Mondragon,[10] Sir Ricaud of Caromb[11] and good Sir Pons of St Just.[12] Now war and battle await Sir Simon de Montfort, his son Sir Amaury and his brother Sir Guy, for Count Raymond, duke and marquis of the house of Alfonso, claims his fief.

Laisse 155
Still a child,[13] the count duke claims his fief, he fights against disinheritance and wrong, he captures castles and towns, walled cities and fortresses.

Count Raymond rides to Spain to seek support

When time and chance offered, the two counts, old and young, with Sir Guy,[14] Sir Dragonet, Sir Gerald Adhémar and his son young Gerald discussed matters together:

'My lords,' said the count, 'I will tell you what you are to do. I am going to Spain,[15] but you will all stay here and young Raymond will stay in your care. He urgently needs your guidance. Remember, if he regains his fief you will win great honour, but if he loses it you will all suffer. Raymond,' said the count, 'trust these lords. Good and bad, joy and sorrow, whatever chance brings you, bear it with them. Always be kind to the lords of Avignon, be generous to them, love and enrich them, for you cannot reconquer Provence without their help. Show the men of Marseille how very grateful you are, reward them with goods and honours; accept decently from them whatever they offer you. You will have support too from Sir Anselmet.[16] Always be careful to give the men of Tarascon the gifts and attention they want, for you

---

1. Now L'Isle-sur-la-Sorgue, Venaissin.
2. For Adhémar, see laisse 12. His son William is described as count of Valentinois in some charters during his father's lifetime.
3. Second son of Hugh of Aix, nephew by marriage of Arnold, lord of Crest.
4. Bernis or Berbo, lord probably of Mureils, canton of St Vallier.
5. Co-suzerain of Montélimar with his cousin Lambert.
6. Raymond, lord of Montauban, was a son of Dragonet le Preux, belonging to the formidable Mondragon family.
7. His name appears on charters of 1218 and 1220 witnessing grants made by young Raymond of Toulouse and his wife Sancha to the inhabitants of Nîmes.
8. Of Aramon, Gard. His widow Decanissa brought plaint of robbery to the king's commissioners on behalf of her children in 1248.
9. One of the famous family holding the lordship of Arles, probably the elder brother of William Porcellet.
10. Youngest of the Mondragon brothers, but holder of the bulk of the Mondragon fief.
11. Knight from the Venaissin, one of the chief nobles of western Provence.
12. Co-suzerain of Pierrelatte.
13. Young Raymond was 19, his father 60.
14. Guy of Cavaillon.
15. To seek reinforcements, especially from Catalonia and Aragon.
16. Not certainly identified; probably belonged to an important Marseille family.

will never conquer Beaucaire without them; cherish them well. And be sure the boats are in position at the foot of the rock,[1] for if you can get command of the water, you can destroy them. Do not let one wall, gate or rampart remain standing, and if they try to offer resistance, break them right down. Either by agreement or by assault you will certainly take them.'

'You cannot fail to do so,' agreed the barons.

'My lord,' said the young count, 'as you are going to Spain, you will make your rights clear to the counts and kings there, who must be distressed by your disinheritance, and you will urge your complaints against the court at Rome, where neither God nor faith, discernment nor law have been any use to you. Send me messengers to tell me everything you do and say, and everything you think as well. And send direct to Toulouse, for they are very unhappy there on your behalf and mine. They are such valiant men, you will get them back again, and with their help you will recover everything you have lost.'

'Raymond,' said the count, 'now you will find out who your friends are, who wishes you well, and we shall see what you can do.' Then the count took leave and through fierce heat and bitter cold he rode fast into Spain. The young count sent sealed letters summoning all his friends to join him quietly and without noise at the siege of Beaucaire.

Young Raymond enters the town of Beaucaire

Laisse 156
The true-born count arrived at the siege of Beaucaire and rode straight through La Condamina[2] to the gateway. The town council, most loyal of them all, handed over the gates to him and gave him the keys, to the great joy of the count and his good friends. And the men of Avignon came down the Rhône in boats, those of Tarascon hurried to take oars, and all crossed the river and came ashore into Beaucaire. All over the town rose the cry:

'Our dear lord is entering the town in joy, and now we shall be rid of the Barrois[3] and the French!' Then amid shouts of joy they quartered themselves in the houses, for refreshment and rest.

Simon's men sally from Beaucaire castle

Very soon, however, mortal combat broke out. Sir Lambert of Limoux, the energetic seneschal, with William of La Motte[4] and false Bernard Adalbert,[5] armed their companies, horse and man, and sallied out through the castle gate and along the ditches. They charged headlong into the streets, shouting, 'Montfort! Montfort!'

Let us describe what happened, as suffering and loss returned. Outcry and battle broke out all over the town, the commons ran to arms, the men of Provence rode out in close array, trumpets sounding and banners displayed.

---

1. There were guilds of boatmen at Tarascon and Beaucaire. The Rhône at that time ran at the foot of the castle rock.
2. A new quarter of the town built to the west, outside the walls.
3. Vassals of the count of Bar and recruits from Lorraine and the Rhineland.
4. Lambert's nephew.
5. Probably from Toulouse, and therefore 'false' in supporting the French.

'Toulouse!' they shouted and launched their attack. Darts, lances and stones they flung, bolts, arrows, axes, hatchets; they fought with spears, with swords, with clubs and staves. They pressed de Montfort's men so hard, levering dressed stones down onto them from the windows, shattering shield-bosses and poitrels, delivering mortal blows, that they put them to flight and forced them to take unwilling refuge in the castle. But the French fought back like heroes, and posted men in the towers, ramparts and brattices.

Young Count Raymond planted stakes and palings to make barricades[1] and stationed his forces in Santa Pasca.[2] Down at the foot of the rock were the boats, so that he and his men had full command of the river, water and chrism too.[3] Then they cried out, 'Before we do anything else, let us attack the redoubt.'[4]

The Provençals take the redoubt

Laisse 157
'Let us attack the redoubt, now is the time to take it!' Then you would have seen them running, leaping, racing, all shouting and striving to outdo each other, never a father waiting for son or son-in-law, and they began to hack down and destroy the walls and the gates. They brought fire too and set the place alight. What crossbows were bent, what quarrels rose up and rocks rained down, what stones were flung and good bows were loosed as the men of Provence attacked and the French fought back! Loudly the attackers shouted,

'You're captured, every one of you!' and the Frenchmen yelled,

'Easily said! You'll have to fight for us!' But the smoke and fire, the flames and burning distressed the French so much that they were forced to come down.

'We can't hold out any longer,' they said to each other. 'Let's ask for mercy rather than be defeated.' Sir Peter of St Prais[5] asked for permission to go out and see the young count. Everywhere you would have heard argument and dissension, some wanting to go up and others down. Loud voices shouted,

'Nothing can go wrong for us now! Glorious Jesus Christ who died on Good Friday, now you are bringing back *paratge*!'

The Provençals besiege the keep

Laisse 158
'Oh God, bring back *paratge*, look kindly on reason, maintain justice and throw down treachery!' Then with one voice they shouted, 'Let us attack the castle, the gateway and parapet!'

'My lords,' said Raymond Gaucelm,[6] 'I'll give you good advice: the castle and everyone in it will be yours, but first let us build a wall, unmortared, with double brattices and a strong bartizan. We'll mount a catapult in each

---

1. Between town and castle, to keep the northerners' cavalry in check.
2. Church and monastery in the north of the town, near the castle.
3. Chrism is the holy oil used in baptism; in Provençal it came to be synonymous with 'baptism', and here means 'every drop of water'.
4. A separate fortification on the castle rock, commanding the castle itself; see plan.
5. In 1230 a man of this name was warden of Lavaur for Raymond VII.
6. From Tarascon.

opening to defend it, ones that can throw both at long and short range, for we have an evil and dangerous man to deal with, ruthless and lion-hearted,[1] and if he attacks us it will give us protection. We shall not need to fear any kind of assault.' And they answered,

'This is good advice.' The chaplain Sir Arbert[2] addressed them briefly:

'My lords, in the name of God and the count I tell you that everyone who helps to build this drystone wall will be richly rewarded by God and by Count Raymond. Upon my holy orders, I promise each one of you salvation.' All together they shouted,

'To the pardon, all of us!' But nightfall was darkening the clear sky and a watch was set. Sergeants, young noblemen and the knights themselves kept guard all round the castle. Then as day dawned they raised a shout calling everyone to work, and no one hung back. They began building the wall, its platform and parapet. Never were such distinguished stonemasons seen at any work! Knights and ladies carried the infill material, noble girls and youngsters the timber and dressed stone, each sang a ballad or verses or a song, and they worked so hard that very soon they had no need to fear French or Burgundian. They pitched their tents and pavilions within the wall and garrisoned Santa Pasca. Next they decided to make a battering ram with which they could attack the keep and force its defenders out. In charge of this they put Sir Guy of Cavaillon and the men from Vallabrègues, who are loyal and true. The besiegers commanded the shore all round the keep; not a single man could creep secretly in or out, no one could water a horse or supply water to anyone else. Goods and provisions came in for the Provençals from all over the countryside, pigs, sheep, cows and oxen, geese and hens, capons, partridges and other game, corn and flour and wine from Genestet[3] - such plenty flowed in, that the place looked like the promised land.

Count Simon rides for Beaucaire

The news reached Count Simon at once: he had lost Beaucaire. Sir Lambert of Limoux, Rainier of Chauderon and the rest of the garrison were all shut up in the keep and would be no use to him ever again. When he heard this, he felt as if someone had killed Sir Amaury or Sir Guy.[4] In rage and distress he rode hard for Beaucaire.[5]

Sir Guy de Montfort sent urgent summons to all his friends to join them.[6] When they were all assembled, he and his nephew Sir Amaury, Sir Alan,[7] Sir Hugh,[8] with Guy of Lévis, Foucaud,[9] Solomon[10] and their fine companies

1. Lambert of Limoux.
2. Not identified, perhaps the priest of Santa Pasca.
3. The best of the Beaucaire wines, killed off by phylloxera in the nineteenth century.
4. Simon's son and brother.
5. From the Ile de France, where he had been recruiting, and in April 1216 receiving from Philip Augustus the duchy of Narbonne, the county of Toulouse and the viscountcies of Béziers and Carcassonne.
6. Guy and Amaury de Montfort were at Nîmes, gathering troops to relieve the crusaders trapped in Beaucaire.
7. Alan of Roucy.
8. Hugh de Lacy.
9. Foucaud of Berzy.
10. Perhaps Solomon of Faugères from Lodève.

all rode fast and straight to Beaucaire, occupied the open fields and drew up their ranks on the sands outside the town.

The Provençals behaved like true fighting men and shouted, 'Toulouse, Beaucaire and Avignon! Vallabrègues! Redessan! Malaucène! Caromb!' And the men of Tarascon crossed the river, while horse and foot occupied the gardens. But neither side struck spurs and charged, only Raymond Belarot[1] and Sir Aimon of Caromb[2] in front of all the rest each encountered an opponent, shattering their lances so that the fragments flew out. Not one other man gave or took a blow, and when night fell the crusaders raised their banners and rode off at full speed to their quarters at Bellegarde.[3]

Laisse 159

Very glad they were to find quarters at Bellegarde, where they took over the stables and ground floor and upper rooms and all the food they needed. They set all the squires to keep watch, for they were afraid of their mortal enemies. Marseille does not love them, nor does Montpellier, and Avignon and Beaucaire were the first to attack them.

They are all very cheerful inside the town of Beaucaire, laughing and making jokes, because their situation has improved so much. Master craftsmen and all the carpenters are at work building ramparts and galleries, erecting barriers, palisades and breastworks as well as mangonels, bitches[4] and quantities of other siege weapons. Present at the foot of the castle are the town's troops, on guard and sentry duty, keeping watch on the gates. In double armour and with sharp steel blades they ensure that no one can creep in or out. Down below by the cliff are picked boatmen, who have cut the French in the keep off from the water and broken down the rocks.[5]

Now the young count sent letters and messengers to the barons of his fief, to his vassals and to every place where mercenaries were known to be: anyone who wants gold or silver or good fast horses, let him come and earn them at the siege of Beaucaire.

De Montfort's besieged men discuss their situation

Sir Lambert of Limoux, in considerable anxiety, discussed matters with his companions. He spoke well and said no less than the truth:

'My lords, we are shut up in towers and solars and they have manned their turrets and gateways against us so that not one of us can get out without turning into a sparrowhawk. I can see them fetching stones for their deadly engines with which they'll mount a full-scale attack. We have all got to work hard and fast to strengthen our outer defences; that is essential. We have suffered one recent setback: they have cut us off from the water, both from the bridges and the steps. But still we have provisions for two full months and after that, if we have to, we'll eat the warhorses. In law the young count is heir to the castle and if he can surprise us and take us prisoner, he'll make it quite clear that he doesn't want us as co-heirs, so that we shall

---

1. From Provence.
2. No doubt related to the Ricaud of Caromb mentioned in laisse 154.
3. Guy de Montfort had taken this place, 10 km SW of Beaucaire, the previous day, 4 June 1216. Simon arrived there on the 6th.
4. *Gousas*, siege weapons similar to mangonels.
5. To block up the stairway going down through the rock from the castle to the river.

do better to die than be taken. But the count de Montfort is a very fine warrior and when he hears what has happened he will come at once. He is tough, he is a clever speaker, he will bring their best laid plans to nothing. Whatever happens, he is our chief hope.'

Rainier of Chauderon spoke last: 'My lords, remember William Short Nose and all he endured at the siege of Orange![1] Living or dying, let us all be true knights, let us bring no disgrace on Montfort or on France, for if the young count captures us, our wages are paid and the man who dies first is the luckiest.'

'It is very right and reasonable,' said Master Ferrier,[2] 'that you and your advice should be trusted.'

Count Simon arrives

But the count de Montfort travelled by roads and tracks, summoned his friends and all his mercenaries, sent to every place where troops were to be hired, and they rode night and day in all weathers till they reached Beaucaire and dismounted on the bank of the Rhône. Sir Guy, Sir Amaury, Sir Alan[3] and Roger[4] were the first to arrive, bringing their fine companies, and trumpets sounded to hasten the latecomers.

And the count de Montfort looked beyond the walls and the siege-towers and saw his men inside there, bold and alert. Up on top of the keep were his standard-bearer, and the lion banner flying from the tower. His face turned quite black with rage. He ordered his men to unload the pack-beasts, pitch the tents and cut down the olive trees. There they encamped in the gardens and orchards.

Now the siege was complete, inside the place and out, with Montfort and Beaucaire face to face. But God can see very well which of them is in the right, he can bring help to the true heir, for good and evil are the combatants in this war, they are the two commanders.

Laisse 160
In this war it is clear that God will restore the fief to those who truly love him, for pride contends with lawfulness, deceit is at grips with loyalty, the conflict is imminent. Everywhere a new flower is blossoming, one which will re-establish worth and *paratge*, for the brave young count, alert and valiant, has taken up arms against the ravagers and disinheritors, so that the cross of Toulouse is raised up and de Montfort's lion brought low.

Count Simon in council

Now the count de Montfort sent for the barons whose advice he trusted, wanting their counsel in this difficult situation. Thirty of them met in a leafy orchard and Count Simon pulled at his gloves and spoke to them like a wise man, noble, intelligent and brave:

---

1. A version of the epic *Prise d'Orange* survives, but not the one referred to here.
2. Possibly the Ferrier who was prior of the Dominicans at Narbonne; an active inquisitor from 1234.
3. Alan of Roucy.
4. Roger of Andelys, included in list of crusaders, laisse 36. There were several northerners of this name.

'My lords, before God and before you all, I claim that the men of this fief are false and faithless. I am racked with sighs, it is a grief and a burden to me that I am robbed by a child of fifteen. He has no power, no strength, no wealth to give away, yet he throws me out of Provence and makes active war on me! What amazes me most of all is that it was the Church who granted me Provence and the right to display my oriflammes, and then these Provençals attack, they hurl their weapons at me and shout 'Toulouse!' although it is the Church's work I am doing, her orders and her commands I am obeying! And as Raymond is a sinner whereas I pray for mercy, it does indeed astonish me that God should support him.'

Sir Alan was the first to respond:

'My lord count, your words and your boastful pride will keep us here pining for success, and you will be an old man, grey, white-haired, before you take this town, its keep or roundwalks. It is clear to me and to others that Jesus Christ does not intend deceit to triumph any longer. Although the count is so young, only a child, his nature is good, he is a fine, tall, handsome boy, and he has power, he has strength and good protectors, so that he is doing us harm, defeating us, forcing us onto the defensive. What is more, he is certainly the sort who will improve his position and succeed, for Sir Richard was his uncle and Bertrand his kinsman.[1] Whoever may call him a sinner, I say he is a boy who at his first throw has thrown a six. And since you ask for advice, it is not right to scorn it: Send him two messengers, good speakers, tell him to give you back your men and all the horses. You are unable to help them, and if you lose so many at this time both the dishonour and the loss will be very damaging. If he is willing to return them, tell him you will let him keep Provence and will make no claim on it ever again, for you have all the rest of the fief and can do very well with that.'

'Sir Alan, I doubt if this advice is well founded. My fist and your blade shall be red with blood before he and I come to any agreement, whether for good or ill. He has killed my men, but I have killed twice as many of his. If he takes these men by storm, it will be no fault of mine, for so help me God and St John, seven years will I maintain this siege till I have the town and can do what I like with it!' Then without a pause he shouted to all his men to break up branches and bring stakes and put barricades and defences across the fields so that sleeping or waking they could not be surprised. And at nightfall with a great noise and outcry and trumpets sounding, sentinels were posted, for inside and out they were all eager for battle.

Count Simon attacks

Laisse 161
So eager for battle are they that they remain alert all night, the horses saddled, and neither side can take the other unawares. As dawn breaks and the day brightens, every man on either side is ready; fine gold gleams on hauberks and helmets; shields and lances glitter across the whole expanse. Now Count Simon spoke out loud enough for all to hear:

---

1. Raymond's mother was a sister of Richard I; on his father's side he was related to the heroes of the First Crusade, Raymond of St Gilles and his son Bertrand, who conquered the county of Tripoli.

'Barons, we must show courage, vigour and good sense, for Christendom has chosen us as the best! And since our opponents have picked their best men, you will all be shamed if you let me lose the fief. Whatever I won with your help, I gave away freely and shared with you, so that no one can say I have failed him. After all I have said and all you have promised me, if I lose this fief, little service have you done me! They have robbed me of the castle of Beaucaire, and if I do not take revenge, little have I ever done! I had seizin of it from the archbishop of Arles;[1] my anger is just, for they have driven me out of my lordship, they have surprised and daunted my men inside there; my banner flies on the keep to tell me my men are at the point of death. I can bring them no help and my heart is fit to break! But this I can tell you, that as they have driven me to this state, the affair will not take long to finish, once I can bring them to battle! Battle is far better than disgrace.' His barons answered,

'We are all pledged to you, your command is our duty.'

But brave young Count Raymond has taken his stand at the gateway; he and the men of the fief, the dispossessed knights, the sergeants and archers, all well equipped and armed, are there. Rostand of Carbonnières[2] spoke to them as follows:

'Barons, we all agree that anyone who runs away is a traitor to his lord, and the rest of us can say so without contradiction. Take care, then, that none of you wears a traitor's hat!'[3] Bertrand of Avignon[4] said,

'Soon we shall know who is to hold the fief and rule it. We have felt the evil, we know how the clergy lied to us, saying we should bring death and the sword, we should spread fire, should drive out our own lord and make him a banished man, that this would be doing Jesus Christ good service! But now we are going to follow our own path to salvation, one where each of us can honestly save his soul. Do not neglect any of your weapons, keep them ready, strike hard! Fight well! We shall reward you, God and the count will be so generous that you will make your children's children rich for evermore.' Sir Gerald Adhémar spoke to them and said:

'Barons, be ready, be alert, stand firm! They are brave men and will attack at any moment. If we can stand their first assault, we shall defeat them, honour and glory will be ours.'

Then came the roar of shouting and the charge; joyfully the horns rang out; trumpets and shrill clarions resounded all along the riverbank and field.

The crusaders spurred, and charged as one into the thickest of the array, but the men of Beaucaire took their assault well. Now came the clash of blades from Cologne and twice-tempered steel, of round-headed maces and chilled javelins, well-honed axes and shining shields, came flights of darts, arrows and polished quarrels, feathered shafts and brandished spears, came brave knights, alert and active, sergeants, archers eagerly advancing, and the other companies, keen to strike hard. On all sides the rush and crash of men and weapons shook the field, the riverbank and the solid ground.

---

1. On 30 January 1215.
2. From Provence.
3. A common expression, deriving from the fact that criminals condemned to the pillory often had to wear headgear indicating their offence, such as a wreath of vine-trimmings for theft of verjuice.
4. A knight from Avignon, several times consul of that town.

Count Simon, Sir Alan and Sir Foucaud with Sir Guy and Sir Peter Mir[1] bore the shock of the encounter. What damaged hauberks you would have seen there, what good shields cracked and broken, what fists, legs and feet cut off, what spattered blood and skulls split apart! Even the simplest mind could not but feel it. But the men of Beaucaire had the upper hand and drove the crusaders down the beaten track; although they resisted strongly and there was not much pursuit. Many were the horses you would have seen running loose, iron-clad, riderless, their masters fallen and killed. Sir Guy of Cavaillon, riding an Arab mount, struck down William of Berlit[2] that day and they hanged him then and there from a flowering olive tree.

At last the mêlée broke and the combatants left the field. How many men you would have seen lying there dead, once the fighting was done!

Count Simon in defeat

Laisse 162

Once the fighting was done and the danger over, many felt joy and others rage. The men of Beaucaire went back into the town, their courage high and tested, and crusaders returned quickly to their tents. The count de Montfort conferred with his close supporters; three bishops[3] were also present and I don't know how many abbots. To both these groups the count complained emphatically:

'My lords,' he said, 'listen and see how I have been driven out and deprived of Provence, and have to watch my men suffering danger and defeat. In his arrogance the young count attacked me and since he left Rome he has been so successful that he has taken my land from me and is robbing me of my heritage. If he now takes Beaucaire from me, I am brought so low that all the rest of the fief seems rubbish. It was holy Church who began this affair, and if she abandons me now, then I have failed and can no longer protect my rents and revenue. A man who fails, a man of honour, will be always be accused, without right or reason. Suffering as I am in so many ways, I want to know what advice you will give me.'

The bishop of Nîmes[4] hastened to speak first, and was heard attentively:

'My lord count,' he said, 'in good and evil I adore Jesus Christ and thank him for everything! It is laid down that in this world you must patiently endure sorrow and distress - although if you are robbed, you must defend yourself well. You are free to chose evil or good, and if you lose in this world, you gain in the other. As for the knight who is hanging on the olive tree, I tell you he has suffered martyrdom this day for the love of Christ, who forgives him his sins, errors and wrongdoing and those of all the others who have been killed or wounded.' But Foucaud of Berzy was prompt to speak:

'For God's sake, my lord bishop, according to your logic, good shrinks to nothing and evil is doubled! And it amazes me that you clerics give absolution where there is no repentance. But if evil were good and lying the same as truth, then where pride flourishes we should find humility! I do not and will

---

1. Peter Mir, here fighting for Simon de Montfort, appears in laisses 54 and 55 as a follower of Peter Roger of Cabaret. No doubt he joined the crusaders when Peter Roger made his surrender and released Bouchard (laisses 63 and 64).
2. Not identified.
3. Of Nîmes, Toulouse and Carcassonne.
4. Arnold, former abbot of St Ruf.

not believe, unless you can prove it better, that any man who dies unshriven deserves salvation.'

'Foucaud,' said the bishop, 'it grieves me that you should doubt that any man alive, even one utterly condemned, is fully shriven, as long as he has fought those men.'

'In God's name, my lord bishop, nothing you can say will ever make me believe, if you'll allow me to say so, that it is not your preaching and our sins which have aroused Christ's anger. What I have seen makes me despair! Courage and the stars have turned against us. Never did I dream that we could be forced into shameful retreat, no, not if the whole of Christendom were ranged against us on the field!' Then he said to Count Simon, 'Remind the whole army: old or young, let none of them disarm. It will indeed be a crowning mercy and a wrong put right if you and we can win the justice you are seeking.'

Then on both sides they kept watch, the horses armoured, swords girded on, helms laced, until it was light, for everyone inside and out was so angry they longed for battle, not for rest or peace.

Harassment continues

Inside the town there were ample supplies, every kind of food they could wish for, but in the keep there was dismay and anger, for there was no plenty there, no bread, no wine or corn. The crusaders besieging the town were so harassed that none of them could rest or undress to sleep, no one had a moment to eat or drink or disarm. They had to fight much oftener than they liked, as the brave young count had catapults set up to attack the keep on all sides and to break down the shelters and crenellated walls.

Ralph of Le Gua[1] said to young Raymond,

'Count, I will tell you what to do: cut their whole force off from the Rhône, and that will finish them.' And the young count said,

'Raymond Gaucelm, order all the armed boats to take control of the river.'

'My lord,' said Sir Albeta,[2] 'the fleet has gone across; we have occupied and closed all the crossing places, every one of them is blocked from here to Arles. And below the castle by the rocks are the men from Vallabrègues with their fast boats, so that no one can drink there and come away unhurt.'

De Montfort has siege engines built

While the young count was discussing matters with his close friends, the great count de Montfort sent for carpenters from all over his fief and domains, and he built a castle and a cat, siting them carefully between the ramparts and the ditches. Built of iron, timber and leather, they were fully equipped and manned day and night. Standing forward near them was a catapult which shot all day long and smashed the big dressed stones of the town's gateway and the square crenellations.

Reinforcements join young Raymond

Then both inside and out the rumour ran that great lords were coming to the help

---

1. 'Del Gua' is a name known in the Dourgne region (Tarn) in the late twelfth century.
2. From Tarascon.

of the town. Raymond of Montauban, clever and respected, Sir Isoard of Dia[1] with many brave companions, William of Belafar,[2] well equipped and armed, Cotignac,[3] Peter Bonassa[4] with many others, Sir Peter of Lambesc[5] with a numerous troop, and Sir Guigo of Gaubert[6] all very cheerfully entered the town to help its defence.

Laisse 163

Valiantly they came to the town's defence; and with great reluctance other men came to attack it, men who would much rather have been elsewhere.[7]

Young Raymond talks with his supporters

In council with some of the greater barons, Sir Dragonet addressed his lord the count:

'My lord,' he said, 'it is clear that God is hurrying to your help, for since you came from Rome he has brought you from twilight into glorious day. We know he wants you to recover the lands your forebears held, for now your deadliest enemies are suffering defeat. Falsehood and treachery only produce dishonour. I have never heard a sermon from a false preacher who did not go wrong in the end. Men of good understanding tell us that the betrayed are more valuable than those who betray them. By the body of St Mary, whom I adore and pray to, if you do not now show wisdom and valour, we can believe nothing any more except that worth and *paratge* are destroyed, both flower and seed. And the count de Montfort is brave and intelligent, he has courage, daring and prudence. He has built a castle and a cat in order to frighten us, but these have no more effect than an enchanter's dream, they are a spider's web and a sheer waste of material. His catapult, though, throws strongly and is breaking down the whole gateway, but we shall place our best men there, our strongest, most daring, cleverest and most valiant.'

'Dragonet,' said the count, 'we shall certainly do well. Gerald Adhémar shall have the honour of defending the gate, he and his companions, Sir John of Nagor,[8] Sir Datil[9] and Sir Austor.[10] You and Raymond of Montauban will be with them day and night, and so will the dispossessed knights, who are good fighting men and skilled in arms. And if you are hard pressed, I myself will be ready to come to your help and bear the danger beside you. And I would like to know who will abandon us!'

'My lords, free knights,' said Ricaud of Caromb, 'if Count Simon dares attack the gate, let us resist! Let us scatter so much blood and brains around us, such lumps of sweaty flesh, that any survivors weep!'

---

1. Isoard, son of William Artaut of Dia.
2. One of the dispossessed knights of the viscountcy of Carcassonne
3. William of Cotignac; his family originally came to Provence with Alfonso I of Aragon.
4. Another Provençal notable in the service of the counts of Provence.
5. One of the great lords of Provence.
6. Gaubert is a village 4 km south of Digne.
7. Auxiliaries recruited in the south by Count Simon; their sympathies lay with their neighbours.
8. Not identified.
9. A name common in Provence in the country along the Durance.
10. Probably William Peter Austorgat of Avignon.

'My lords,' said Peter Raymond of Rabastens, 'the count de Montfort is doing us a kindness by not retreating. He is going to lose his mind, his wealth and his luck. Look at us: here we are in comfort and plenty, we have rest and repose, coolness and shade, as well as wine from Genestet to cheer our hearts. We can eat with pleasure and drink with delight. But they, wretched sinners, are out there with no rest or comfort, nothing but exhaustion and distress, suffering heat, dust and misery. Day and night their companies are so harried that they lose many swift warhorses, ravens and vultures hover above them. And the dead and wounded stink in their nostrils so that the daintiest among them turns pale.'

De Montfort's trapped men signal to their lord

The men in the keep went out onto the viewing platform and flew a black flag from the tower to tell the count de Montfort that they were in distress.

Reinforcements arrive by water from Marseille

Trumpeters summoned all men, great and small, from every house and ordered them to arm themselves and their thousand-shilling horses because the men of Marseille were now arriving with great joy. Out on the waters of the Rhône the rowers sang at the oars; at the prows were the captains who controlled the sails, the archers and the seamen. Horns and trumpets, cymbals and drums rang across the riverbank under the dawning sun. Shields, lances and dancing waves glittered red and azure, green and white, glanced gold and silver, as sun and water shone and the mist dispersed. Along the shore Sir Anselmet and his horsemen rode merrily in the clear light of day, their horses richly clad and the oriflamme going on ahead. On all sides these brave men shout, 'Toulouse!' in honour of the count's son, who is winning back his fief. And so they enter Beaucaire.

Laisse 164
In great delight they entered Beaucaire and each man rejoiced and blessed his good fortune.
   The news that reinforcements had arrived was reported in the crusaders' camp. They made ready, therefore, and kept alert, for in preparation and battle lay their joy and happiness, in shrilling clarions and the sound of trumpets at daybreak their pleasure and refreshment.

Further attacks on the keep

The townsmen kept up a fierce fire that severely damaged the keep and the viewing platform, shattering timber, stone and lead. And at Santa Pasca they set up the battering ram. This is long, straight, sharp and shod with iron; it thrust, carved and smashed till the wall was breached and many of the dressed stones thrown down. When the besieged crusaders saw that, they did not panic but made a rope lasso and used a device to fling it so that they caught and held the ram's head, to the rage of all in Beaucaire. Then the engineer who had set up the ram arrived. He and his men slipped secretly into the rock itself, intending to break through the wall with their sharp picks. But when the men in the keep realised this, they sewed fire, sulphur and tow together in a piece of cloth and let it down on a chain. When the fire caught and the sulphur ran, the flames and stench so stupefied them that not one of them could stay there. Then they used their stone-throwers and broke down the beams and palisades.

Up on the main tower above the pointed merlons, de Montfort's lion fought and struggled with the flames and was almost brought down. The captain of the tower shouted and yelled, crying out,

'Montfort has lost us, but it's not his fault, no shame to him, the brave young count has caught us all by surprise.' Then he waved napkins and a gleaming bottle to show that their food was finished, they had eaten and drunk all their bread and their wine. And when the count de Montfort saw this, he sat down on the ground in rage and anger and shouted out, aloud and furious,

'Knights, to arms!'

This brought swift response: word ran through the camp and not a man remained there, old or young. They armed themselves and their good chargers; trumpets and shrill clarions spoke. Then they rode up Hanged Men's Hill.[1]

'My lords,' said the count, 'I've suffered a set-back, my lion complains of hunger, he's hard pressed and starving. But by the holy Cross, today's the day he'll feed on blood and brains!'

'A welcome day, brother!' said Sir Guy. 'If we lose Beaucaire, the lion will be silenced, your glory and ours thrown down for ever. Let's ride, let's fight until we've beaten them!'

And as soon as they saw them, the men of Beaucaire took their equipment, their weapons, iron hats and shields, sharp swords and keen-edged axes, took javelins, maces and good strung bows, and in the fine open ground along the trodden road both sides moved in to the attack and fought hand to hand.

Further conflict at Beaucaire

Laisse 165
Under a clear bright sun the attack began. It started with jousts and encounters in front of the tents, and the men of the town came up in strength, for no one, not one lad or youngster, wanted to stay behind. More than fifteen thousand of them came through the gates, good, skilful fighters and very swift. Gerald Adhémar, loyal and alert, and Sir Peter of Lambesc with Sir Alfan Romieu[2] and Sir Hugh of La Balasta[3] took command.

Such were the shouting and the uproar, the moving pennons and the rush of wind, that the green leaves trembled, so loud the horns and trumpets that the earth re-echoed and the heavens shook.

Count Simon's charge defeated

Now Sir Foucaud, Sir Alan, Sir Walter of Préaux, Sir Guy with Sir Peter Mir and Sir Aimon of Corneaux[4] led the charge across the open ground. The

---

1. *El poi dels pendutz* - probably Margailler, a hill NW of Beaucaire, part of which was known as Haute-Justice in the late nineteenth century.
2. A baron of Provence.
3. Vassal of the counts of Valentinois.
4. Foucaud of Berzy, Alan of Roucy, Guy of Lévis; Walter may be from Préaux, Normandy; Aimon from Thiérache, Aisne.

count de Montfort, hard, evil, cruel, drove his black charger straight into the fray, shouting,

'St Peter and St Michael, give me back the town before I lose the castle! Give me vengeance on these new enemies!' Into the mêlée he rode and the struggle began. The sergeants and young men threw many down. But the townsmen came on in such numbers that very soon the charge so strongly begun lost impetus and stopped. Sir Imbert of L'Aia,[1] swift and valiant, struck Gaucelin of Portel,[2] shattered his shield, hauberk and laces, and flung him and his bay charger dead to the ground. Broadswords and maces came into play, hangers and knives; danger and death returned. Stones, darts and lances came in a blizzard like snow, arrows and bolts, halberds, pikes, javelins and axes flashed through the air. Bucklers were smashed, both rims and crystal bosses, hauberks and mail, helmets and iron hats, shields with their banding, bridles and bells. Lance-heads and javelins crashed and clattered - a storm, a downpour of pelting hammer-blows.

So close and bitter, so deadly was the conflict, the crusaders reined back their Arab mounts and turned away and the townsmen pursued them with blows and shouts, they struck and wounded both horses and men. Slashed off and scattered you'd have seen legs, arms and feet, men's guts and lungs, jawbones and heads, scalps and spilled brain-matter. So hard they fought and struck and slew, they drove them off, drove them from roads, hills and open places, from grassland and reedbeds. The battle ended, the remains left lying there made a feast for dogs and birds. Great was the joy, great the rage on one and the other side, when the fight was done.

Laisse 166
On one side was joy, on the other rage. Under an olive tree Count Simon disarmed, and squires and young noblemen took his equipment. Sir Alan of Roucy spoke bitterly:

'By God, Sir Count, we can set up a butcher's shop! Our sharp swords have won us so much meat, it won't cost us a penny to feed the cat, we're far better supplied than we were yesterday.' But the count had so proud and black a heart that he would not answer, and Sir Alan said no more.

Count Simon sets up his siege engines

All that day the crusaders stayed where they were. Then their best fighting men rode out to scout, and the sergeants and bowmen opened an attack. Workmen prepared the cat and the castle, and in front of these they had a catapult which smashed and struck and broke down the Vine Gate and its protecting wall. Meanwhile inside the town they used lime and mortar to build barricades with outlets and cross-passages in which their best knights massed in force.

The trapped men discuss their position

Inside, though, in the keep they were all so anxious that Sir Lambert of Limoux climbed up and addressed his whole company:

'My lords,' he said, 'we are all together in this. Good or bad, we shall all

---

1. Not identified.
2. Perhaps from a family of that name in Sigean, Aude.

share alike. God is causing us such pain, we are suffering worse torment than a money-lender's soul! Night and day the siege-engines strike at us from every direction, and so do their crossbowmen. Our stores and granaries are empty, we haven't a sack of any kind of grain, and our horses are so hungry they're eating wood and the bark of trees. We can get no help from the count de Montfort and there's no hope of an arrangement with the young count. We can see no way, no path or route at all, out of this mortal danger. Now in this great distress, in this anxiety, I ask counsel first from God and then from yourselves.'

William of La Motte was the first to speak:

'By God, fair uncle, as hunger presses us, the only remedy I can think of is that we eat our horses and chargers, for the mule-flesh we ate yesterday was excellent. We've enough for one quarter between fifty every day. When that's finished and we've eaten the last one, then let every man eat his comrade! And the one who fights worst and gives way to fear, it makes sense to eat him first.'

Raymond of Rocamaura[1] beat his hands together and cried,

'My lords, I who the other day left my own lord for the count de Montfort, I will accept this reward! It's only right I should suffer, as I've done so wrong.'

Rainier[2] spoke next and said:

'By God, Sir Lambert, we'll do this differently! William of La Motte's suggestion is diabolical. I have never thought human flesh would taste good. But when the Arab coursers are eaten, we have a single loaf and a little wine left in the cellar; in the name of Jesus Christ, the righteous lord, let us receive his most true and holy body and then, armed in double mail, we will sally out through the gate and down the stairs and begin the fighting, the struggle and the blows! Red shall be the stonework, red the ground! It's better we should all die together, killed by iron and steel, than live disgraced and captive.'

'This is the advice we'll follow,' said Master Ferrier, 'for death with honour is better than life in prison. Now let's put our minds to it and defend ourselves!'

Laisse 167

'Now let's defend ourselves, let none of us hang back. Every day our mortal foes attack us and we grow weaker as our supplies fail. We have no lord, no friend or kinsman who can help us here, and so it's better to die than be crucified alive.'

Then into the hall ran a beggarman shouting,

'My lords, to arms! This is the truth I'm telling you: I've seen the weasel[3] so close against the wall, I think it's gripping it.' Then there was uproar as the meeting separated and each man ran to his post. There came the weasel, about to drive home a pike, but the chief engineer, a man of firm and antique heart,[4] took burning pitch and put it in a pot and hurled it against the weasel, striking it exactly where he intended. The pitch burst into flames and the fire spread so fast it could hardly be put out.

---

1. Vassal of the count of Toulouse, owned property in and near Beaucaire.
2. Rainier of Chauderon.
3. A wheeled shelter built to be moved up against the walls, like the cat but smaller.
4. *Ab fi cor e antig*; brave as the heroes of classical times.

Fresh conflict outside Beaucaire

In the fine open space where the French had built the cat, both armies made ready. Trumpets rang out and clarions blew; castle and riverbank gave back the sound. Out before the others rode Philippot,[1] who lowered his steel-clad head and shook his sword. Any man he ever struck fell dead at once. William of Belafar rode to encounter him, and struck him so straight and hard that he drove through shield and hauberk, overthrew him and burst his heart. From every side men struck at Philippot, who never got up again but died where he was, he and his horse together.

Now up rode Count Simon with Sir Guy, Sir Amaury, Sir Alan, Sir Foucaud, Sir Hugh and Sir Aimery.[2] Men swarmed out from their camp, filling riverbank and field; the ground shook under their tread. Out of the town came every man who could thrust his way forward, and brave young Raymond galloped out along the street. Dragonet, meeting him, seized his rein and shouted:

'The courage which gives you strength will defend *paratge* and mercy against all attack!' At that the gate opened and they sallied out together, followed by the dispossessed knights, each man striving to outride the next.

'My lords,' said Sir Peter Raymond of Rabastens, 'fear never won fame, I can tell you that. Let's defend our good names and avoid disgrace!'

'That's how we'll survive, my lords!' said Arnold Feda.[3] He made ready to defend himself and them.

Loud was the clash of steel as the two forces met, many the helmets shattered and lances smashed, many the hands, arms, feet cut off, much the blood shed and brain-matter spilled. Bernard of Rocafort[4] held the cross-passages; Sir Peter of Mèze,[5] great-hearted, he was there; and in the thickest of the press Sir William of Minerve hacked, cut and slashed till the blood ran, himself receiving such wounds that he scarcely recovered. Fighting continued until daylight failed and darkness put an end to the struggle. They bore Philippot away and Sir Guy buried him. Then they kept watch till dawn.

Now the count de Montfort sent for certain chosen barons, fifteen loyal friends whose advice he wanted.

Count Simon consults his advisers

Laisse 168

The count moved aside to consult his barons. With sighs and groans he said to them:

'My lords, it's with you, my good friends whom I respect, that I must discuss what we are to do, whether to raise the siege or stay. If we raise it, we shall be disgraced. If we stay, we shall suffer double the disgrace and loss. As I see the position, I am afraid we shall never recover the keep by force,

---

1. One of the crusaders, not identified.
2. Probably Aimery of Blèves, who appears below in laisse 202.
3. One of the dispossessed knights, held a fief in the viscountcy of Béziers until declared a heretic and expelled by the crusaders.
4. A dispossessed knight formerly holding fiefs in the viscountcies of Carcassonne and Béziers.
5. The lordship of Mèze was a fief of Béziers.

we shall lose the men, their weapons and their mounts. I should be very sad to lose them without a fight. But these are both great evils, and I want us to choose the lesser.' The barons crowded close to catch his words.

'My lord,' said Sir Foucaud, 'hear my opinion. If we abandon the siege, that will certainly be wrong. Yet if we stay here, I think we shall lose so much that your name and ours will be blackened for ever. Trust me, though, and I'll tell you what we should do: we should stay where we are, quiet and calm and careful, making no move of any kind against the town or its men - though if they come and attack us, we'll defend ourselves. Then very soon we'll choose a day, and holy Mary, maiden mother, we'll be shamed for ever if we can't give battle and get into their town along with them! We'll pick one hundred of our knights, the best and most experienced fighters, and place them in ambush behind the cat, with the castle and the catapult in front. Then at noon, when we know the defenders are resting, we on the contrary will arm and sally out all together to the Lists Gate. In all sorts of ways we'll incite them to attack us, and we shall attack them! We'll raise such an outcry and clash of steel that the townsmen will all flock to it. And then when the conflict's at its height, we'll turn our horses' heads and make for the other gate, us and our men in ambush together, and if we find it undefended, we'll all ride in. Once inside, we'll use swords and maces till they've killed us or we've killed them. If this doesn't succeed, we've neither sail nor oar, no hope but to abandon Beaucaire and the whole of Provence, unless we try to get our men back by negotiation.'

'Sir Foucaud,' said the count, 'we'll do as you suggest. If it fails - and it won't! - we'll send a message direct to the young count saying that he must return our men and we'll then go away. If he refuses, we'll pay enough money to all his advisers to get them on our side. In this way we shall get our men back and later we'll recover all our losses. We'll ride straight for Toulouse and share out the property there; for what's still outstanding, we'll take hostages. Then with all that wealth we'll ride into Provence, we'll take Avignon and Marseille and Tarascon and we'll recover Beaucaire.'

Laisse 169
'We'll recover Beaucaire, castle, crenels and all, and as for the traitors who surrendered it, they'll hang from the palisade. If I don't seize them, nothing's of any use!'

But Sir Hugh de Lacy spoke up against him:

'By God, fair sir count, you have good judgment! You'll need to put salt and pepper to it, though, before you can recover Beaucaire and its great castle. It's a hard task to take a castle from its natural lord, and these men here, they love the young count with all their hearts, they'd rather have him than Christ himself. If ever they were unfaithful, they mean to be loyal now. When they swore on the missal, it was because they were forced to it and could do nothing else.[1] Force and wrongdoing triumph where law is helpless, and in law a forced oath has no validity. If a man conquers lands and seizes another man's home, if he debases law and employs deceit, he'll lose the fief he has conquered and all its revenues as well. If you'll take my advice, we'll discuss other matters. I have never seen a siege like this one:

---

1. This refers to the oath of loyalty to Simon de Montfort which the townspeople were compelled to take after the archbishop of Arles granted him Beaucaire, 30 January 1215.

the besieged are happy, sheltered and at ease, they have good bread, fresh water, good beds and lodging, and Genestet wine on tap, whereas we're out here exposed to every danger, with nothing to call our own but heat, sweat and dust, muddy watered wine and hard bread made without salt. We stand to arms all day and all night to defend our camp and we wait for them to raise their warcry again and renew their attack. If this hellish situation lasts any longer, we'll suffer worse torments than St Martial's fire!'[1]

'By God, Sir Hugh,' said the count, 'don't complain! You'd better not, for by the holy mass the priest blesses, you won't see Castelnaudary, nor Sir Alan Montréal, until I've got Beaucaire back, rents, revenues and all.'

'Sir count,' said Sir Alan, 'you have the heart of an emperor, so help me God! Listen, and I'll give you advice that will reduce your glory and your wealth day after day: work out how to get us enough bread and meat and wine. Get horses too and chargers, for the ones we have are getting weaker. We'll have kept Easter, Pentecost and Christmas here, before you rescue Sir Lambert the seneschal or recover Beaucaire.'

'Sir count,' said Sir Guy of Lévis, 'let's consider another point, that as they want to avoid a set battle, they are free to go in and out quite safely.'

15 August 1216, the French set an ambush and attack

They continued talking and planning until the feast day of the Virgin Mary, the heavenly mother. Then secretly and all at the same time Count Simon and all the lords and captains and every man of the crusading host put on their armour, each in his own quarters; Count Simon's sons and his brother armed in the count's tent. One hundred knights they were, mighty men, brave and ruthless, men of valour and wisdom, active and courageous, with arms and equipment second to none: Sir John of Berzy, Sir Robert and Sir Theobald with Sir Peter Mir, Sir Aimon and the marshal.[2] Inside the cat and the hospital[3] they hid their men, and laid their ambush between the wall and the gate.

At midday when the sun drank up the shade and the men inside the town were resting without a care in the world, the French spurred forward all together in a single body. Their ringing horns, the trumpets and clarions shook the whole riverbank, the castle and outworks. Ahead of them all, spurring hard through the gardens, rode Count Simon, with Sir Amaury, Sir Alan and Sir Foucaud and the other companies. In close and fast formation they rode for the Cross Gate.[4] Across all the lists and in the brattices rose the cry:

'Holy Mary, be strong and save your people from harm!'

Now the French entered straight through the middle of the palisaded area and the men of Provence ran to arms and all armed themselves in the market place. They shook and groaned and were so frightened that many of them ran to the river and fled downstream. But the best of them, clever and brave as hawks, sergeants, archers and all the workmen rallied to the gateway to defend the place and they held the passage, the wall and the rock. Behind

---

1. Like St Anthony's fire, ergotism or erysipelas.
2. Robert of Picquigny; Theobald, a close associate of Count Simon, probably one of his household knights; Aimon of Corneaux; the marshal was Guy of Lévis.
3. The hospital, possibly that of St Lazarus under the walls of Beaucaire.
4. In the NE part of Beaucaire; see plan. The gateway bore a carved cross of Toulouse.

them came a great throng of ordinary people. And when the French saw that their stratagem was not working, they turned their horses' heads and rode hard between the wall and the camp, along the edge of the ditch, making for the other gate.[1] Now the men hidden in the cat and the hospital sallied out of ambush and took up their ground; they smashed through the barricades, trenches and palisades and arrived together, fast and alert.

But the standard was flying in the gateway and Sir Hugh of Laens, Sir Imbert, Sir Ricaud, Sir Hugh of La Balasta, Sir Rostand of Pujaut[2] with Sir William of Minerve and the barons and captains defended the passage, the entrance and approach.

'To the other gate, true knights,' cried Sir Ralph of Le Gua, 'and take our share of blows, for the French are winning the outworks!'

Thereupon the local men drew together, rapidly filling the parapets and embrasures; crenels and merlons bristled with arms and men; brave companies and good bowmen with wound crossbows stood ready. Then the two sides encountered and again the deadly clash of arms began: lances and swords rang upon heart-of-oak shields; darts, maces, knives and axes, halberds and pikes, fire-brands and clubs, with shining hatchets and slung stones, sharpened stakes, cudgels and hand-flung pebbles, scythe-blades, arrows and hand-bow shafts, water and hot lime thrown from the ramparts into the ditch - all these came from left and right, from straight ahead, so thick and fast that they shattered helms, mail hoods and nasals, hauberks, chainmail, laces and crystal, shields, saddles, bridles and poitrels, clasps, buckles and goldwork all at once; heads too and jawbones, arms and skulls. Cold steel and slaughter, pain and fury, unbelievable carnage raged across the threshold of the gate and dyed the pennons red with blood and brains. They fought and struck so hard that each man there said he had had enough, more than enough, of grievous wounds.

The crusaders withdraw

When the French saw that they could not succeed, they withdrew to their tents, and the townsmen went back to their homes. Then doctors and farriers on both sides required eggs,[3] water, tow and salt, ointments, plasters and linen bandages, to treat the wounds and blows and deadly pain.

But Beaucaire must not, need not be afraid, for the count de Montfort and his captains will not recapture it.

Count Simon in council

Laisse 170
They will not recapture it, for all the danger and torment, the strife, evil, suffering and death have given way to discussion. This is because the count de Montfort is angry and wretched, he has called his barons and summoned his kinsmen to the silk tent above which the eagle glitters, and there in private they deliberate.

---

1. The Vine gate, south of the Cross gate.
2. Hugh and Imbert, not identified; Ricaud of Caromb; Pujaut is near Villeneuve-lez-Avignon.
3. Egg-white was used for surgical dressings; M.-C., ii, p. 193, n. 7.

'My lords,' said the count, 'God has shown me by the clearest evidence that I am out of my mind. Once I was rich, great and valiant, but now my affairs have turned to nothing, for now neither force, cunning nor courage can rescue my men or get them out of Beaucaire. Yet if I abandon the siege so shamefully, all over the world they will call me recreant.'

'Brother,' said Sir Guy, 'I can tell you for certain that God does not want you to hold the castle of Beaucaire and the rest any longer, for he is watching and considering your behaviour. As long as you can get your hands on all the money and the property, you do not care in the least how many people die.'

News from the besieged crusaders

At this point a messenger came hurrying straight to the count's tent and spoke to him angrily:

'My lord count de Montfort, your drive and determination, your valour and courage have all vanished. You are losing your men, they are in their death agony and their souls and spirits are knocking at their teeth. I have got out of the castle, and the distress and terror in there are such that I would not stay in it for all Germany and its wealth. I tell you it is three weeks since their water gave out, and the wine and corn too. I have been so frightened, God and the saints help me! that my whole body shook and my teeth chattered.'

Count Simon admits defeat

Dark with rage and grief, Count Simon listened to this, and then with his vassals' advice and approval he sent a private letter into Beaucaire to Sir Dragonet, an experienced and thoughtful man, saying that he wanted to see the young count; he would make a bargain with him: he would raise the siege at once if Raymond gave him back his men, not one must be missing. Sir Dragonet, good, valiant and wise, talked with the besiegers, talked with the besieged, until in due course the count de Montfort did recover his men, but nothing else. The count of Toulouse kept all their horses, armour and equipment. And when day dawned and the sun shone Count Simon abandoned the siege.[1]

Count Simon's losses

Laisse 171
In rage and fury Count Simon abandoned the siege. He regained his men but lost their equipment, as well as their mounts, packhorses and Arab mules. His losses of all kinds were so heavy that there was plenty of carrion left lying for birds and dogs. And Beaucaire castle remained in the hands of Raymond, count, marquis and duke, for he was a valiant, wise and clever man, courteous, of excellent lineage and powerful kin, related to the noble house of France and to the good king of England.

---

1.   On 24 August 1216 in the thirteenth week of the siege.

Count Simon turns on Toulouse

Now the count de Montfort summoned the men of the Toulousain, the Carcassès, the Razès[1] and many other districts: no one, sergeant or peasant, must stay behind, but all must come to Toulouse; and from the Lauragais district as well. The count and his companions rode so hard that they did five days' journey in three days, and quartered themselves in and around Montgiscard.

In the clear light of dawn Count Simon and all the French armed themselves, arrayed their ranks and rode straight along the good level highway to Toulouse. Out from the town in twos and threes came some of the best knights and chief citizens. As soon as they saw the count they said to him with great courtesy:

'My lord count, may it please you, we are astonished to see you here bringing swords and deadly steel. A man who injures his own possessions achieves nothing, and if we were to quarrel with you, we should suffer. There ought to be nothing between yourself and us which could cause any kind of trouble. In all kindness you promised us that you would never hurt us. But now we can see no kindness, nothing good, for you have come against the town in arms. You should enter it, my lord, riding your palfrey, unarmed, weaponless, wearing a gold-embroidered tunic, singing and garlanded like the lord of the city. No one would dispute any order you might give, and here you come bringing fear and a lion's cruel heart!'

'Barons,' said the count, 'you may like it or not, but armed or unarmed, along the road or across it, I am coming into the town and shall see what is happening. You are in the wrong, you began this trouble: you have robbed me of Beaucaire, it's your fault I could not take it, robbed me of the Venaissin and Provence and the whole Valentinois. In a single month more than twenty messengers have told me that you had bound yourself by oath against me and had sent word to Count Raymond, so that he should regain Toulouse and I should lose it. And by the true cross on which Christ hung, I will not take off my hauberk nor my Pavian helmet until I am given hostages, your most important men. I shall be glad to know whether you'll refuse them.' And they replied:

'My lord, have mercy on us, on the town and on its people! We have done you no harm or wrong, not so much as a *malgoire*[2] pennyworth! None of us have ever taken an oath against you, and anyone who told you we did, is trying to get the fief away from you. Christ the true God well knows what the facts are. May his holy body and our own good faith avail us!'

'Barons,' said Count Simon, 'you are too much my enemies, and too eloquent! Never since I conquered you, nor before, have you rejoiced at any honour or success of mine.'

Then he called to him Sir Guy, Sir Hugh de Lacy, Sir Alan, Sir Foucaud and Sir Aldric the Fleming.[3]

'My lord count,' said Sir Alan, 'you need a bridle to keep your anger in check, for if you bring down Toulouse, you yourself will sink past recovery.'

---

1. A county on the upper Aude.
2. A coin common in Montpellier, struck originally by the counts of Melgueil.
3. Perhaps related to Raoul Le Flament, lord of Canny-en-Beauvaisis.

'My lord,' said Count Simon, 'I am fully committed, I have pledged all my rents and revenues. My company tells me they are suffering such want and poverty, that if I don't succeed here, I don't know what they will do to me. Now, these men who came out here,[1] I want them arrested now at once and put into the Narbonnais castle. We shall hold all property and all silver at our disposal till we are rich enough to return to Provence.'

Laisse 172

'We shall return to Provence when we have the means to do so, but first we shall destroy Toulouse and leave nothing good or beautiful inside it. They have robbed me of Provence and they shall pay for its recovery.'

'My lord brother,' said Sir Guy, 'I'll give you good advice: if you take no more than a fifth or a quarter of their wealth, the green shoots will grow with better hope; but if in your rage you destroy the town, all Christendom will blame you, you will earn Christ's anger and the reproach of holy Church.'

'Brother,' said the count, 'every one of my companions wants to leave me, because I have nothing to give them. And if I destroy Toulouse, it's with good reason, for they hate me here, and always will. Then with the money I get out of it, I can hope to recover Beaucaire and take Avignon.'

Now Master Robert[2] spoke:

'My lord count, I have good reasoning to offer you: Since the day the pope chose you, it has been your duty to observe reason and law, so that you bring no trouble upon the Church. As Toulouse has committed no treason against you, you must not destroy it except by due judgment of law. If you abide by the law, they should not suffer loss or harassment for the sake of an unproved accusation.'

The bishop of Toulouse addresses the inhabitants

Talking like this, they approached the town. The bishop[3] spurred his horse and rode in through the streets, giving his blessing. Then he at once ordered his hearers, he begged and commanded them:

'Barons, go out now to the good and dear count! Since God, the Church and I gave him to you, it is your duty to welcome him with a great procession; you will win rewards in this world and the joy of true confessors in the next! For he seeks nothing of yours, no, on the contrary he will give you what is his, and under his protection you will flourish.'

'My lords,' said the abbot of St Sernin,[4] 'the lord bishop speaks sense. Accept the pardon, go to meet the count and welcome his lion! Lodge his men in your houses as they require, do not say no to them, and sell them all the goods they need. They will not cheat you of so much as the cost of a button!'

---

1. From Toulouse to beg for mercy.
2. Robert, described in laisse 174 as a wise lawyer, is thought by M.-C. to be one of those few inhabitants of Toulouse who accepted Simon's rule in order to avoid worse trouble, and identified with a *Raimundus Rotbertus* who was a member of Simon's court of justice at Toulouse between 1216 and 1218; M.-C., ii, p. 205, n. 5.
3. Fouquet.
4. Jordan, abbot 1212-33.

Count Simon's exactions

At that they went out into the countryside[1] and the man who had no horse went on foot. But all through the town ran a rumour, saying, and with reason,

'My lords, turn round, go quietly home! Count Simon wants hostages. If he finds you here outside, you'll look very stupid.' And round they turned and went promptly home again. But while they were talking and wondering, the count's sergeants and young men broke open their strongboxes and took their wealth. 'Pay up,' said these lads and squires, 'or else be tortured. My lord Sir Simon is angry with you.' And between their teeth and low-voiced the Toulousains murmured,

'God, you have delivered us into the hands of Pharaoh!'

The Toulousains resist

But now a cry arose through the whole town:

'Barons, to arms! Now is the moment to resist the lion and cruelty! Better to die in honour than live as prisoners!' From every side they came in haste, running, spurring, knights and citizens, sergeants and the town's militia, each with his full equipment, be it shield or iron hat, tunic or leather jacket, with sharpened axe, scythe-blade or javelin, handbow or crossbow, good lance, knife, gorget, mail-hood or padded jacket. Once they had assembled, fathers and sons, ladies and noble girls, all striving to do their utmost, they built barricades in front of their houses. Benches and chests, staves and palings, rolling barrels and beams and rafters, they built them up from the ground to stall-height and from the ground to the stair-landing. All over the town they resisted so vehemently that streets and sky re-echoed to the noise, the outcry and the trumpets' sound.

Fighting breaks out

'Montfort!' shouted the French and Burgundians, and 'Toulouse! Beaucaire!' and 'Avignon!' cried the defenders. Both sides with furious hatred attacked any enemy they could find: lances and swords, spear-hafts and stumps, arrows, stones, clubs, firebrands, shafts and halberds, blades and pennons, pikes, wooden beams, rocks, planks and quarrels flew fast on every side, shattering shields, helms and saddlebows, shattering skulls and brains, chests, chins, arms, legs, fists and forearms. So violent was the fighting, so fierce the struggle, the townspeople drove them off, drove them and Count Guy away.

Count Simon orders Toulouse to be burned

Seeing nothing else for it, the count de Montfort shouted,

'Fire the place!' Instantly firebrands and torches blazed. But conflict was raging near St Rémézy, in the Jewry and in St Stephen's Square. The French

---

1. Under the south-facing ramparts of the town, now the Faubourg St Michel.

held the church, the Mascaron tower and the bishop's palace;[1] ours fought the blazing fires, and piled up timbers at every corner to withstand attack.

Laisse 173
To withstand attack and defeat the enemy, to uphold their right and destroy the foe, they thrust themselves in amongst the flame and fire and brought felled timbers to reinforce the barricades. Some fought off the attacks, others quenched the flames, others again moved fast to seize and capture the French who had first quartered themselves in the town. These were terrified and in fear for their lives; the Toulousains blocked them into the count of Comminges' town house[2] and stopped them getting out. But loudly for all to hear, the count de Montfort shouted:

'Barons, let's try again elsewhere! Straight to St Stephen's,[3] that's where we'll hurt them!' And the count and his men spurred in such anger that the ground shook at the Santas Carvas elm tree.[4] They sallied out through the cathedral square, but failed to reach any of the townsmen. Hauberks and helmets rang and banners waved, horns blared and trumpets shrilled; earth, sky and air gave back the sound. Straight along the road from Sir Baragnon's cross[5] they charged with such force as to break down the barricades and timbers; from all sides they gathered there to fight, knights, citizens and sergeants rushing pell-mell, and with swords and clubs each side attacked the other. They took blows from darts, lances, arrows, knives, they brandished spears, javelins and scythe-blades. Such crowds were engaged, no one knew which way to turn. What brilliant encounters you would have seen, what mail hoods ripped and hauberks torn, what chests split open, helmets dented, fighting men overthrown and horses killed as blood and brain-matter ran in the square! So hard did the townsmen fight, they forced the French to abandon the conflict and draw off.

'My lords,' said Count Simon, 'I can tell you for certain, we'll never defeat them here. But follow me, and I'll go round and take them by surprise.' Away they spurred together, not one wanting to retreat, and tried to enter the town by the Cerdana Gate.[6] But the men there received them bravely; the streets were full of fighting; with clubs and stones and swords, with axes and halberds they drove them off and cleared the streets.

Count Simon withdraws into the castle

Fighting continued until darkness fell. Then the count withdrew, anxious

---

1. Rémézy is the local form of Remigius, St Rémy, patron saint of the church of the Hospitallers. The Jewry was in the same area, and St Stephen's Square in front of the cathedral stood some 500 m north of these. The Mascaron tower, named after the cathedral provost appointed in 1205, probably stood between the cathedral and the bishop's palace. M.-C., ii, p. 212, nn. 1 and 2.
2. Its site is not known but is indicated by a street, bridge and gate all called 'de Comminges' at the SW end of the present Rue des Moulins.
3. To St Stephen's cathedral.
4. The square where this elm tree grew, now Place Saintes-Scarbes, is some 150 m from St Stephen's Street.
5. This stood where St Stephen's Street crossed a main road consisting of the Rue Tolosane and Rue Baragnon (now des Arts). The Baragnons were a well-known Toulouse family.
6. This gate stood between those of Vilanova and Matabiau.

and very angry, into the Narbonnais castle, where there was great dismay. Vindictive and furious, he went and spoke to the townsmen he was holding captive there:

'Barons,' he said, 'you cannot escape, and by the most holy cross on which God hung, no riches in the world can stop me cutting your heads off and throwing you from the battlements.' And when they heard him swearing and raging, there was not one who did not shake for fear of death.

But the bishop in great anxiety tried hard to think of a way to win over the town and the townspeople. All night he sent messengers to and fro to explain to them, to persuade and convince them of the supposed remedy they hoped would help them, till in the end his words tamed them. Next morning at first light, he said, they must come out to Vilanova,[1] just at dawn.

Laisse 174

Just at dawn, as day was breaking, most of the town's best men were gathered inside the town hall,[2] men of wealth and honour, knights, citizens and commons. When they were all assembled and the noise died down, the abbot of St Sernin spoke to them first, also to the prior and the provost[3] there beside him, and to Master Robert, a wise lawyer.

'My lord barons,' said the abbot, 'We have been sent here by God, the true Trinity, by the Virgin Mary who bore him, and by the lord bishop who is sad, distressed, and very anxious at the confusion and danger now prevalent in Toulouse. Both sides, though, have sheathed their swords; may the Holy Spirit therefore bring his light, may he establish good will and peace between yourselves and the count, and do it in such a way that neither party is injured or deceived. And if you wish it, such an agreement shall be discussed and settled, for the lord bishop has urged so much on your behalf that he and holy charity have overcome the count. The bishop spoke up so strongly for you that he quite displeased the count!

Now Count Simon and the bishop have agreed that the bishop should order you to place yourselves in the count's mercy. The bishop promises by God and by his own spiritual and temporal powers and by those of the pope and all other clergy, that you shall lose neither life nor limb, property nor lands, nor any building in the town or any other inheritance. And if you now humble yourselves before the count, his love and kindness towards you will increase twofold. Moreover if anyone, stranger or resident, prefers not to acknowledge him as lord, he has full leave to depart freely and neither the count nor his men will arrest or injure him.'

But the men replied:

'My lord sir abbot, may it please you, we find your loyalty terrifying. You and the count and the bishop have taught us to be careful, for you have tested us again and again and you have never stood by anything you have told us. And the count is ruthless and arrogant, he will break his word to us the moment he has us in his net.'

'My lords,' said the abbot, 'listen to this: holy Church has promised you safety, and the count is neither so stupid nor so arrogant as to do anything to you

---

1. *Lai fors a Vilanova*; outside, east of the town. The present Rue Rempart-Villeneuve preserves the name.
2. *La maizo cominal*; between the Cité and the Bourg.
3. The prior either of the Hospitallers or of the monastery of Notre-Dame-la-Daurade; the cathedral provost, Mascaron.

for which he could be blamed. And if he did injure you, the Church would shout so loud that Rome and all Christendom would hear it. Don't be afraid of the next step; honour the count, and you'll win honey and wax together.'[1]

Master Robert spoke:

'My lords, listen to me. The count de Montfort certainly does not blame you at all and does not want to harm your bodies or your town - except for one man, rich and respected, who is guiltier towards him than the rest.'

'My lords,' said Sir Aimery,[2] 'it is I who am threatened. But I would rather go away than stay here, and am ready to do so. We shall go, my lord abbot, I and some of the best and noblest of the town, if you and yours will guarantee our safety.'

'No, Sir Aimery,' said Master Robert, 'don't do that.' But in his ear he said, 'You would be wise to go, for you and the count will never be friends.'

The townsmen attend the count's meeting

That is how the discussion began and ended. Afterwards they went straight to Vilanova where the meeting was to be held - but some go there free men, who will return in chains, if God does not help them.

Laisse 175

If God does not help and succour them, they will find they have walked into the trap and into the jaws of death, for the count and the bishop have planned secretly together to conquer worth and *paratge*.

When morning came and the sun rose in splendour, the bishop went out to the meeting. Knights, citizens and the chief lords came from the town and gathered at the viewing platform.[3] Bishop, abbot, provost, prior and Master Robert, they all went and stood before them, and with soft words, sighs and what seemed to be tears the bishop spoke:

'My lords,' he said, 'my heart grieves to see your distress and I pray to Jesus Christ and adore him with a true heart, begging him to drive out the evil sap and harmful humour, to give you good courage and such strength that there may be true affection between yourselves and Count Simon. And as God has chosen me to be a master and teacher, has given me as a shepherd to his sheep, let them trust me, let them not turn elsewhere, for I will protect them from the wolf and the wicked robber. I will lead them to feed on sweet grass and they shall win God and the highest glory. For if I lost or drove out one of them, how should I render account to my holy commander? However eloquent my defender, my lord would send me to seek the one I had lost, and I should not know where to look for him. Shake the blossom from a tree and you'll have no fruit that year. If I lost you or sent you astray, I should lose fruit and tree and all the labour; Jesus Christ would think me a false deceiver. May wild beasts and vultures consume me, blood and flesh, strength and vigour, if I cannot protect you from violence and wrong, if I cannot set you shining in glory

---

1. That is, it will be all profit, you cannot lose.
2. There were two men, uncle and nephew, called Aimery of Castelnau, both consuls of Toulouse. This one must have gone to join Raymond VI in Spain, as we find him in laisse 181 accompanying the count on his return to Toulouse.
3. Part of the town's defences, here used as a platform from which to address the meeting.

with the apostles and holy confessors! Accept light and the spirit, and I will show you the way to holiness!

Do me this honour, I beg you - enable me to make peace and love between you and the count, free from any damage to land, property or your own persons. Place yourselves in his power, don't be afraid, so that he may love and pardon you and you may accept him as lord. And if any man here has a changeful heart and fears the count's rule, he can depart freely and unafraid.'

And they answered him:

'My lord, you are our father and governor, and so we accept you in sincere love as our protector and adviser. Tell us, we beg you in the name of justice and the Redeemer, is this good advice you are giving us or should we be fools to take it?'

'Barons,' said the bishop, 'I take God to witness, and the Virgin Mary and our holy Saviour's body, I take my holy orders, the abbot and prior, that the advice I am giving you is good, the best I have ever offered. And if Count Simon were to do you any harm and I heard your outcry, God and I would come instantly to your defence.'

Such were the words they exchanged. Caught between force and persuasion, they were trapped in a running noose, and the bishop and Sir Guy immediately led them to Count Simon.

Count Simon takes more hostages

Laisse 176

When they saw the count, their grief and alarm intensified.

'My lord count,' said the bishop, 'here are some hostages for you, and you may take any more you want out of the town. We can tell you which ones to choose. Take my advice and call them in at once.'

'Barons,' said Count Simon, 'you will give me back all my captured men!'

'You shall have them at once,' they answered. And they were brought to him, not a leather strap missing. Then the count immediately sent in men bearing staves,[1] who went rapidly up and down every street and told the chief citizens:

'Don't try to hide! My lord the count commands you to go and join the hostages in the Narbonnais castle. Go now, this moment, don't stop to say goodbye to your friends. If you don't go at once, you'll be no better off, he'll never let you stay here in future.'

Then you would have seen women and children weeping, and little ones saying,

'Sir, when are you coming back?' And by ones and twos the men went up to the castle. The count locked them all away till the castle would hold no more.

Count Simon in conference

Next he ordered his barons to come to him at once, quietly.

'My lord count,' said the bishop, 'speak to us, we are listening.'

'Barons,' said Count Simon, 'I require your advice. I intend to destroy Toulouse. You may not like this, but all the property in the town is yours to share between you, and so now you will be able to recoup your losses.'

---

1. As a sign of authority.

'Brother,' said Sir Guy, 'by the faith I swore to you, you shall not do this! If you destroy Toulouse, you destroy yourself, but if you hold the town, you hold the fief as well. Lose this, and you lose the world and your good name. Reason, right, custom and honour all demand that as the town has shown you humility, so should you do to the town; since it is not arrogant, neither should you be arrogant. And I can tell you how to succeed: unite the two courts, theirs and your own;[1] put right all wrongs, all acts of injustice and injury; let them forgive you and do you forgive them. Place us and yourself and the town in their hands, generously give them back their fiefs and estates, grant them their own laws and good customs, and if they ask for more than that, give them more. Take nothing from them in taxes or forced levies. Then explain to them what your losses have been and decently accept from them whatever they give you. A small sum freely given is worth more than great wealth which brings trouble. If you'll take my advice, that's how you'll win Toulouse.'

'Sir count,' said Sir Alan, 'trust Count Guy, and you can be sure you'll make no mistake. They are men of rank and you must treat them honourably. Suppose they profit, you'll profit more, for if you strip them of their wealth now, they will never support you in future.'

'By God, Count,' said Sir Foucaud, 'now we shall see whether you're a wise and valiant man or going to act like a fool. If you destroy Toulouse, you may rise as high as you like, but God, honour and the world will bring you down again.'

'Barons,' said Lucas,[2] 'you are giving the count bad advice, and if he takes it, you will lose him his fief.'

'Lucas,' said Count Simon, 'you and the lord bishop shall advise me, for I can trust your judgment, you want me to succeed. You won't tell me lies.' They drew aside and spoke privately.

'My lord count,' said Lucas, 'listen: if you bring down Toulouse, you'll win honour, but if you honour Toulouse, you'll bring down yourself and us. The proverb tells you and the law confirms it: don't trust a man you've injured. That's why you must be on your guard against them. You've killed their fathers, their sons and kinsmen - that's an anger you can never dispel. And since they have no love for you, it is wrong for you to love them. Secretly they are longing for the other count and he loves them, so that you'll never hold the place for any length of time unless you take advice that will crush them permanently.'

'My lord count,' said the bishop, 'I will show you how to subdue them. I took them into my mercy so that you could attack them. If anyone reproaches you, explain to them why you have broken the protection offered by myself and the Church. Destroy all their barricades and defences, immediately confiscate all their arms and equipment; if anyone tries to hide his weapons, have him killed. Disperse the hostages, send them off to different parts of your lands, and in one way or another get hold of all the wealth which you and we know they possess. Then with these funds you will confound your enemies, win power for yourself and all your kin, capture Provence, Catalonia and Gascony and retake Beaucaire.'

---

1. The Toulousains' court consisted of the consuls and the communal council; Simon's of his marshal, Guy of Lévis, his castellan Gervase of Chamigny and his other officials.
2. Lucas 'filius Johannis'; one of Count Simon's entourage.

Laisse 177

'With this you'll retake Beaucaire, be sure of that.'

'I will be revenged,' said the count de Montfort, 'on the men of Provence for the disgrace they have put on me.' Proudly he addressed his lords, saying,

'This is the advice I hold good: to reduce this town to nothing.'

'My lord count,' said Theobald, 'you're not a fool, you know who's lying and who's telling you the truth. Subdue Toulouse and its dependencies, and you'll keep safe hold of all the rest of the fief.'

'Theobald,' said Count Guy, 'you're talking nonsense! The advice you're giving the count won't work, for if he burns Toulouse, if not even a third of the population is left there, he will never be able to hold the place for long without very great trouble.'

'Sir count,' said Ferry,[1] 'I'll tell you what I think: if you leave the men of Toulouse as they are, rich and comfortable, they will remember their sons and brothers and kinsmen whom you killed, whom they mourn, and then when they have the other count inside their ancient walls and are encouraged by his presence, they will bring you and the rest of your lands to ruin. Remember the reply made by the evil snake, the one who spoke to the villein about an agreement between them: Whenever I see the axe-mark, whenever you see the cradle, we shall hate each other and therefore I shall go.'[2]

'My lords,' said Sir Foucaud, 'let's end this discussion. Anyone who advises the count to destroy Toulouse for the sake of its gold and silver, who tells him to tear down the city and its wonderful buildings, is seeking the count's death, his misery and destruction. In losing this city he would lose the best tooth in his head! But if he treats it with honour, handles it so that it's ready and willing to obey him, then he could conquer all the kings of Spain.'

Notables of Toulouse exiled or imprisoned

At this point Sir Aimery came rapidly out of the town under safe-conduct, together with many other notables and the dispossessed knights.[3] The rest stayed behind, so harassed that many sons of good fathers groaned in agony, for the count de Montfort sent his sergeants into every street to take hostages. They took them off with threats and blows and herded them into the Count's Farm,[4] until they had four hundred of them. All night they stayed there in the wind and rain with no joy at all and no change of clothes. And at dawn when

---

1. Ferry of Issy (Seine), knight and member of Simon's court.
2. In this story, as told slightly differently by Marie de France, the snake accepted regular bowls of milk from the villein and in return gave him silver and gold and useful advice about farming. The villein's wife, however, feared the creature and persuaded her husband to attack it with his axe. He missed his blow, leaving an axe-mark in a stone; and the snake retaliated by killing the couple's child in its cradle as well as all their sheep. The terrified couple begged the snake's forgiveness and future help, which it granted on condition the villein kept his distance, as the mark on the stone and the empty cradle would always remind them that they could never trust each other (Marie de France, *Lais*, LXXII, ed. K. Warnke).
3. Who had found refuge in Toulouse when driven out of the Carcassès and the Biterrois.
4. A farmhouse west of the town which belonged to the counts of Toulouse, later known as the Château de la Cépière.

the sun rose in splendour, the count and the bishop ordered all the inhabitants to gather at St-Peter-in-Cozinas.[1]

Once they were assembled, an able lawyer spoke first, raising his voice so that all could hear:

'My lords, my lord the count commands you to withdraw from the mercy and from the whole agreement granted you earlier by the bishop. You shall not call on the Church or the clergy for protection. You shall all throw yourselves upon the count's kindness, with no fear of harsh imprisonment or death. Either you do him right by accepting the judgment he will deliver in his own court, or you leave his land and simply go, your freedom guaranteed by his safe-conduct and appended seal.'

'My lords,' they said to each other, 'now we can escape death by accepting torture! But what heart could imagine such strange talk, so cruel, so hard and so false?'

One of the townsmen called out to them:

'My lords, I wish to leave, and I'll abandon my property here. But give me a pass so that I can travel safely.'

'You shall have it at once,' they said. But they put him in prison, and with no gentle hands, they bound him in chains which were not made of silver, until God and his good stars should set him free. When the rest saw this they were terrified and asked for no further pledges or guarantees. Angry and wretched, sad and suffering, they are all at the count's mercy.

Laisse 178

At the count's mercy, the people of Toulouse suffer worse sorrow yet from cruel slaughter and lying tongues. Count Simon sent his murderous servants to hunt up and down the streets, swift as running messengers, and seize weapons and equipment. Next he ordered the trumpeters to proclaim that every knight and lady, every man of substance, rank or worth, should leave the town.

....

'Sir count, God has exalted you, so why do you not take revenge on your enemies, enemies worse than anyone ever had? Kill any survivors and confiscate their goods.'

'This is nonsensical!' said Sir Guy of Lévis. 'You are sending your men in to destroy the town.'

'First, though,' said Count Simon, 'I'll shift them elsewhere.'[2]

Then he sent his fluent speakers to tell the townspeople that they must pay him enough money to conquer heresy, and must pay it before next All Saints' Day.[3] Miserably, they promised to do so. Next he ordered them all out of the town. Out came all the best and the flower of its people, knights, citizens and money-changers, driven out with blows, with threats, abuse and insults, by armed ruffians who hustled them along like running footmen. Such grief and anger, such heat and dust, distress, anguish, danger and burning rage brought tears to mingle with their sweat, made hearts and guts ache with a pain that increased their agony and reduced their strength.

---

1. A parish church in the Bourg often used for meetings.
2. *'Pero,' so ditz lo coms, 'ans mudarei alhors.'* The meaning is not clear, as there is no object for the verb *mudarei*.
3. 1 November.

All over the town rose shrieking and lamentation from men, women and children, from sons and fathers, from mothers, sisters, uncles and brothers, from rich citizens in tears.

'Oh God,' they cried to each other, 'what wicked rulers! Lord, you have delivered us into the hands of robbers! Give us our own lords back or give us death!'

Count Simon orders Toulouse to be razed

But the count de Montfort sent orders to every part of the fief: let no man stay away or fail to bring every mattock and spade, every pick, fork and good splitting wedge; they must join the count and help him destroy Toulouse, which now had no defenders. And he ordered his officers to send men with picks all over the town to break it down so flat that a man could run straight into it without a pause. Then you would have seen solars and towers knocked down, ramparts, halls and tall crenels overthrown. Workmen demolished roofs and workshops, passages and fine painted chambers, doorways, vaults and lofty pillars. Such was the noise, the dust and damage, the confusion and heat in every quarter of the town,[1] such the mingling of sun, air, haze and fog, it was felt like an earthquake, like thunder or the beat of drums.

In every street many were in tears, their distress renewed by the turmoil, their hearts and spirits overcome by the darkness, for Toulouse and *paratge* were in the hands of traitors, as their deeds made plain.

Laisse 179
Very plain their deeds make it, and the way they are treating these wonderful rich palaces, the costly buildings, ancient towers and new constructions, the ramparts and defences which they smash and throw down, levelling every part so smooth that men or animals can run straight in. And they lead away the hostages, heaping them with threats, with foul taunts, affronts and insults, and disperse them to foreign lands. In heavy irons they go, in chains, suffering grief, distress and pain, the living and the dead all bound together.

Count Simon summons his counsellors.

The count de Montfort summoned his council to come at once. The bishop, provost, barons and the count's kinsmen talked privately inside the ancient tower.[2]

'My lords,' said Count Simon, 'both logic and feeling tell me the town must be sacked and then set alight and burned, for its people are arrogant past all comparison. If it weren't for the bishop, who's a clever and subtle man and managed to talk them into that agreement, my whole following would be slaughtered, I myself disgraced and my name made worthless. I should be sorry to take no revenge for this!'

'Sir count,' said Theobald, 'sentence has already been passed: any vassal who attacks his lord must die a painful death.'

---

1. *Per totas las partidas* - Toulouse was divided into twelve sections, six in the Cité, six in the Bourg.
2. *La tor antiqua*, no doubt the Narbonnais castle, described in 1556 as possessing two towers dating from Roman times.

'Theobald,' said Sir Alan, 'your reasoning will do the count great harm, if God does not protect him. Did my lord the count not promise them on holy relics to be their good and true lord and to rule them with kindness? And they certainly swore a similar oath to him.[1] As it was a mutual pledge, it is important to see who broke it first. Suppose I am your vassal and your loyal captain, giving you sincere affection and obedience, doing you no wrong or injury, wishing you no harm, but you are a bad lord to me, you break your oath and come to destroy me with sharp shining steel, am I not to defend my life? Indeed I am! A lord has only this much due to him as lord: that his vassal must never make a first attack on him.'

'Brother,' said Count Guy, 'you are so worthy and valiant, your own good sense should calm your anger and enable you to show them mercy. You should do no harm to them or their town, but take a general subsidy.'

'My lord count,' said the bishop, 'be harsh to them, strip them to the skin! Let all wealth belong to you, both silver and coin; let them pay you thirty thousand marks, not a penny less, between this All Saints and next. And let that be only the beginning! What they have left shall be as nothing. And keep them all the time like recreant serfs, so that they are never able to bare their teeth at you in anger.'

'My lord,' said Sir Theobald, 'give me a moment's hearing! They are so proud and so obstinate, so perverse and intelligent, that you and we ought to be afraid of them, for if you don't crush them, then you, we and the Church will have trouble.' With such words as these, Count Simon and his advisers reached agreement.

Toulouse sacked

Now the count de Montfort sent his brutal sergeants into Toulouse to begin their exactions, their filthy bullying affronts and atrocities. All through the town they went, threatening and clubbing their victims, seizing whatever they wanted in every quarter. In every street you would have seen unhappy men and women weeping and in pain. Bitter tears they shed, bitterly their hearts mourned, as de Montfort's men took and the townspeople gave. Nothing could they keep, no flour or wheat, no brocades or purples or good clothing of any kind. Ah, noble Toulouse, God has given you into the hands of wicked men so that they may break your bones!

The count de Montfort stayed there a long time[2] in order to do what he intended and destroy Toulouse. Then he crossed the Garonne and rode to St Gaudens and straight into Gascony.

Count Simon rides to Gascony and Bigorre

Laisse 180
Straight into Gascony he rode, full of joy at having wreaked his fury on Toulouse, where he had slain *paratge*, destroyed and banished it, driving all

---

1. On 7 March 1216 the Toulousains did homage to Simon de Montfort and his son Amaury; next day Simon and Amaury promised to be true and loyal lords to them, to protect them and make good any wrongs they might do them; M.-C., ii, p. 251, n. 6.
2. From mid-September till the end of October 1216. In early November Simon is at Tarbes.

the town's best men out into danger and holding the rest captive in sorrow and dismay.

Count Simon went to Bigorre where he married his son[1] and gave him that county, but not the whole of it. It was trimmed off near the Gave, for the young man could not take possession of the castle of Lourdes.[2]

Then Simon returned to Toulouse and redoubled its agony. Good men and sinners, everyone paid the price of his wickedness, for he demanded the contributions of those who had left the town[3] and any who did not pay were tormented in body, goods and inheritance.

February 1217, Count Simon besieges Montgrenier

Next the count gathered his troops and with an angry heart laid siege to Montgrenier.[4] Inside was the capable Roger Bernard of Foix[5] with many good knights well armed and equipped, youngsters of good family and experienced sergeants. But the defenders suffered an irreplaceable loss in the death of Baset of Montpezat,[6] a man of powerful lineage and noble kin, courteous, pleasant and excellent in every way. Count Simon kept up the siege until the defenders were forced to negotiate for lack of water.

Summer 1217, the crusaders campaign in lower Languedoc and the Rhône valley

Then Count Simon subdued the length and breadth of the country. He rode to Posquières[7] and did all he intended there; next he wickedly destroyed Bernis, where he killed many good honest men, men who gave alms and sowed corn, and many innocent knights as well.[8] After that he took the Bastida and many a fine young nobleman, by which means he and Dragonet[9]

---

1. In November 1216 Simon de Montfort married his younger son Guy to Petronilla of Comminges, countess of Bigorre in right of her mother Stephanie, and widow of Gaston VI of Béarn. Soon after Gaston's death in 1214 Petronilla had married Nunyo, son of the count of Roussillon and cousin of the late Peter II king of Aragon, but Simon succeeded in getting the Gascon bishops to annul this marriage.
2. The castle of Lourdes, Bigorre's main fortress, was garrisoned against the crusaders by Nunyo and his ally William Raymond of Moncada, which earned them a sentence of excommunication from Honorius III.
3. Those who were still there had to pay up on behalf of those who had fled or been driven away.
4. This castle towered above the Ariège valley some 4 km south of Foix. Simon undertook this siege in the depths of the Pyrenean winter, February 1217, out of anger and fear because Honorius III had just returned Foix castle to its count, Raymond Roger. The pope ordered Simon to abandon the siege, but he paid no attention.
5. Son and heir of the count of Foix.
6. Baset, lord of Montpezat; the ruins of his castle can still be seen on a peak above the Garonne between Mancioux and St Martory.
7. This commanded the town of Vauvert (Gard). Rostand, its lord, did homage to Simon in April 1215, but later supported young Raymond.
8. Simon stormed this town and hanged many of its inhabitants as relapsed heretics.
9. Dragonet of Mondragon held lands in Bollène (Vaucluse); the Bastida may be a castle in that area belonging to the Reynaud family.

were reconciled. Next, as he and Sir Adhémar[1] were at odds, he sent to tell the bishop of Viviers[2] to provide him handsomely and quietly with boats on the Rhône, and they crossed over. The brave young count was very angry at this, for they destroyed the Valence vineyards. If only, he declared, he could get to grips and fight them!

Count Simon entered Montélimar, to which Lambert[3] brought him. He rode to Crest Arnaud[4] and laid siege there. This place was garrisoned by many good men, including William Artaut of Dia, a tried and true heart, and Sir Berbo of Murel[5] with a strong company. But the bishop of Dia who held the castle gave it up and surrendered it out of sheer wickedness.[6]

August 1217, Raymond VI returns from Spain

These were serious setbacks for the Provençals, but then God caused a kindly light to shine upon them from Toulouse, one that blazed across the world, restored vigour to *paratge* and splendour to worth, for their lord the count,[7] so much endangered, so wrongly disinherited by the mighty pope and the other clergy, arrived in a fief where he found loyalty, that of Sir Roger of Comminges.[8]

Count Raymond confers with his supporters

Laisse 181
Sir Roger of Comminges is a man of true valour, wise, generous and full of goodness. Count Raymond reached his fief without trouble and talked and took counsel with his close friends:

'My lords,' he said, 'advise me, for you know very well how wrong and how shameful it is that I have been disinherited for so long. But pride has been cast down and humility raised up, blessed Mary and the true Trinity do not want me to remain disgraced and brought low for ever. I sent messengers to Toulouse, to its most powerful and respected men who love me from their hearts and whom I love, to ask if they would welcome me, and what they think. And in their good sealed reply they tell me that the count de Montfort has taken hostages from the town, but that there is such love and friendship between them and myself, so true and loyal are they, that they would rather lose those hostages than have me remain in exile, and they will give me back the town if I can get there undiscovered. Having found them so devoted to my service, I want to hear what you advise.'

---

1. Adhémar of Poitiers.
2. His name was Bournon.
3. Lambert, co-suzerain of Montélimar, supported Simon; the other co-suzerain, Gerald Adhémar, fought for Raymond.
4. Crest (Drôme) belonged in part to Adhémar of Poitiers.
5. Probably the same as the Bernis of Mureils in laisse 154.
6. He had taken over the part of Crest belonging to the other co-suzerain, and now forced Adhémar's garrison to surrender.
7. Raymond VI count of Toulouse.
8. Viscount of Couserans and count of Pallars, nephew through his mother of the count of Foix and on his father's side of the count of Comminges. His lands were situated in Catalonia and on the northern side of the Pyrenees, linked by the Salau pass. Raymond had had messengers from Toulouse who told him how desperately he was wanted there, and that Simon de Montfort was away campaigning beyond the Rhône.

The count of Comminges[1] said,

'Listen to me, my lord. If you can regain Toulouse and keep it, *paratge* will shine in splendour once again, you will shed glory upon yourself and on all of us, for if you recover your heritage we shall all have enough land.'

After the well respected count, Roger Bernard[2] spoke:

'My lord count, I tell you that if you get Toulouse back, you'll hold the dice, you'll have the keys to your whole inheritance. Worth and *paratge* will be restored, for if you can only get into the town, we can hold it well enough. It's better for you to be its lord and die there than to wander the world in danger and disgrace.'

Bernard of Comminges[3] said,

'My lord, believe me, my whole heart is resolved, it is my firm intention always to do and say what you wish. If you have neither wealth nor land, then I want none. But if you regain Toulouse and are fortunate there, it will be essential to defend it so strongly that no one can ever take it from you again.'

'Fair nephew,' said Count Raymond, 'God willing, so we shall!'

'Push forward, my lord count!' said Roger of Comminges. 'I have many enemies and must garrison my fief against sudden attack, but I shall reach Toulouse as soon as you do.'

Roger of Montaut[4] said,

'A good plan can turn to disaster if it is not followed up, but a good beginning can lead to victory.'

'My lord count,' said the Abbot of Montaut,[5] 'don't be afraid! Don't turn back, ride till you see Toulouse, for even if you had no one with you but ourselves and the men of Toulouse whom you trust so well, we shall certainly be able to defend it, just so long as you don't flinch from entering the place.'

Sir William Gerald[6] said:

'Be sure of this, my lord count: you will regain Toulouse! We shall recover our heritage, we shall use all our wealth and power and our strong arms so that you can defend the place and live there in peace.'

William Unaud[7] said, 'And if you find Frenchmen in there, the town loves you and longs for you so much that nothing can stop you taking them all prisoner.'

'My lord,' said Sir Aimery,[8] 'choose messengers to tell them what you are planning, so that you find them ready and able to fight for you the moment you arrive.'

---

1. Bernard IV. Protected though he was by his oath of obedience to the Church (April 1214), he now had Simon on either side of him, in Toulouse and Bigorre, which must have increased his anxiety to help his cousin Raymond, as he had already done in 1211 (laisses 87 and 88).
2. Son of the count of Foix.
3. Son of Bernard IV, count of Comminges.
4. There were four Montaut brothers, Bernard, Roger, Isarn known as the Abbot, and Odo. The castle of Montaut stood on a hill above the Garonne 10 km NE of Carbonne.
5. Isarn; see the previous note.
6. Not identified.
7. The Unauds were an important and wealthy family of the Toulousain. William was a son of Raymond lord of Fourquevaux and his wife Marquise.
8. Of Castelnau.

'See to that for me, Sir Aimery,' said Count Raymond.

Men in attendance on the count, members of the best families of Toulouse,[1] cried out with one voice, saying,

'For God's sake, dear lord, enter Toulouse! Even if you sent in no one but these armed men here, you'd never find one man to oppose you. Those who have to beg for other men's kindness are better dead, better unborn!'

'Barons,' said the count, 'God be praised that I find your hearts so firm and strong! You are all determined to enter Toulouse - then since you are all agreed, let us go and take it!'

Raymond and his friends ride for Toulouse

Thus was the discussion begun and agreement reached from which fire blazed and light sprang, for the mighty count now rode fast and joyfully straight for Toulouse. Up hill and down dale he rode, across deep combes and through leafy forests, and came to the Garonne and crossed it. Ahead of him rode Roger Bernard of Foix with a small troop on the strongest mounts, he and three other Rogers,[2] banners flying. These rode straight on and came to La Salvetat,[3] where they encountered Joris.[4]

A skirmish on the way

Laisse 182
At the encounter with Joris there was uproar and shouting and many of ours were alarmed. But Sir Roger of Montaut attacked them bravely, fought and challenged them with his sharp-edged sword, and Sir Roger of Aspet,[5] riding well ahead, spurred and struck Sir Ainart of La Becha[6] on his fine-woven hauberk and overthrew him so forcefully that his heart burst. Roger Bernard[7] heard the encounter and rode straight to it; well his Arab courser bore him! He struck Richard of Tournedos,[8] shattering his shield and the hauberk that could not save him; down to the ground he flung him and smashed his skull. Hand to hand was the fighting, men hacked and slashed wherever they could reach and many of them were wounded. But when Joris felt their strength, he took fright, withdrew from the conflict and made his escape. Fast as they pursued him, he fled faster still.

Now Count Raymond came up, spurring full tilt; he saw the dead men lying there and was delighted. Bernard of Comminges, a man of great good sense, said,

---

1. They had fled from Simon's reign of terror in the autumn of 1216 and joined Raymond VI in exile.
2. Roger of Comminges, Roger of Montaut and Roger of Aspet who is mentioned in the next laisse.
3. La Salvetat-sur-Garonne, Rieux canton, on the left bank of the river.
4. A knight called Joris (the Languedoc form of George) is mentioned in 1262 as having received the property of Payan of Ladern in the Carcassès 'du temps de Simon de Montfort'. M.-C. concludes that he was a local man who joined the crusaders when they arrived in the south; M.-C., ii, p. 271, n. 5.
5. Lord of Bérat (Haute-Garonne) and nephew of the count of Comminges.
6. Not identified.
7. Son of the count of Foix.
8. A knight from Normandy.

'God is guiding us, my lord! We have beaten them at the river crossing, and we shall win back Toulouse, this omen tells us so.'[1]

'Fair nephew,' said the count, 'you won't be proved wrong!'

Count Raymond sends word into Toulouse

All that day they rode along smooth highways till darkness fell. Then the count chose good faithful messengers and briefly told them to tell his sworn friends in the town that he and the other dispossessed men had arrived outside; let them come without fail to welcome him. At sunrise when the day began to brighten and they saw the dawn, the count was anxious in case he should be seen and the news of his arrival be spread all over the country. But God worked a miracle for him - the weather darkened and a grey mist filled the air, so that the count got safely into woodland and was soon hidden.

Count Raymond is welcomed

Ahead of all the rest Sir Hugh John[2] came out, together with Sir Raymond Belenguier[3] both longing to greet the count, and they found him where he was sheltering. Great was their joy when they met.

'My lord,' said Sir Hugh John, 'thanks be to God! Come and retake Toulouse! They are so ready for you there and all your kin will be so instantly obeyed that even if you put no one but these armed men into the town, you will defeat and kill all your enemies and restore yourself and us to power for ever. But do not let us go in across the bridges, for if they saw us, they would man them at once.'[4]

'I tell you truly, my lord,' said Sir Raymond Belenguier, 'they long for you here as for the Holy Spirit. You will find us full of courage; never again will you be driven out of your lordship.'

With that they rode on, still talking, and when they saw the town, the eyes of even the boldest among them filled with heartfelt tears. Each in his own mind said,

'Virgin Empress, give me back the home where I grew up! Better I should live or be buried here than wander any more about the world in danger and disgrace.' They rode up out of the water and reformed in the meadow, ensigns displayed and banners flying, and when those inside Toulouse distinguished the blazons, they came to the count as to one risen from the dead.

13 September 1217, Count Raymond enters his city

When the count entered through the arched gateway all the people flocked to him. Great and small, lords and ladies, wives and husbands, they knelt before him and kissed his clothing, his feet and legs, his arms and fingers. With

---

1. La Salvetat-sur-Garonne is less than 40 km from Toulouse.
2. Leader of Raymond's supporters in Toulouse; member of an important Toulousain family, consul more than once, *viguier comtal* under Raymond VII.
3. Several members of this family, also spelt Berengarius, were consuls of Toulouse during the thirteenth century.
4. They forded the Garonne below the mill-dyke at Bazacle.

tears of delight and in joy they welcomed him, for joy regained bears both flower and fruit.

'Now we have Jesus Christ!' they said to each other, 'now we have the morning star risen and shining upon us! This is our lord who was lost! Through him worth and *paratge* are freed from their graves, are healed and restored, and our whole kinship regains power for ever!'

The Toulousains slaughter the French

So strong and valiant were their hearts now that they took sticks and stones, lances and sharp javelins, and with shining blades they went through the streets and cut down every Frenchman they could find.

'Toulouse!' they shouted. 'Today the false lord must go, he and all his brood and his evil spawn, for God defends the right! The betrayed count comes with a handful of men and he is so strong he has won back Toulouse!'

Laisse 183

The count has won back Toulouse which he so passionately desired, but in all the city there is no tower or hall, no gallery or solar, no high wall or bastion, no protective merlon, no gate, no rampart, no watchman or gate-keeper, no hauberk, armour or full equipment. But everyone there was so overjoyed to welcome him that each man felt brave as Oliver,[1] and they cried out,

'Toulouse! God has given us back our rightful lord, now we shall triumph! We may need weapons and money, but we shall regain the fief and its true heir. Daring, courage and good luck challenge us all to attack our enemy and crush his arrogance.' Clubs, pikes, an applewood cudgel, each took what he could; banners flying and warcry resounding, they ran through the streets. What Frenchmen they could find, they slew; the rest fled hurriedly into the castle,[2] where the townsmen pursued them with shouts and blows.

Now out from the castle rode brave crusading knights in double mail, but they were so frightened of the townsmen, not one of them spurred forward to give or take a blow.

Alice countess de Montfort in the Narbonnais castle

High up in a vaulted archway of the great rich palace stood the countess,[3] in desperate anxiety. She sent for Sir Gervase, Sir Lucas, Sir Garnier and Sir Theobald of Nouvila[4] and briefly asked them:

'Barons, what are these troops who have taken the town from me, and who is to blame?'

'Lady,' said Sir Gervase, 'it can only be Count Raymond, who claims

---

1. The legendary hero who died with Roland at Roncevaux.
2. The Narbonnais castle, held by the crusaders since the spring of 1215.
3. Countess Alice was in the castle together with Guy's wife Briande, Amaury's wife Beatrice of Vienne, the younger Guy's wife Petronilla, countess of Bigorre, her own youngest son Simon, and her nephew and nieces.
4. Gervase of Chamigny, Simon's castellan and seneschal of Toulouse; Lucas, see laisse 176; Garnier, reported killed in laisse 205; Theobald, laisse 169.

Toulouse, with Sir Bernard of Comminges - I can see him among the first, I know his banner and his standard-bearer. And Sir Roger Bernard is there, son of Raymond Roger, and Sir Raymond At of Aspet, Fortanier's son,[1] and so are the dispossessed knights and the legitimate heirs, and many more, more than a thousand. Toulouse loves these men and longs for them, they will set the whole fief ablaze. And we have kept them out and kept them poor - now we shall pay for it.' Hearing this, the countess beat her hands together and struck herself.

'Alas!' she said, 'and yesterday all was going so well for me!'

'Lady,' said Sir Lucas, 'we must lose no time. We must send Count Simon a sealed letter and a messenger to let him know our danger; let him make agreement if he can with the whole of Provence, and come to help us, he and his companions; let him not count the cost of sergeants or hired troops. If he is slow in coming, there will be no second chance. There's a new heir just arrived who won't leave him one quarter of the fief.'

Countess Alice sends word to Count Simon

The countess sent for a man skilled in languages.[2]

'Friend,' she said, 'take bad news to the count: he has lost Toulouse, his sons and his wife. If he makes the slightest delay in passing Montpellier, he'll find neither me nor any of his sons whole; if he loses Toulouse while he is over there trying to win Provence, it's a spider's web he's spinning, not worth a penny.' The messenger received these words and set off.

The townspeople build defences

The men of Toulouse stayed where they were on the fine open ground by the ramparts and there they built lists and barricades and a strong cross-wall, with brattices, arrow-loops and an opening to the left, so as to provide shelter at the rear against bolts shot from the castle. Never in any town have I seen such magnificent labourers, for the counts were hard at work there, with all the knights, the citizens and their wives and valiant merchants, men, women and courteous money-changers, small children, boys and girls, servants, running messengers, every one had a pick, a shovel or a garden fork, every one of them joined eagerly in the work. And at night they all kept watch together, lights and candlesticks were placed along the streets, drums and tabors sounded and bugles played. In heartfelt joy, women and girls sang and danced to merry tunes.

Town councillors are chosen

Count Raymond and his commanders consulted together and selected men to form a Capitol, which was essential for the rule and good management of the town. They chose a chief magistrate[3] to defend their rights, a good, wise and

---

1. Raymond At was the second son of Fortanier of Comminges, lord of Aspet; the youngest, Roger, is mentioned above in laisse 182.
2. *Un sirvent latiner* - a messenger needed to know several languages, for travel as well as for the delivery of his messages.
3. 'Chief magistrate' translates *viguier*. In September 1219 this post was held by William of Roaix.

valiant man, able and pleasant. Both the abbot and the provost handed over their church buildings, and the roofs and bell-towers of these were well garrisoned.[1]

Guy de Montfort brings troops to attack Toulouse

Count Raymond is in Toulouse, his own place, head of his lordship, but his fiercest foes are riding to battle with iron and steel: Sir Guiot, Sir Guy[2] and the other captains, on the Friday morning, very early.[3] May God look his way and defend him!

Laisse 184
May God defend him, for now is the time. Count Raymond has had loving welcome in Toulouse, worth and *paratge* rejoice. But Sir Guy and Sir Guiot ride on in wrath with their fine companies, the baggage trains following. Along the familiar roads towards Toulouse Sir Alan and Sir Foucaud[4] ride their bright-maned horses, standards displayed and banners fluttering. Helmets and shields rich with beaten gold crowd thick as drops of rain, hauberks and blazons glitter across the whole wide scene.

At the Montoulieu ditch where the rampart had been demolished, Guy de Montfort cried out, and was clearly heard:

'Free knights, dismount!' He was obeyed; at the trumpets' sound, each man dismounted. Squadrons arrayed, swords drawn, they forced their way into the streets, smashing down and destroying all the barricades. Old and young, knights and citizens, the townsmen withstood the attack; the people, active, valiant and so dearly loved,[5] offered fierce resistance; sergeants and archers, bows bent, gave good blows and took them too. The attackers were encouraged, however, by their initial success in taking the wooden barricades, they fought hard in the streets and very soon set fires blazing; but the defenders put these out and did not let them spread.

The attack repulsed

Now in through the thick of it rode Roger Bernard of Foix, bringing his whole company, and when the townsmen saw who it was, they were greatly encouraged. It was Sir Peter of Durban, lord of Montégut,[6] who bore Roger Bernard's banner, and gave them confidence. Sir Roger dismounted and advanced. 'Foix!' cried his men and 'Toulouse!' Brisk was the conflict wherever these appeared: darts, clubs and keen-edged swords, stones, arrows and slender bolts came showering thick as rain. From the housetops the Toulousains flung sharp stones to shatter helmets, crystals, shields, fists, bodies, arms and legs. Strongly and in every way they could, they fought off their attackers. But they were daunted by the blows and knocks, the uproar and

---

1. The abbot of St Sernin and the provost of St Stephen's cathedral. These were fortified buildings, with roundwalks and arrow-loops at roof height.
2. Young Guy, Simon's second son, with his uncle Guy, Simon's brother.
3. Possibly 22 September.
4. Alan of Roucy and Foucaud of Berzy.
5. By their lord the count.
6. From Durban-sur-Arize (Ariège), he was co-suzerain of Montégut.

shouting, and the French smashed down and captured the entrances and passages.

But then they were driven off; fighting for their lives, overcome, beaten, fleeing, they were repulsed by the defenders' united strength, they fled disarmed and defeated. Such was the townsmen's renewed vigour that they drove the French right out of the town, where they remounted and rode fast to the garden of St James;[1] here they retreated. But inside Toulouse lay their dead; marshland and ground afterwards showed red with the blood of men and horses who did not escape.

Sir Bernard of Comminges behaved very well: alert and valiant, he and his good company defended the entrances and passages on the castle side where the enemy had left their baggage train;[2] for this he has indeed won praise.

'Well, my lords,' said Sir Alan in retreat, 'I see you are thoroughly beaten! Knights, who can have defeated us? France is disgraced, our glory lost, we are conquered by a beaten enemy! Better unborn, better not to have lived, than to be defeated like this by unarmed men!'

The Frenchmen retreated. Some did not leave, but were dragged through the town and hanged.

'Toulouse!' cried its people, 'salvation is here!'

Joy now blossoms, sorrow now flourishes on one and the other side.

Laisse 185

On one and the other side the strife is sharper, for pride and vainglory have been flung out of Toulouse and Count Raymond directs and sustains the town. Many long years have he and his kin been here, and clearly it is God who has given the place back to him. Unprovided, weaponless, with only a few men and a handful of foreign troops, but with steadfast hearts, Count Raymond with God's help has driven out the Normans and the French. The Lord God is merciful to sinners who show mercy, he has given the town back to Raymond whose flag now flies there - may he look well on right and reason, on wrong and treachery, may he hear the cries of his faithful flock, defend Toulouse and guide those who love him!

The crusaders discuss the situation

Sir Guy and Sir Guiot talked with Sir Foucaud and Sir Alan, with Sir Hugh, Sir Guy of Lévis and others, more than I know. Sir Foucaud took the lead, saying:

'My lords, I am neither Breton, English nor German, so I tell you to listen and understand my Roman tongue.[3] Every one of us must grieve, for we have lost honour and glory, we have disgraced the whole of France, parents and children, she has suffered no more appalling shame since Roland died. We have plenty of weapons, good blades and swords, hauberks and mail, shining helmets, we have strong shields, maces and fine swift chargers, yet a defeated people, half dead, suffering, unprovided, unarmed, under attack and crying

---

1. Gardens close to the city wall (at that time demolished), where the Rue St Jacques now runs.
2. That of the crusading force under the two Sir Guys, arriving in haste from the Carcassès.
3. *Que aujatz mo romans.* Foucaud of Berzy is speaking French and expects non-French crusaders to listen carefully.

out, these have driven us out of Toulouse with sticks and stones and cudgels, have killed Sir John, the best fighter in my whole company. My heart will be heavy, my mind bitter, until my strong spear and I can take revenge! Well may the whole world stand amazed that an unprotected town can put up such a fight.'

'Sir Alan,' said Count Guy, 'you must remember how the men of Toulouse came to us to beg for mercy. It's clear that God does listen to grievances, for my brother Count Simon is such a harsh tyrant that he has always refused to take them back into favour, and so they have a strong claim. If he had only laid aside his hatred, we should not be defeated or have lost Toulouse, for a man who injures his own people does very wrong and is rightly blamed. Whatever anyone may swear to the contrary on the bones of the saints, I shall always believe that our sins have turned God against us. And it is clear that the situation is getting worse, for they are prospering and we are not. If God does not come to our help, this one throw can lose us all we have gained in ten years.'

Then Count Guy at once summoned his swift messengers and said,

'Go into Gascony and take my orders to the lord archbishop at Auch, tell him to go [to Sir Gerald of Armagnac and to Sancho];[1] they must come to our help at once. Tell them to bring all their men from every district, and hired troops too, so as to attack the town from all sides. Any man who does not come will never again hold land worth a pair of gloves; let him not doubt this for a moment.'

Count Raymond explains matters to his supporters

The count of Toulouse, a gifted speaker and intelligent, made clear to his barons all the difficulties they would face, the labours, guard duty, tax payments and edicts. He sent a messenger with sealed letters into Provence to tell his son about their glorious victory.

Reinforcements come to join Count Raymond

To the town's help came galloping the respected count of Comminges, wise and eloquent, the brave and upstanding Sir Esparch of La Barta, Sir Roger of Comminges, righter of wrongs, Bertrand Jordan and Sir Odo, claiming their rights, Sir Gerald of Gourdon who holds Caraman, Bernard of Montégut and his brother Sir Bertrand with all their vassals, Sir Gaillard, Sir Armand, Sir Estève Sa Valeta who can both take and give, Araimfres and his brother who refuses requests, Sir William Amanieu, a young man beginning well, Sir Amalvis and brave Sir Hugh of La Mota, Sir Bertrand of Pestillac who gives

---

1. There is a lacuna in the manuscript here; prose versions of the *Canso* indicate that the archbishop was to summon the count of Armagnac and an unidentified Sancho to Count Simon's help.

more than is asked, and Sir William Arnold.[1] With joy and glory they rode in, with fine companies and trumpets sounding. Great and small rejoiced, noise and uproar spread across all the town.

The countess Alice watches her enemies

Very anxious was the countess as she stood high at a window in the tower gallery. She watched them as they came and went, the men and women building the defences, she heard their dances and the noise and singing. Weeping, she shook and trembled, and exclaimed,
'I can see that my happiness is over and my sorrows must increase. I am afraid for myself and for my children!'

Her news reaches Count Simon

Her messenger rode hard, travelling fast over long stages, till he reached Count Simon[2] and spoke to him in the Roman tongue.[3] He knelt down before him and handing him the sealed letter, he sighed.

Laisse 186
Sighing, he gave him the letter, and Count Simon looked at him and asked,
'Friend, tell me the news: how do my affairs stand?'
'My lord,' said the messenger, 'it is painful to speak of it.'
'Have I lost the town?'
'Yes, my lord, undoubtedly. But if you go there at once and don't let them get settled in and fortified, you will be able to recover it.'
'Friend, who took it from me?'
'My lord, this is clear to me and to others, for I saw the other count return in great joy and the men of Toulouse bringing him in.'
'With a strong force, friend?'

---

1. On the names in this list, see M.-C., ii, 297 ff. for more details and surmises. Some we already know; others cannot be identified. Those that can include:
   Sir Esparch, who belonged to the family of the viscounts of Labarthe;
   Bertrand Jordan and Odo, younger sons of Jordan III, lord of La Isla Jordan, and of Esclarmonde of Foix;
   Gerald of Gourdon who fought the crusaders when they besieged Lavaur in 1211; did homage to Raymond VII for lands in Quercy, 1230.
   There was a Gaillard of Beynac in Périgord whose castle Simon de Montfort took and demolished in 1214.
   Armand is probably Armand of Mondenard; Araimfres probably of Montpezat.
   William Amanieu: in 1214 Simon de Montfort confiscated a fief in the Agenais from a man of this name and granted it to another Amanieu, Pons.
   Amalvis is probably the *Amalvinus de Pestillaco* whose name witnesses a donation made by young Raymond in 1219, and who in 1249 swore fealty to Alfonse count of Poitiers.
   Hugh of La Mota, perhaps related to William of La Mota and his son Raymond, from Montauban.
   Bertrand: the ruins of Pestillac castle command Montcabrier village, Puy-l'Evêque, Lot.
   William Arnold of Tantalon was seneschal of Agen, 1222-47.
2. Simon was besieging Crest.
3. *E dit li en romans*, i.e. in French.

'My lord, that I can't reckon. But the men who came with him do not seem to love you, for they at once attacked the Frenchmen they found there and pursued those who fled.'

'What are the townspeople doing?'

'My lord, they are working hard to make moats, ditches and brattices. As far as I can tell, they mean to besiege the Narbonnais castle.'

'Are the countesses[1] inside it?'

'Yes, my lord, they are. They are sad and in tears, weeping in terror of death and destruction.'

'Where was my brother Sir Guy?'

'My lord, I heard that he was bringing back the good troop you usually command and hoping to take Toulouse by storm, but I don't think he can succeed.'

'Friend,' said the count, 'be sure you keep this secret. If anyone sees you doing anything but laugh and crack jokes, I will have you burned, hanged or cut in pieces. If anyone asks you for news, speak sensibly, tell them no one dares enter my lands.'

'My lord,' said the messenger, 'there's no need to tell me this.'

Count Simon hides his anxiety

Count Simon came back from hearing the letter and joined the prince and the other lords.[2] He was a clever man, able to control his manner, hide his anxieties and make the most of success, and so now his lips smiled though his heart was groaning. They asked for news, and he at once began to boast:

'Indeed, my lords,' he said, 'I promise you I owe fear and thanks to Jesus Christ, for never before, I think, has he granted such good fortune to anyone. My brother has sent me the most cheering letter: no one, anywhere, can stand against him, and Count Raymond has gone off adventuring in Spain, for he has no safe refuge here. And the dispossessed lords have fled towards Bordeaux, to the sea, because they don't dare set foot in any part of my land. And the king of England[3] wants to make an agreement with me and will give me more land if I will let him alone. And my brother has entered Toulouse to collect the payments they wish to make me there; he will have it all sent to me so that I shall have plenty to use, to keep and to give away. And he tells me to concentrate on winning victories, to win land and defeat my enemies; but when I return to my own fief, he says, if I can arrange a useful treaty, I shall at once receive the strong castle of Lourdes, with Béarn and Bigorre and every part of that fief as far as its boundary with the kingdom of Navarre. And as God wills my success, I shall be glad to accept such an agreement for the sake of the rule of law, if I can arrange satisfactory terms without any loss to myself. Then I shall go and take possession of Lourdes and the whole of that fief as far as the coast.'

The barons who supported him were pleased, but many others felt their hearts shake within them, for fear they would lose their lands.

---

1. Alice, her sister-in-law Briande, and daughter-in-law Petronilla, countess of Bigorre.
2. William of Les Baux, prince of Orange, and Count Simon's Provençal supporters.
3. John, who in fact had welcomed and was expected to help his brother-in-law and his nephew, the two Raymonds of Toulouse.

Alliance made and a marriage planned

Then they discussed the agreement to be made. Between the hands of the bishop and on the holy relics of the altar they made a settlement between him and Sir Adhémar by which their son and daughter were then and there betrothed, and neither party would be able to deceive or outwit the other.[1] Then Count Simon made ready and had his horse saddled; the whole court was astonished that he said so little when he took leave. Many rode after him as he left. But when the news came, and it could not be hidden, that Count Raymond had entered to relieve Toulouse, to destroy the French and raise up worth, tongues were loosened all through the country and people cried out:

'Toulouse, God guide and save her, may he aid and help her, guard and defend her! May he give him strength to rebuild what's destroyed, to rescue *paratge* and rekindle joy!'

Count Simon rides for Toulouse

Now, full of anger, Count Simon rides night and day to enforce wrongs, to overthrow rights and exalt evil. He has sent his messengers and sealed letters in every direction, summoning to his help every man the archbishops and the cardinal[2] can find.

They rode hard by long stages and on a following Sunday at nightfall Count Simon reached Baziège,[3] but not to stay there. At dawn on a fine clear morning he had his troops make ready and his trumpets sound, the horses armoured and banners raised. Angry and ominous, he rode straight for Toulouse.

The cardinal advises extreme measures

'Count,' said the cardinal,' how glad you must be that the day of your enemies' defeat has come! You will of course take the town. As soon as you enter it, have the men hanged and the counts[4] put to death. Take care that no one escapes.'

'My lord,' said the bishop,[5] 'the Church must save all who are in a church within sight of the altar.'

'No,' said the cardinal. 'This was decided when sentence was passed. I abandon them to you, Count. Never fear that God will require them of you or exact repayment!' But the cardinal was wrong, for the king who rules, who sees straight and clear, who gave his precious blood as a remedy for sin, he wills to defend Toulouse.

Laisse 187
He wills to defend Toulouse, the king of heaven, the judge, the ruler who sees right and wrong.

---

1. The marriage of William of Poitiers and Amicia de Montfort agreed by Adhémar of Poitiers, count of Valentinois, and Simon de Montfort, did not take place.
2. Cardinal Bertrand, sent by Honorius III early in 1217.
3. Twenty-four km from Toulouse.
4. The counts of Toulouse, Comminges and Foix.
5. Presumably Fouquet, bishop of Toulouse.

Lion displayed and crystal bright, Count Simon rides. Up and down combes and valleys he follows the river bank straight for Toulouse,[1] and so they reach the meadows. His brother and many captains rode to welcome him and they met with warm affection.

Count Simon joins Guy before Toulouse

'Brother Guy,' said the count, 'and all of you, why have you not hanged these perjured traitors, burned the houses and destroyed the town?'

'Brother,' said Count Guy, 'everything we could do, we did. We attacked the town, got into the ditches and into the streets, and there we met them, knights, citizens and working men, and fought them hand to hand. With clubs, pikes and sharp hatchets, with shouts, yells and great deadly blows they paid us the rents and dues which were owing to you. Your marshal Sir Guy[2] can tell you how many marks of silver they flung at us across the ditches! By the faith I've sworn to you, there was not one of us so brave he wouldn't rather have suffered fever or a full battle when they were driving us out through the gates.'

'Brother,' said Count Simon, 'it is disgraceful to have let unarmed men defeat you! May God and St Martial never help me more if the barrels and equipment are unloaded from the pack-beasts before we get them into the town and in the market-place!'

'My lord count,' said Sir Alan, 'don't think in that way, for your oath is mere morning dew. By the faith I owe you, we have other things to discuss! If you wait till we get into the trenches, we shan't unload till Christmas, for by St Peter's body if these men weren't false to us, you never saw better fighters.'

Next came the throng of great barons and commanders, the lord cardinal ahead of them all, bishop[3] and archbishop in his train, with all their mitres, rings, crosses and croziers and missals.

Cardinal Bertrand exhorts the crusaders

He addressed them, a learned man speaking:

'My lords, the spiritual king tells each one of you that the fires of hell are in this town! It is brimming with guilt and sin, for there inside it is Raymond, their overlord. Whoever attacks this place will be saved before God. Recapture the town, seize every house! Let neither man nor woman escape alive, no church, no relics or hospice protect them, for in holy Rome sentence has been given: the sharp sword of death shall touch them. As I am a good and holy man, worthy and loyal, as they are guilty, wicked and forsworn, let sharp steel strike down each one of them!'

The crusaders muster to attack

His speech finished, the riders dismounted, and a finer company no mortal man ever saw. Crystals shone, helmets and hauberks gleamed, blazons glowed

---

1. Coming from Baziège, he would be following the River Hers.
2. Of Lévis.
3. Cardinal Bertrand, Garcias, archbishop of Auch, and Fouquet, bishop of Toulouse.

blue and scarlet, and all the countryside and the Saracen rampart[1] rang and re-echoed to the jingling of poitrel bells. Handsomely the squadrons mustered in the gardens; and on the castle walls and at the arrow-loops stood men with wound crossbows and steel-tipped bolts.

The defenders prepare

But the men of the town and their natural lord manned the lists and occupied the levels. Wherever they could they displayed their devices, the two scarlet crosses,[2] and the count's banner. On the sentry-walks and in the brattices stood valiant men, strong and secure, bearing halberds and stones. Down below on the ground others held lances and boar-spears to defend the lists and prevent any approach to the barricade. Within the arrow-loops and embrasures were the archers, defending the galleries and outworks with all kinds of bows, both arbalests and handbows. The tubs were filled with arrows and crossbow bolts. And all around stood the people, grasping axes, clubs and cudgels, the women and ladies bringing containers full of gathered stones, large ones and fist-sized pebbles. Toulouse stood to its defences. Outside, the attackers in good array brought fire, ladders and heavy rocks, and in different ways occupied the outlets.

The conflict begins

In full armour Sir Guy, Sir Amaury, Sir Sicard[3] and Sir Foucaud ride forward, they lead their fine companies close to the ditches. Battle and the day of danger approach - God guard the right!

Laisse 188

God of all truth guard the right! That distinguished legate the cardinal, the bishops, the abbot, provost, bishop[4] and clergy are praying to Saint Mary and the true Trinity to protect the town by damning it, to defend right and their loyalty, to cherish the count de Montfort and his noble barons, his banner and its sculpted lion. The breeze blowing through the patterned pennons, the jingling bells and glinting golden shields steady the knights' courage and enhance their joy.

The men of Toulouse are well prepared and resolute, ready to give blows and take them. Through the streets go the armoured horses. Both outside on the castle's crenellated ramparts and inside in the lists skilled bowmen keep up a rapid fire of slender steel-tipped shafts. The two sides are engaged. Shouting, trumpets and the mingled horns shake the Garonne, the castle and the meadow. 'Montfort! Narbonne!' they yell, they hear. French and de Berzy's men draw so near that only the lists and the ditch hinder them. Stones come flying in from the sides and find their mark.

---

1. The 'Saracen' invasions began in the eighth century, but part of the town's defences dated back to late Roman and Visigothic times.
2. On the banners of the count of Comminges and his kinsman Roger, whose arms were: Argent a cross patée gules.
3. Sicard of Montaut in Razès; no relation of the four Montaut brothers. Foucaud and John of Berzy commanded crusaders from the Soissons area.
4. The abbot of St Sernin, the cathedral provost and Fouquet, bishop of Toulouse.

Sir Imbert of La Volp[1] thrust so far ahead he managed to throw filling into the middle of the ditch; but as he turned back towards the patterned banner Sir Armand of Montdenard drove six inches of steel into his side. In the town the defenders set up a mangonel which cut and smashed and shattered both left and right. And the great count of Comminges, tried and true, had a crossbow bent - gladly they brought it him! - set to it a point of fine-tempered steel, drew, considered, took aim and hit Sir Guy de Montfort[2] whom he could see in the front ranks. So hard did the bolt strike the damascened mail that it drove in through silken surcoat and ribs and out the other side. Down fell Sir Guy and they carried him away.

'I reached you there, I think!' jeered the count. 'But as you're my son-in-law, I'll let you have the county!'[3] 'Toulouse!', they shouted, as they saw pride take a fall, 'Comminges!' for the count, 'Foix!' for Sir Roger Bernard, 'La Barta!' for Sir Esparch and 'St Béat!' for Sir Odo. 'Montégut!' they cried, 'La Isla! Montaut! Montpezat!'

Now with these warcries, every man is engaged. Sharp fly the javelins, the lances and feathered quarrels between the opposing sides, fast the inlaid spears, the rocks, shafts, arrows, squared staves, spear-hafts and sling-stones, dense as fine rain, darkening the clear skies. How many armed knights you'd have seen there, how many good shields cleft, what ribs laid bare, legs smashed and arms cut off, chests torn apart, helmets cracked open, flesh hacked, heads cut in two, what blood spilled, what severed fists, how many men fighting and others struggling to carry away one they'd seen fall! Such wounds, such injuries they suffered, that they strewed the battlefield with white and red.

The crusaders retreat

Privately Sir Guy the Marshal said to Count Simon:

'Alas, my lord, that ever you set eyes on Toulouse and its lands! Your brother's killed[4] your son's wounded, and so are many more who will be wept for ever!'

'By God, Guy,' said the count, 'today will finish it!'

'Count,' said Sir Hugh de Lacy, 'we are cut to pieces, we shall die here. Today will finish it, for I'm sure we have lost a third of our men. Let us withdraw, or they'll destroy us. Any more of this, and we're all dead men.' Great was the conflict, extreme the danger, until the best of the attackers turned away with their banners and withdrew in defeat.

'Toulouse!' cried the defenders. 'Checkmate and death to the madmen![5] All alone the cross has given the lion fresh brains and blood to eat! The star shines in the darkness, worth and *paratge* blaze out in glory!'

---

1. Not identified.
2. Simon's son.
3. The county of Bigorre. In November 1216 Simon's second son Guy married Petronilla, countess of Bigorre, daughter of Bernard IV of Comminges (laisse 180).
4. Simon's brother Guy did not die until January 1228. This lapse on the part of the poet or the scribe may indicate the date of the poem's composition, or its copying.
5. There is an untranslatable pun here: *Toloza! que los matz a matat!* The *matz* are madmen, and they have been *matat*, killed.

Count Simon's men rebuke him

Then they said to the count,

'It is because your mercy is dead and rotten that we have achieved so little, because you and your officials have deliberately treated these people with extreme arrogance; they are as badly off as a money-changer who gives Toulousain coin for rubbishy pence from Le Puy. And now they have got their natural lord back, in future the hare will have an open field.'

Angry and wretched, Count Simon went away, and under his bowed helmet he shook with rage. But the Gascon barons he had summoned, who had joined him in anger and out of compulsion - weep or complain who might, these men laughed and joked and said to each other,

'We are all saved! Ah, noble Toulouse, full of goodness, *paratge* blesses you, mercy gives you thanks, for you have used righteousness to drive out pride!'

Sad, angry and raging, the French depart, and the men of Toulouse remain there in honour, with God and righteousness in command.

Joy in Toulouse

Laisse 189
God and righteousness command in appearance and in fact, for law and loyalty have cast down arrogance and boastful pride, they have overthrown falsehood and treachery. That is how the count of Toulouse with his few men, so ill equipped, through good fortune regained Toulouse and accepted their oaths; and its men, joyfully labouring and defending the town, live in delight under true lordship.

Wounded crusaders are treated, the dead buried

The count de Montfort sent for wise physicians who make plasters and ointments and restore moaning and wounded men to life, and the lord cardinal summoned lettered priests to bury the dead.

Grief and discussion in the Narbonnais castle

All night long their sorrow grew. When it was almost morning and daylight came, they met on the paved floor of the Narbonnais castle's ancient tower[1] to discuss their plans. Guy de Montfort lay there, badly injured,[2] and near him Count Simon, the clergy and valiant lords, together with the countess, talked in private.

'My lords,' said the count, 'I must indeed grieve, for in the space of a few hours I have seen my kinsmen, my noble company and my son wounded. If I lose my brother here and am left alone, I shall be doubly sad all my life long. I am defending holy Church and her commandments; Provence and its lands were my own; I am amazed that God agrees to this! I am doing his service, obeying him, and yet he is pleased, he allows and wants me to be disgraced, he has let his own enemies destroy me!'

---

1. *La tor antiqua*, late third or early fourth century, demolished in the sixteenth century.
2. Guy recovered from this wound, but was killed on 20 July 1220, besieging Castelnaudary.

'Count,' said the cardinal, 'you must not be afraid. Your spirit is holy and patient, you will recover the town, you will recapture it very soon. And then let neither church, hospice nor saints avail them, let them all find martyrdom together! And if one man of yours dies in that struggle, the blessed pope and I promise them crowns like those of the holy Innocents.'

'My lord count,' said Sir Alan, 'I know you are a conqueror, but you are not looking at this matter as you should. God sees men's conduct and their hearts. It was pride, it was anger and arrogance that turned the angels into serpents.[1] And since it is pride and cruelty that control you, since you do not love mercy or find pity sweet but delight in causing pain, this great fang has grown up, a fang which both you and we will find hard to grind down. And the Lord, ruler and true judge, takes no pleasure in the destruction of the people of Toulouse, does not intend it. My lord cardinal, though, argues that we ought to be harsh and vindictive - but as he also says that he will be our guarantor, I suppose we can fight from now on in safety. Let us thank him for describing us as holy! And as our well-being is so dear to him, we can all tell which is his shaky tooth - when any of the knights die, their money goes to him. God and St Vincent never help me more, if at this time I lead an attack against Toulouse!'

'My lord count,' said Gervase,[2] 'I will tell you what I think: it is useless to attack the town, because there valour is flourishing, whereas we have nothing but loss and trouble. We are not at war with beginners! When we attack, they resist stubbornly, their defence is fierce and resolute. We have wounded them to their hearts' blood and so they prefer a decent death to a dishonoured life. By the faith I have sworn to you, let's look and see how much they love you, what their feelings are, and whether we've found them angry and resolute! There are one hundred and sixty of our men who won't bear arms again during these forty days.'

Foucaud of Berzy offers a new idea

'My lord count,' said Sir Foucaud, 'in my opinion you were never in more urgent need of a wise plan. And as we now face fresh losses and disasters, and so that we can destroy every man in there and kill them all, let us now discuss and implement a strategy so effective that men will still talk about it when we are dead. Let us create a new town with new buildings, newly provided with new roofs, and put up new barricades with newly felled timber. Then we will newly occupy these new positions, and new people and new forces will come and join us there. New Toulouse, it shall be called, and there shall be new oaths. Never has such a venture been tried! Swords will cut flesh, sharp blades shed blood, and Raymond's Toulouse and ours will harass each other till one sets the other on fire, and the survivor will hold the fief.

But for us it is pure gain, as men and provisions will come in to us from every district. We shall get bread, meat, wine and corn, money and rents, cloths and clothing, merchandise and goods for sale, buyers and sellers. By force or freely, they will give us handsome gifts, and pepper too, wax, cloves and spices.

We must work out how to maintain a long siege so as to destroy the town

---

1. That is, into devils; angels cast out of heaven for the sin of pride.
2. Of Chamigny, castellan and seneschal of Toulouse.

and get our revenge, for you cannot possibly hold it long by force, no place has ever been so strongly garrisoned. And every day we must mount raids across the whole country so as to deprive them of corn and grain, of trees too and vines, both the grapes and trimmings, of salt, timber and other provisions. In this way we shall force them to surrender. And if you manage to destroy them, the glory will drive all your sorrows out of your head.'

Count Simon approves of the plan

'My lords,' said Count Simon, 'I like this plan. It is good, forceful and clever, attractive and practicable.'

'My lord count,' said Bishop Fouquet, 'it has one drawback - if they can move freely on the Garonne, with no siege there and nothing to fear, they will be so well supplied from Gascony that they can hold out in comfort all the rest of your life.'

'By God, my lord bishop,' said the count, 'tomorrow I will go myself with plenty of good men and we will hold the river bank and the crossings so that nothing can come in by river but the wind. And my son and my brother will hold the other bank.'

Thus they decided to set two sieges.[1]

Laisse 190
They would set two sieges; that was the advice given by the barons and accepted by the count; and then the cardinal, wisest of learned men, with abbot, bishop, prior and legate would go into every land and preach peace and the expulsion of heretics and clog-wearers,[2] and in this way they would attract crusaders to join them.

The archbishop of Auch said,

'My lord, listen to me. When you set the second siege, you can be sure of wine and corn from Gascony; we shall send you both men and meat in plenty.'

'My lord,' said Count Simon, 'a hundred thousand thanks! But it is no wonder I am unhappy when I have been so unexpectedly defeated and have seen so many of my men dead and wounded that my mind, my heart and purpose are affected. Just when I thought I was safe ashore in a good harbour, I have been thrown into the waves and there I have to toss. Under what conjunction can my fate have been formed, when my stars so suddenly turn against me and everything I thought certain is but dew and vanity? It doubles my distress - I am sure it must be witchcraft! - for us all to be defeated by these beaten men!'

Alan of Roucy rebukes Count Simon

'My lord,' said Sir Alan, 'thought is vanity, poverty a shame and shame virtue.[3] A man who does harm, who arrogantly chooses to sin, must suffer loss.

---

1. One based on the Narbonnais castle in what is now the Faubourg S Michel; the other across the Garonne, based on the new town near the St Cyprian suburb; see plan of Toulouse.
2. *Los ensabatatz*, Vaudois heretics, see laisse 8.
3. *Cuidars es vanitatz / E paubreza vergonha e vergonha bontatz.* Sir Alan's laconic style tends to conceal his meaning.

Mercy sees that you hate pity, and so she and righteousness challenge you to fight them. Any earthly prince whose pride is excessive, who makes Jesus Christ his enemy, must obviously be unhappy, must lose the world's approval and stand condemned. And as I sincerely love you and suffer with you, it is my duty to speak out and tell you when you do wrong. If you treat Toulouse badly, you will be acting stupidly. Chance can go either way, but loyalty will regain the town. And there inside the town are *paratge*, courage and wealth; it is the head of the lordship, long possessed of rich lands.

But I don't say you won't take it, seeing you have begun so well! With the whole of Christendom to help you, it won't be surprising if you succeed. But by St Mary, glorious in light, before you capture it, paradise and hell will be filled afresh and many souls left orphaned and alone!'

'Sir Alan,' said the count, 'your reproach is too strong! It is not as if my losses could do you any good. Well, I have lost Toulouse, but I still hold the dice, and by the holy chrism with which I was baptised, as long as I live I will keep them under siege, until my days are done and they are beaten!'

'My lord count,' said the holy and consecrated bishop, 'may the Lord who gave you birth and whom you should therefore honour, observe your righteousness and perceive their sin!'

'That will do admirably,' said the count de Montfort.

Count Simon creates a second Toulouse

He then orderd his envoys:

'Go to all my lands, proclaim that any man who does not join me, has defied me.'[1] And he had the new town fortified and barricades built all round it, with ramparts, levels and ditches, loops, gates, salients and chain-barriers. Rights of residence within the town were granted, and along the metalled[2] roads from all around flowed in goods for sale and purchase, foodstuffs, market wares, satins and silks, purples and scarlets, money-changers, stalls and stocks of coin. And the Narbonnais castle was well equipped and defended with every sort of bow and feathered arrows.

Then the count de Montfort divided his forces into two and led one half across the Garonne. Handsomely arrayed, they rode along the bank, ensigns, banner and the lion flying. Sunlight danced on helmets, on painted colours, twin blazons and nielloed scabbards, on splendid shields and golden fringes, and set all the riverbank, the meadows and the water glittering.

Count Simon led his fine companies into St Cyprian's town[3] and quartered them all over it. As he was doing this and occupying the levels, one of the knights entering with him rode right on into the river, but what a fool it proved him to be, for before he could rejoin the others he was killed and cut to pieces. The men of Toulouse from both town and citadel, well armed and equipped, had crossed the bridges and were holding the barbicans.

Skilled archers and sergeants, well positioned, shot night and day at these two sets of besiegers and harassed them continually, allowing them no respite.

---

1. A formal defiance between lord and vassal broke the bond between them and entitled the lord to reclaim the vassal's fief.
2. *Pels camis ferratz* - this phrase was used of Roman roads, built of dressed stones on a pebble base.
3. That is, the newly built town.

The count of Foix arrives

As night fell and the stars shone in the sky, the count of Foix and Sir Dalmas[1] rode into Toulouse. Sir Dalmas is a good man, able and intelligent, so that his and the brave count's arrival doubled the defenders' courage. What candles you would have seen lit, what light cast by tapers and burning torches! Drums, trumpets and well-tuned tabors resounded through the town and the rejoicing grew louder still. The besiegers outside heard the uproar, a perfect storm of noise and shouting, so loud that the troops trembled and Count Simon put on his armour. Hastily he told the rest,

'Stay calm!' and then at once asked why the townsmen were rejoicing and who had arrived. Robert of Beaumont[2] answered,

'My lord count, I believe it is the count of Foix bringing them support. You can be sure he has brought strong reinforcements, knights from Catalonia, from Aragon and many more, and the men in Toulouse are all arming as well. That is why he has moved up so quietly, to give you battle if you'll wait for him.'

'Wait?' said the count. 'You don't think much of me!' And being a hard man, bold, clever and experienced, he said to them all: 'Listen to me! I must win back Toulouse now, today, or be left lying there in honour. If all the kingdoms of Spain came on with one shout, they should have immediate battle, unless you are afraid, for I would rather fight than be stripped of my lands.'

Count Simon's advisers do not recommend attack

'My lord,' said Sir Manassès,[3] 'no, don't do that. Take my advice and act sensibly. Fortune favours the count of Toulouse, and as for that excellent knight the count of Comminges, the good count of Foix and Roger Bernard his son, Sir Bernard of Comminges and all those others whose dearest kin you have killed, and the men of Toulouse, united as they are - when all these remember the sword with which you shed their blood, they will take any risks to kill you and to raise the siege on the other side.[4] Not one of us, therefore, recommends or wishes you to fight.'

'My lord,' said the count, 'the planets at my birth forbid me to fight alone, but I detest retreat. My courage is chilled, my heart saddened because my reach is so much less than my desire, because fortune hates me, you force me to despair and I am compelled shamefully to give up this siege.'

The crusaders retreat in haste

Meanwhile knights, citizens and many others sallied out in arms together from the town and the crusaders raised the siege so fast that no one waited for anyone else, only saying, 'Come on, hurry!', and the swiftest man there thought himself well out of it. Count Simon retreated in close array, his best-mounted men guarding the rear. The boats were tied up along the river bank,

---

1. Dalmas of Creixell, a great noble from Catalonia; fought at Muret (laisse 140).
2. Payment to a knight of this name in the French army is recorded in 1231.
3. Manassès of Cortit appears in laisse 193 but cannot be certainly identified; from Picardy or Champagne.
4. The siege based on the Narbonnais castle, on the east bank of the river.

and the men reached them all together and rushed on board, the ones at the back knocking over those in front. The count rode up so fast to check this rush that he fell into the water and was almost drowned. A man close by saved him, but his horse, wearing armour, was drowned there .... and kept the horse-covers, the flower, fruit and grace, so that joy shone and pride was brought low.

Crossing the Garonne, Count Simon returns to the Narbonnais castle

The count de Montfort rode to Muret[1] and then back to the other siege, astonished at his bad luck.

Count Raymond confers with his supporters

Then the count of Toulouse summoned his barons, for he wanted to consult his close friends as to how they should defend the town.

Laisse 191
To defend the town and repel attack, the count of Toulouse conferred with his supporters: the count of Comminges, a man beyond praise, the great count of Foix, deservedly famous, and his sister's son Sir Roger of Comminges,[2] as well as the brave and clever Roger Bernard, with Sir Bernard of Comminges, rich in renown, in generosity, joy and honour, as well as Sir Dalmas of Creixell, brave son of a noble Catalan house, and many distinguished barons and counsellors. Present too were the best and most powerful lords of the town, both knights and citizens, and the members of the Capitol. They met in the lesser St Sernin[3] and the count of Toulouse called for silence. He spoke well, and said to them:

'My lords, I adore Christ Jesus, almighty God. Let us thank him for his help and comfort and for bringing us out of pain, helplessness and distress. He has sent us a blaze of glory to restore life and colour to us all, for he is holy, worthy and full of loving-kindness. May he hear my complaint and give ear to my cry, may he behold the righteousness of his sinful child and give us the power and strength, the energy and courage honourably to defend this town! Most urgently do we need him to shelter us from sorrow.

By St Mary and the blessed Saviour there is not one baron, not one count, knight or lord who in arrogance or folly does any injury to a religious house or on a pilgrims' way, whom I shall not hang, burn or fling from the tower. And since God has given me back the head of my honour, may he if it be his will take me as his servant for ever!'

The count of Comminges said,

'This policy seems good to me, for it will bring us approval from God and from the world. Holy Church and her preachers may damage us, but let us never injure them, let us rather ask Jesus Christ, our father and redeemer, to give

---

1. He had to go upriver in order to cross the bridge at Muret, and then come back to Toulouse down the east bank.
2. Roger of Comminges, viscount of Couserans, whose mother was a sister of Raymond Roger, count of Foix. See also laisses 180 and 181.
3. The church built on the spot where the saint died. His body was later reburied in a larger church some 300m away. See p. 147 and n. 3.

heretical?

us an advocate before the pope who will win peace for us from holy Church, and we will appoint Jesus Christ to enquire and judge of the right and wrong between us and them.' All the greater barons accepted this recommendation.

The count of Foix encourages his hearers

Now the great count of Foix, fresh complexioned, followed Count Raymond, saying with courtesy:
'Barons, men of Toulouse, hear my true word: How you must rejoice in your ancestors who were loyal to God and their lord, and in yourselves who have done honour to their name and your own! Through you a flower has blossomed, has restored light and made the darkness shine, through you worth and *paratge* have been brought into the light of day instead of wandering the world, uncertain where to go, while you good men wept for them. If you have among you a tree that stinks, root it up and fling it out! You take the proverb's meaning - let us have no turncoats or traitors among us! And as Count Simon is threatening to attack us, you need knights - you must go and look for them elsewhere - and with them we shall destroy his pride and his threats.'

Other speakers voice their opinions

Dalmas of Creixell said,
'A sensible man must be offered good counsels, and then he will choose the best. As God has given us back our great commander, you must count all of us[1] as true friends, since from now on you need not fear for the town, we can defend it well against all its enemies. I came to Toulouse from my own fief in order to avenge my lord[2] and here I will stay until you have defeated them or raised the siege.'
'All of us on both sides,' said Roger Bernard, 'are ready and eager to fight, so let no one set up any stalls or workshops, let every one of us stand to it all day long out there on the levels and make trenches and shelters, so that the sergeants, archers and stone-slingers can get into them easily when they are hard pressed, for those men out there are fierce in attack. They will make their first assault and our javelins, arrows and sharp quarrels will kill both men and good thousand-shilling horses, enough to delight the ravens and vultures! And if any friends come in to join us, we shall go and attack the French in their quarters; but with so few weapons,[3] our forces must stay on the defensive.'
Sir Bernard of Comminges said,
'The French are fierce fighters, but they are afraid of us, and that cuts their strength by a third. That is why they raised the siege so shamefully; it is the worst disgrace the count de Montfort has ever known.'

One of the Capitol has several points to make

Now a good and wise lawyer stood up among these valiant counts, a fine

---

1. He and his companions are not local men, but from Catalonia and Aragon.
2. Peter II, king of Aragon, killed at Muret.
3. In 1216 Simon had confiscated the weapons in Toulouse (laisse 178).

speaker and learned man known as Master Bernard,[1] a native of Toulouse. He spoke courteously, saying,

'My lords, we thank you for your good and honourable words about Toulouse. But we complain to God about my lord the bishop, the shepherd he gave us, for he has led his sheep astray and tried to bring them into a place of destruction where for every sheep there are a thousand robbers. And since we have Jesus Christ, almighty God, to defend us, we shall slay with the sword all who attack and try to kill us, and they will die in pain. We must be brave, therefore, and determined, for we have a good town and will make it better. Night, day and dawning we'll guard it well, around it we'll build mangonels, catapults and a trebuchet to shatter the Narbonnais castle's Saracen wall, with its tower, watch-tower and all. And since the members of the Capitol are good men and govern well, I who am one of them, say in my own name and theirs and in that of the whole people from greatest to least, that we will risk our flesh and blood, our strength and vigour, our property, power, minds and courage for the sake of my lord the count, so that he may keep Toulouse and the whole honour.

And we wish to tell you privately that at All Saints[2] our comrades will go to hire knights, and we know very well where to find them.'

Sir Arnold of Montégut[3] said to them:

'I will ride with them and see them safe to Rocamadour;[4] Sir Bernard of Cazenac[5] will receive them on their way back; and you'll see us back again, God willing, at Easter. You fortify the town while you still have time.' And the meeting broke up in joy and cheerfulness, as the work clearly showed.

The Toulousains refortify their town

Laisse 192
Clearly the work showed it, as did the other activities, for men worked inside and outside the town fortifying its gateways and levels, its walls, bastions and double brattices, its ditches, lists, bridges and stairways. Inside Toulouse so many carpenters were busy building strong fast-firing double trebuchets that no tower or hall, rampart or merlon was left undamaged in the Narbonnais castle confronting them.

Conflict at Montoulieu

Sergeants and archers of both sides divided the field of Montoulieu[6] between

---

1. Identified by M.-C. with the 'wise lawyer' of laisse 133; Master Bernard, many times consul of Toulouse; M.-C., iii, p. 57, n. 5.
2. 1 November.
3. Montégut or Montaigu, 'pointed hill' is a common place name, but M.-C. identifies this Arnold with a 'miles Albiensis' who was lord of a castle of Montégut on the right bank of the Tarn between Gaillac and Rabastens; M.-C., iii, p. 60, n. 2.
4. Defenders were now being sought, successfully, from districts north of Toulouse, the Albigeois, Quercy and Périgord.
5. A noble of Périgord; accused jointly with his wife Elise of brigandage, in 1214 he was attacked in the name of the papacy and dispossessed by Simon de Montfort, who granted his whole property, along the Dordogne river and elsewhere, to Raymond, viscount of Turenne, brother of Elise. Bernard later received the town of Castelsarrasin from Raymond VII.
6. Outside the Montoulieu gate to the east of the town; see plan.

142

them. Battle and fierce fighting began. Swords, steel and blood coloured the green grass rose-red, for no one was taking prisoners.

The count of Foix recovers his fief

The great and pleasant count now left Toulouse to go and receive Foix. This fief was returned to him by Sir Berenger, to improve and strengthen the situation and to re-establish *paratge*.[1]

Sir Arsius of Montesquiou,[2] a valiant knight from Gascony, staunch and true, rich in all good qualities, arrived of his own free will to help Toulouse and its count.

Count Simon discusses his plans

Now the count de Montfort, who is a clever speaker and a hard man, powerful, cunning and devious, summoned his chief advisers to a conference. He spoke well, addressing these commanders:

'My lords,' he said, 'I am in great anxiety and increasingly beset by problems, by anger and wickedness. I thought I had beaten my enemies, conquered Provence and become a man of peace, but instead I am forced back to war. Count Raymond arrived like a whirlwind; he brought the count of Comminges, he brought Count Raymond Roger and his son Roger Bernard and the young man's cousin Sir Roger,[3] Sir Bernard of Comminges and many other fighters; with all these as well as the men of Toulouse, their sergeants and hired troops, he has taken my town and killed my comrades. My rage, bitterness and passion mount, and it is no wonder I cannot be cheerful when I see the hares turning on the hounds!'

Bishop Fouquet expresses optimism

'My lord count,' said the bishop, 'what are these bitter words? He who loves you best must check you, for you have no reason to be angry or apprehensive, as very soon now the checker-board will double.[4] My lord cardinal, who is a light and a beacon, has sent clerics and speakers into every land to preach in kingdoms, counties and the empire, and other messengers

---

1. Raymond Roger, count of Foix, had put his castle of Foix into the Church's keeping in 1214 (see laisse 144). Berenger, abbot of St Thibéry, was given charge of it. Innocent III promised to return the castle; his successor Honorius III received oaths of loyalty from the count, his eldest son and Roger of Comminges, and in December 1217, anxious to keep Innocent's promise, he restored the castle to its lord, on condition that he should remove his troops from Toulouse and stop helping the Toulousains against the crusaders. Count Raymond Roger left Toulouse for Foix in January or February 1218, and did not take up arms against the crusaders again until early 1219 (see laisse 210 and following). His son Roger Bernard, however, did not leave Toulouse.
2. Lord of Montesquiou, one of the four baronies of the county of Armagnac.
3. Roger of Comminges, nephew of the count of Foix, was cousin to Roger Bernard, the count's son.
4. I.e. we shall soon have overwhelming numerical superiority. M.-C. quotes a fifteenth-century manuscript explaining the *escequier double* as geometrical progression: place one grain of wheat on the first square, two on the second, four on the third and so on, rising very soon to millions; M.-C., iii, p. 66, n. 2.

to the abbeys as well, to tell them to send us money to hire troops. And when the date comes and January is past you will see hundreds and thousands of crusaders and mercenaries arriving from all directions, so that if Toulouse stood as high as the bell-tower not one rampart, wall or cross-wall should remain whole. And every man, woman and suckling child shall be put to the sword, except any inside churches, and then an agreement will be settled for all time.'

[handwritten margin note: bloodthirsty bishop]

A distinguished Frenchman disagrees

Robert of Picquigny,[1] a valiant mercenary, worthy and wise, pleasant and powerful, who came from France, said to him very sensibly,

'Ah God, my lord bishop, your rebuke is unjust! It seems to me that the fire is blazing hotter since Count Raymond began his venture. A man who with unbroken courage conquers a fief will lose it once he becomes arrogant. His courage is shattered and the true heir retakes the honour. And a Frenchman must by his very nature conquer immediately, and he goes on conquering till he soars higher than a hawk. There he stands on Fortune's wheel and behaves with such arrogance that his pride smashes the ladder and tosses it away; and the man himself falls, tumbles and lies level with the rest. He has lost all he won, for he is not a good lord. It was French pride and pettiness that killed Roland and Oliver in Spain.[2] The count has lost the fief because he has not been a good lord to it. Yet he swept from La Réole port up to Viviers[3] and won it all with cross and steel, nothing escaped him but Montpellier.[4] He took all the revenues, both marks and pence;[5] then he handed the fief over to demons who are devouring and wantonly destroying its inhabitants.[6] But God is light, he is holy, worthy and true, and readily hears the outcry at these ceaseless crimes. That is why he has sent us these new partners who have made us throw a splint we did not need![7] Toulouse has suffered mortal agony; no wonder we have lost it. By giving it boys and bullies for its lords, Count Simon has earned trouble for himself and for us, for all our kinsfolk wherever they go. A man who robs and kills a fief's natural lords must expect anger, fire and pain. It is not likely, therefore, that our position will improve.'

---

1. He had already fought for the crusaders in 1209 (see laisse 36). His fief in Vernon (Eure) obliged him to serve the king of France for forty days, but now he is serving for pay.
2. 'French' means 'of the Ile de France'. Roland and Oliver died in Spain with Charlemagne's legendary rearguard because Roland was too proud to accept reinforcements or summon help.
3. La Réole on the Garonne, with an English garrison, taken by Count Simon 1214; Viviers in the Rhône valley where he was campaigning in 1217.
4. Montpellier took care to get a bull from Pope Innocent in 1209 protecting it against attack from crusaders. It had belonged to the king of Aragon since Peter II married Marie of Montpellier in 1204.
5. *E los marcs els diners* - pence, *deniers*, were actual coin; a mark was a unit of account.
6. Fortune-hunters from the north who were glad to accept lordships in the conquered territory and meant to exploit them.
7. 'Partners' is used ironically; the splint, *sobros*, a bony growth on a horse's leg, is a natural metaphor for a cavalryman.

A surprise assault suggested

'Count,' said Sir Guy of Lévis, 'talking is easy, and while losses increase, funds are shrinking. This siege is nothing but delay; and whatever you and your clergy may do, you'll still have enough fighting for the next ten years. But if you'll take my advice, we'll finish quickly: in the morning, just at dawn when the look-out blows his bugle on the tower, you'll have armed all your knights and the good companies and your squires, the horns, trumpets and all the standard-bearers ready - and it's winter, sharp, bitter, cold and dark, and men are in bed with their wives - so while they are looking for their clothes and their shoes, we put ourselves and our warhorses at risk. We ride into the passages and along the paths straight to the gate and kill the gate-keepers. Conflict will spring up all over the town, shouting and uproar, fire and killing, death, swords, blood and flame! Tomorrow shall be our last day or theirs, for a decent death is better than captivity.'

'By God, Sir Guy,' said Sir Alan, 'as you are the count's servant and his good friend, I will let you go first, and if the count rides second, I will come third!'

Count Simon approves

'Sir Alan,' said Count Simon, 'it shall be done as he suggests, and in no other way.'

Laisse 193

'In no other way shall it be done: at daybreak we shall be fully armed, with all our weapons and our good Arab mounts. We'll have prepared our stratagem secretly, and our best men, our picked troops will begin the attack, until the defenders ride out. Then when they are out and dispersed across the field, we shall charge together in great strength, spurring, fighting, striking, right in amongst them; with steel and sword we shall be so scattered about that before they realise it or take alarm, we shall ride into the town with them in such numbers that we shall hold Toulouse or lie there dead. Better we should live or die together than continue this long and shameful siege.'

'Very well said, my lord!' said Sir Amaury.[1] 'I and my company will begin the engagement.'

Assault on Toulouse

Leaving the conference, they ate and slept; then as dawn broke they laid their trap while some of them spurred across the level ground. But when the townsmen heard and saw this, waking to hear noise and shouting all about them, they hurried into their armour, not troubling with shirts or breeches. Banners and horns, trumpets and battle-cries filled all the open space and into the field rode the French in a single body.

Sir Bernard of Comminges took command of the defenders to prevent defeat and at once called out to tell them that no one could stand against them.

---

1. Simon's son.

Count Simon de Montfort, Sir Amaury, Sir Alan alert and ready, Sir Foucaud, Sir Robert, Sir Peter of Voisins,[1] Sir Robert of Beaumont, Manassès of Cortit, Sir Hugh de Lacy and Sir Roger of Andelys spurred all together, followed by such numbers that wherever they rode fine blows were struck and the defenders were overthrown; some fell into the water in full armour. And the Frenchmen drove on so hard they crossed the moat and the water and made a way in. The defenders cried out,

'Holy Mary, help us, save us from defeat!'

Sir Roger Bernard drove in his spurs and manned the passage, where he put up a determined and successful defence. The townsmen and the dispossessed lords gathered, and with knights, citizens and brave sergeants they resisted the attack, the tumult and the uproar. On both sides men struck and struck again so hard that town, field and castle shook. Javelins, lances, brandished spears, bright maces and shining axes, sharp hatchets, tempered steel, stakes, stones and polished bolts, with broadswords, arrows and handflung setts, came flying from both sides, smashing hauberks and breaking helms.

The French are forced back

The defenders endure, they strike down and conquer; they pursue and beat off their attackers and fling them into the moat, hard hit and wounded. With steel, with clubs, with strong blows dealt and taken, the French fight in defence and in retreat. They must withdraw, and in the ditch lie their horses held fast under the ice - horse-cloths, pennons and good Arab mounts, double mail and flowered shields, saddles, bridles and shattered poitrels, this way and that, trapped and held. The two sides draw apart. After such blows and counterblows there's not a man or a limb unhurt. Attacked and attackers draw off, and into the town ride its defenders, full of joy, while the French retreat with heavy hearts.

When Count Simon had returned and disarmed, the cardinal and the bishop, robed and vested, joined him and gave him greeting and blessing.

'My lord count,' said Bishop Fouquet, 'if Jesus Christ does not pay some attention to these stubborn men, they will not be easy to convert.'

Count Simon despairs

'Bishop,' said the count, 'sure as I am that God raised me up, I am just as sure that you and the clergy have betrayed me! I won this great city with the cross, now by bad luck and the sword I have lost it.'

'Count,' said the cardinal, 'pray to the holy Spirit that he may not have heard your bitter words! A man who welcomes anger into his heart .... and mercy, justice and good sense. Where mercy is diminished and good forgotten, mercy loses its name, and lordship its rule.'

'My lord,' said Count Simon, 'I am wrong, forgive me. I am in such fury, such a rage, I don't know what I am saying. I have every right to be out of my mind with anger, thrust out of my lordship by this puny people! Never as long as I live shall I repay that! But by holy Mary who suckled her fine son,

---

1. From Voisins-le-Bretonneux in the Ile de France. Took part in the later war of reconquest with Guy of Lévis and Lambert of Limoux; succeeded Lambert as lord of Limoux in 1231.

unless I can discover some way to defeat these men, your affairs and mine are so desperate that mere chance will decide the issue.'

Laisse 194

'Chance will decide. How could this happen, just when I thought I was free from any more trouble or fighting! Except for Provence,[1] of course, but I would soon conquer that and defeat all my enemies. I was going to rule my lands and become so powerful that everyone would obey me, whether out of fear or friendship, they would love holy Church and serve Jesus Christ. But now I don't know what to think, I don't know who can have defeated me, for he seems to understand all the marvels Merlin ever mentioned.[2] Never did I think to see my judgment so astray! I thought I knew for certain that Count Raymond had gone to the Saracens or some other land and I would never see him here again. Now he comes blazing forth and I know I must have misjudged him, for look at him, there he sits securely in his capital, and he's had no help except that small troop of his and those rebels who are disgracing and destroying me. He's defending the place, fighting back, he's getting stronger and doing me harm. But by the holy Virgin to whom Christ came, if I were to be given Spain with all its *marabotins*[3] and all the land held by the king of Morocco, I would not stir from here until I had taken and destroyed Toulouse and smashed its count!'

Cardinal Bertrand offers advice

'Count,' said the cardinal, 'God sent me to you so that I should rule and lead you and you should obey me. As we cannot defeat these men, if you'll take my advice we should make another plan. We should send the bishop straight to Paris to the lord king of France and ask him to take pity on us and fulfil his promise. The countess will go with him, and Master Clairin,[4] and she will ask her brother,[5] her kinsmen and cousins to come to our help, and they shall have Quercy. I shall send to Rome, as is already in hand, to tell them to send preachers and speakers all over the world. If it cannot be settled now, we shall try to get Louis[6] to come next year to destroy this town, the breeding ground of evil! Yet if the prince were unable to take it, I don't know what else to suggest, except to make an end of it all. What God directs, St George defends.'

'My lord,' said Bishop Fouquet, 'as you ask me to do so, I will take your message straight to St Denis,[7] and at Pentecost when the leaves grow green I will bring you plenty of pilgrims and crusaders, who will bring money, both marks

---

1. The marquisate of Provence, taken by young Raymond after his capture of Beaucaire.
2. Merlin, see p. 81, n. 1.
3. Gold coins in imitation of Arab dinars first struck in 1172 by Alfonso VIII king of Castile. With their Arabic name corrupted to 'maravedi', they were still minted, although worth less and less, until 1854.
4. Priest; chaplain and then chancellor of Simon de Montfort.
5. The countess' brother was Matthew of Montmorency, Constable of France.
6. Eldest son of Philip Augustus, king of France. He did intervene in this war, but not until after Simon de Montfort's death; see laisse 212.
7. St Denis, first bishop of Paris and patron saint of France; his abbey stood just north of Paris and its name was often used as a synonym for the capital city.

and sterling[1] - men from Germany, from France, Brittany and Poitou, from Normandy, Champagne, Flanders and Anjou, and many others too, rich as well as poor. Then the siege by land and water will be so great there'll not be a single mill left working on the Garonne![2] And we shall not stir from there till we have taken them all prisoner, and then the town and the whole of this country will be ours.'

'My lords, I don't know what to say,' said Sir Hugh de Lacy. 'It looks to me as if St Sernin[3] is on their side and they and their country have his protection, or so it appears.' And so they talked on together till nightfall.

Countess Alice and others go to France for help

In the dawn of a fine day the bishop and Sir Foucaud of Berzy set off, taking the countess and Sir Peter of Voisins with them. They travelled through the woods for fear of the dispossessed knights.

The situation inside Toulouse

In the town were Raymond, the great count palatine, with Sir Bernard of Comminges, Sir Bernard of Montaut, valiant Roger Bernard - who gave me gold and glory - Sir Dalmas of Creixell who commands and leads, Bertrand Jordan with Sir Odo and active Amalvis, good Sir Hugh of La Mota, in whom renown delights, and Sir William Arnold, faithful and true. Sir Bernard of Comminges took leave of them and went to make war in Gascony and attack Sir Joris[4] there. And the men of Toulouse with steadfast hearts rode about the country and searched the roads, the castles, towns and boroughs; every day their convoys brought in meat, bread and wine.

In the field of Montoulieu there grew a garden which sprang new and blossomed every day, a garden set with lilies, but the white and red which flowered there were flesh, blood, swords and scattered brains. Spirits and souls, sinners and saved, the newly killed repeopled heaven and hell.

All in Toulouse rejoiced together and told each other,

'Now we can laugh and be happier still, because Sir Pelfort has arrived. He is valiant and wise, grim, good and clever and our dear friend.'

Inside the town and out, all strengthened their positions. But the losses from bows and crossbows were so severe that for a long time neither side challenged the other, not until Easter.[5]

Count Simon confers with his advisers

Laisse 195
At Easter when pleasant weather came, Sir Amaury and Sir Guy de

---

1. *Els marcs els esterlis*. Both these were units of account, not coins; there is no connection with English sterling coin.
2. Mills stood on the right bank of the Garonne and floated on the water on pontoons; if milling could be stopped, there would be famine in Toulouse.
3. St Sernin or Saturninus, sent in AD 250 to bring Christianity to Gaul, reached Toulouse and became its first bishop; died a martyr there, dragged to his death by a bull.
4. This is the Joris who was defeated at La Salvetat (laisse 182), now making war in Comminges.
5. In 1218 Easter fell on 15 April.

Montfort,[1] Count Simon, the cardinal and a number of other lords left the main host and met for private discussion.

'My lords,' said Count Simon, 'this siege is costing me a great deal of money and I am losing my companions. Night and day I am anxious and worried because I cannot make the gifts I have promised. The whole of Christendom ought to be ashamed to see us resisted by unarmed men!'

'Count,' said the cardinal, 'don't be afraid! I have sent preachers all over the world, and at Pentecost with the fair weather all Christendom will come to you. So many pilgrims, such great prayerful processions, will arrive from distant lands that if we had nothing but their halberds, their fine hoods and felt hats, their gloves and staffs, we could fill up these lists, these moats and ditches! We shall take Toulouse and welcome you into it. And its men, women and noble buildings shall feel the fire's heat and be burned to ashes.' All the barons listened to him but none of them replied, except Robert of Beaumont, who opposed him:

'By God, dear father, there is no point telling us about this salvation and promising us pardons. By holy Mary, mother of the Glorious, before we take the town with speeches and sermons there'll be enough blows and grappling, wounds and anger, for God and the devil to sort out good souls from bad.'

The Toulousains attack

While the French were talking, the men of Toulouse came spurring to the attack, hard-hitting and brave: William Unaud, Sir Gerald[2] and good Sir Hugh,[3] agile Sir Amalvis, Sir William Arnold, brave Sir Hugh of La Mota with his scarlet lion, and the noble companies, young and joyful men. Swift Sir Hugh of Pontos[4] bore the banner and flew his pennon at the besiegers' gate. Inside their quarters arose such shouts and yells that the whole host trembled from top to bottom. 'Holy Mary, help us!' they cried and ran for their armour and weapons. There was savage fighting outside in the fields while de Montfort and his men were arming; the Toulousains hacked and slashed the Normans and Bretons and cut Sir Armand Chabreus[5] into several pieces. Sharp steel met flesh: noses, scalps and chins, arms, legs and feet, guts, livers and kidneys lay strewn on the ground in lumps and gobbets.

Count Simon leads a defensive charge

Now through the gateway sallied valiant Count Simon with Sir Hugh de Lacy, Sir Lambert of Limoux, Robert of Picquigny, Sir Evrard of Villepreux,[6] Sir Peter of Voisins, Rainier of Chauderon, Sir Guy the Marshal, Sir Walter the Breton,[7] Sir Sevin Gorloin[8] and Sir Rainier the

---

1. Simon's son and his brother.
2. William and Gerald Unaud, cousins or brothers; and see laisse 181.
3. Hugh of Alfaro.
4. Not identified.
5. Not identified.
6. From the Ile de France; one of the original crusaders, as in 1215 he held the lordship of Lanta in the Toulousain, confiscated from its 'heretical' lord. A brother of Robert Mauvoisin.
7. Not identified.
8. From the Ile de France, son of Philip Gorloin, castellan and in 1215 seneschal of Carcassonne.

Frisian;[1] and out through the other gates came the lesser troops. 'Montfort! Montfort!' they cried. 'Free knights, attack!' From every side the French and Burgundians charged, so that the men of Toulouse turned back in haste, hotly pursued by the French. But as they fled, Sir Hugh of La Mota called to them,

'Handsomely, knights! My lords, let's defend ourselves! Better to die well than live disgraced in prison!' And he aimed his lance at the leading crusader and knocked him deftly off his charger and down onto the dusty ground; then, reining back, he drove his lance into one of the men-at-arms, dyeing his white pennon red. Sir Amalvis shouted,

'Knights, turn again!' and he gave and took great marvellous blows in defence of himself and his comrades. Sir William Unaud spurred his strong warhorse and struck a knight so that he ripped his silk tunic and snapped off the lance, leaving its head in his body. Good Sir William, fine knight that he is, used his mace on Sir Robert of Beaumont.

Reinforcements from the town join in

Then the townsmen, anxious to make a sortie, shouted out, 'My lords, let's follow them!' and knights, sergeants, citizens and men on foot poured out of the trenches and onto the grassy plain. Outside and in, the struggle intensified. Water, town, castle and the sky itself shook at the noise of trumpets, horns and bugles. Wherever they could find each other, there they fought. 'Beaucaire!' they shouted, 'Toulouse! Avignon!' Swords and halberds, quarrels and fire-brands, lances, maces, stones and setts, javelins, axes, pikes and clubs, broad arrows and slender children's bolts came at the French from all sides, from front and back. None could remain unafraid, not the fiercest man among them.

Eagerly Sir Peter of Voisins charged, but the Toulousains knocked him off his horse, and he got back to his own men. Up rode Peter,[2] took it by the reins and cried, 'Toulouse! Barons, stand up to them!' and struck a knight, piercing his armguards and flinging him down so hard that the battlefield shook. But Sevin Gorloin, a strong and handsome knight, son of the brave seneschal, shouted, 'Montfort! Montfort!' and hit hard about him, striking down sergeants and young men. From all sides the Toulousains struck at him there on the killing ground and left him in pieces. Bertrand of Pestillac, thrusting eagerly, drove lance and blazoned pennon into and right through an archer, and the grass and sandy ground showed red. Fierce and grim, the count de Montfort charged into the thick of battle and threw down two men. All around men struck at him; his horse slipped, the saddlebow broke and he fell. But he kept his feet, fought back, turned and remounted. William Arnold was taken and held in the mêlée, but cleverly he dropped down onto his knees and the Toulousains hid him; he abandoned his horse and got back to his friends.

---

1. Not identified.
2. Not identified.

When the fighting was done, many were sorrowful. The defenders lost, wounded, William Peter of Maurens,[1] the Wolf of Foix[2] and many other men in that dangerous garden on the field of Montoulieu where red and white bloom fresh each day, where blood, brains, flesh and hacked off limbs are the flowers, the leaf and the dolorous fruit for whose sake so many fair eyes are full of tears.

Count Simon in defeat

The count withdrew, angry, raging and sad. In his fury he said,

'Christ Jesus, glorious Lord! Where is my good star, my kind, strong, lucky star that's famous by land and sea? Never did I think I could be so accursed that neither weapons, saints nor prayers were any use! Holy Church defends neither herself nor us, she blackens her glory and her precious name. Beloved Saviour, in grief and distress I beg you: now give me death or let me take and keep this town!' Away rode the count, raging and wretched, but the men of Toulouse went home rejoicing, and told each other, 'Jesus Christ is with us, he guards and directs us.'

The Toulousains' creed, and their complaint

Laisse 196

'Jesus Christ directs us, he gives us good and ill and we must thank him for it and bear it patiently, for he can rightly support us, as we intend to live and die in his faith. We believe in the God who saves us from wrongdoing, who made heaven and earth bear flower and fruit, who made the sun and moon shed light on the world, created man and woman and gave life to souls, entered into the Virgin to fulfil the Law, accepted bodily death to save sinners, gave his precious blood to lighten the darkness and made himself an offering to his Father and the holy Spirit. And by receiving and fulfilling holy baptism,[3] by loving and obeying holy Church, we must indeed win Jesus Christ and his love. But the lord pope, who ought to care for us, and the prelates of the Church who condemn us to death - may God give them the sense and courage, the knowledge and judgment to understand what is right, to repent, for they are ordering our death and destruction at the hands of foreigners who quench the light, from whose dominion we want to be free. If God and Toulouse had let them, they would have buried worth and *paratge* deep, past recovery. May the Lord who rules and does not lie, who threw down pride and cast out the angels, give us power to support our lord,[4] whose nature is such that with wisdom and clear sight he must love the Church and hold the fief!'

---

1. Maurens, Revel canton, Haute-Garonne. A deposition of December 1243 testifies that William Peter of Maurens and his mother Argentella had once been seen talking with Guilabert of Castres, 'bishop' among the heretics; M.-C., iii, p. 100, n. 6.
2. Son of Raymond Roger, count of Foix, not named in his will, probably illegitimate.
3. By fulfilling the promises made at baptism.
4. Count Raymond VI.

May 1218, Count Simon has siege engines built

In the kalends of May when the fine weather began, the cardinal and the count sent for carpenters to begin the cat with which they meant to destroy the town, and to build their castles, catapults and mangonels.

The countess de Montfort brings troops from France

Now a messenger arrived bringing them joy; courteously he said to the count,

'Go quickly to welcome the bishop and the countess who are coming as fast as they can, welcome Sir Michael of Harnes,[1] leader of men, Walter Langton[2] and Sir William of Mello.[3] Toulouse cannot hold out, and you'll make them pay dear for all your losses. There's a crusade on its way which will daunt them all, a good hundred thousand men who'll shake their resolve!'

'Nothing,' said Count Simon, 'can hurt me now!' And he went to welcome them and offer his services. Great was the joy when they arrived.

'My lords,' said the count, 'here you will want for nothing, for if you take Toulouse I don't know what more I can give you, you will drink from a fountain that never dries up.'

'They cannot stand against us,' they answered, and went to strengthen and complete the siege. (But very soon they met the Toulousains hand to hand!)

The whole army rejoiced as Count Simon went to meet Sir Amaury of Craon, Sir Gilbert of Les Roches and Sir Albert of Sentlir,[4] who brought a more splendid company than I can tell you.

Toulouse sees to its defences

But the men of Toulouse ran to prepare, no able-bodied man waiting for anyone else, and they manned the lists and ditches, deploying sergeants and bowmen outside in the gardens. And as the crusading forces turned and came back,[5] the plain, the levels and all the ground shook. What hauberks you'd have seen shining there, what bright helmets and splendid shields,

---

1. Michael, lord of Harnes in Artois, had distinguished himself at the battle of Bouvines, 1214, and was famous enough to feature in an early thirteenth-century epic poem, the *Roman de Guillaume de Dôle* (ed. Servois, lines 2710-52).
2. Walter Langton, brother of Stephen Langton, archbishop of Canterbury. The manuscript reads: *gauter de la betona*, but Walter Langton is known to have been present on this and other occasions, and M.-C. considers *de la betona* to be a phonetic rendering of a name heard by the author but never seen written; M.-C., iii, p. 107, n. 3.
3. The manuscript reads: *W.lmes Melir*, and *Melir* is the rhyme word, probably altered from *Mello*. William of Mello was a son of Drogo, Constable of France. His younger brother Drogo appears in laisse 200.
4. Amaury: a young and brilliant knight, later seneschal of Anjou, son-in-law of William of Les Roches, died 1226. Gilbert of Les Roches, not certainly identified, probably related by marriage to Amaury. Albert, perhaps of Senlis, perhaps of Santilly. This contingent arrived some days after that brought by Michael of Harnes.
5. Presumably the crusaders already encamped outside Toulouse had gone to greet the newcomers and now they all came back together.

what fine banners and pennons fluttering! Not a man but looked at the town, and then they said to each other,

'By God, I can tell you it doesn't look to me as if they want to run!'

Count Simon addresses his troops

Now the count de Montfort ordered the whole host to gather and listen to the discussions. A fine clever man was the count, and knew how to give them heart. He unlaced his helmet and began by saying,

'My lords, you have come here to serve the Church, to take Toulouse and bring me victory. What you must do now is to push forward and set up a fresh siege down at the bottom of the town[1] in order to strengthen the blockade so that none of them can get out anywhere. Then we will keep them hungry and helpless. If I can take the town and defeat its inhabitants, you shall have all its wealth and land to share between you; I want nothing that's in Toulouse, nothing but the destruction of the place and the people.'

The newcomers disagree with Count Simon

All the barons listened to him and began to murmur. Finally Sir Amaury of Craon answered him:

'By God, fair my lord count, we should be very grateful to you for offering us such a speedy victory! But first of all we must ask you not to lead us into disappointment or disgrace, for those who act in haste repent at leisure. We and our horses are all tired with travelling and could not endure the stress of battle, for when a man is weak, he does not know which way to turn. But as you are so anxious to be kind to us, give us the new town you have had built and we can rest there and eat and sleep without being driven out of it by the men of Toulouse. You know their town, the ways in and out and how we can deal with them, you are maintaining this siege which you order us to support; for by holy Mary, I've heard that the men of Toulouse are not easy to tame, that if anyone tries to attack or enslave them, they can hit very hard and fight extremely well. Therefore we ask you, fair lord, to let us recover; then you and we will go together and attack them and get directly to grips with them in every way we can, and so we'll make them fill their lists and ditches with their dead. And if we succeed in conquering the men and the town, let it all belong to you and let us go away. That is the only way it can be done.'

When the count realised that he could not set them against each other,[2] he shook and groaned and fell into a rage. But the crusaders rode on together and went to settle into the new town.

The new arrivals take up quarters in St Cyprian's town

Laisse 197
In the new town they promptly took up their quarters and pitched their tents and pavilions on the well trodden ground.

---

1. On the west, St Cyprian, side, where the ground level was lower than on the east bank.
2. I.e., that he could not persuade any of the newly arrived crusaders to disagree with Amaury of Craon.

Discussions inside Toulouse

The men of Toulouse held their parliament, and present at the council were all their best minds. Gently and softly Sir Roger Bernard spoke, for he is noble, intelligent, has courage and sense and is son of the good count who holds and defends Foix. He smiled at them and spoke well, saying:
'My lords, there is no plan but defence, for we shall never find mercy or kindness there. But don't be discouraged, for we have every reason to be cheerful, as we have a good town, a good right, a loyal lord and Jesus Christ to defend us. He guides and directs us and proves it to us constantly. And so that our enemies can see how strong we are and that we're at their throats[1] night and day, we'll strengthen the town with new work and reinforce the ancient defences, we'll build such fortifications that we shall be quite unafraid and they will be terrified.' Sir Dalmas of Creixell said,
'What you say is quite right. Such a reinforcement will improve us a hundredfold, we shall be less anxious and much better able to fight.'
'My lords,' said Sir Pelfort, 'undoubtedly we and the whole town will benefit by it, we shall be more firmly based and more secure. I have no better suggestion to offer. In the name of Jesus Christ, let us make a start.'

Toulouse strengthens its defences

Then and there they went to work all together, fathers and mothers, children and parents, no one waiting for anyone else nor the poor for the rich. But it was Sir Roger Bernard who began to build. They made foundations, walls and ramparts, ditches, lists and defensive crenellations. All over the town rose a feeling of joy, and they told each other,
'Let's be happy, for Sir Arnold of Villemur has arrived, and he is a brave man, strong and intelligent.'

Count Simon addresses the army

But the count de Montfort assembled his men, more than a hundred thousand of them,[2] making them gather round so that they could all hear, and he pointed to Toulouse and its appurtenances.
'Look there, my lords,' he said. 'There is the great fang that resists Christendom and all salvation. Those people are so wicked and evil, so insolent and spendthrift, that the whole world finds battle and contention there. I am so angry, so furious, it breaks my heart! As my power increases, their audacity grows to match it. For their own glory and to humiliate me, they have just strengthened their town. If I cannot find some way to confound them, much good is my valour or your help! But trust me, they are near the end. To destroy the town and be revenged, we'll set another siege on the far side of the running river so that not a single one of them can go out or in, and we shall maintain both these sieges as long as we need to, until we take them by assault or else they surrender.'

---

1. This translates *sus la dent*, literally 'on the tooth'. This text is rich in dental metaphors.
2. A figure not to be taken literally.

The crusading force divides into two

The whole army agreed to this decision. Leaving a strong force to keep up the first siege, the rest of them crossed over at Muret, with ample supplies of food and other essentials. At dawn Count Simon rose, had his trumpets sounded and everything well prepared. Out they rode, filling all the open space with hauberks, surcoats and fine painted shields, with the glitter of helms and silver bosses, with Spanish chargers and gleaming morions, silk banners and coloured pennons. Horns, trumpets, bugles and the fresh wind blew, shaking the riverbank, the air and the Garonne. Out in a single body rode the knights, with such splendour that the men of Toulouse saw them at once.

The Toulousains also divide

These also split their forces into two groups. That fine captain the count of Comminges, with Sir Dalmas, Sir Pelfort and Sicard of Puylaurens[1] and their excellent companies, all young men, manned the lists and the defences; while the rest, knights, citizens, archers and sergeants, rode out fast across the bridges, and all crossed the river, none of them waiting for anyone else. In command of the defence was Roger Bernard; Sir Roger of Montaut rode in the lead; with valiant Sir Odo of Tarrida[2] and their good fighters they occupied the riverbank, the gardens and houses.

Count Simon attacks

Now the count de Montfort came galloping with all his men through St Cyprian's town, full tilt across the trenches, straight onto the riverbank and into the gardens. Sir Michael of Harnes began his charge, Walter Langton and Sir Philip of Aiguilent[3] spurred fiercely among the foremost. Valiant Sir Arnold of Villemur, alert and staunch, watched them come; he cried his warcry, bent low, charged, struck a knight and flung him bleeding to the ground.

With shouts of 'Toulouse!' and 'Montfort!', attackers and defenders met. Wherever a man could find an enemy, there he fought. Polished lances and flashing swords, javelins, pikes and razor-sharp steel, round pebbles and brandished spears, slender arrows and sharp quarrels flew thick from the town's defenders, shattering shields, helmets and armour. The French broke off and withdrew; in great danger they rode for the Garonne and in hot pursuit the townsmen followed, triumphant and hitting hard, till they were fighting among the waves, wounding the horses and overthrowing the knights. The count de Montfort with his biting lion twisted and turned and

---

1. Lord of Puylaurens, which he abandoned after Simon de Montfort took nearby Lavaur in 1211, and burned its lady and inhabitants. Simon at once occupied Puylaurens and granted it to one of his knights, but the inhabitants soon opened the gates to Sicard again. His mother and sisters were Cathars, and he himself had been seen listening to a heretical preacher, but in 1226 he and the knights, citizens and people of Puylaurens made formal submission to the Church and to the French king.
2. The same Odo as in laisse 185, third son of Jordan of La Isla Jordan and Esclarmonde of Foix, brother-in-law of Pelfort of Rabastens.
3. Not identified.

hit out with such energy that he rescued his men from this danger, but none the less they crossed, struggling and fighting, over one arm of the Garonne onto the other bank.[1]

Count Simon wants to make a stand in St Cyprian's town

The count retreated, furiously angry. Gathering his men, he said to them bitterly,

'Barons, I don't know how anyone could blame me or what they could say. I find it intolerable that a false people, men who took oaths to me,[2] should be heaping shame and dishonour upon me every day! For my honour's sake and to get revenge, we shall enter St Cyprian's and base ourselves there, so that they cannot possibly get away in any direction.'

But Walter Langton immediately replied,

'By God, my lord count, they have shown you their quality well enough! You have never seen better men anywhere, or any stronger in attack or defence. How savage and fierce they are, how deep they stab and bite! Their snake has got a good grip of your lion, and unless you are Goufier[3] and can set it free, we and you and all the others are going to suffer. We should have to take appalling losses if we quartered ourselves so near Toulouse.' And all the barons agreed to abandon their hundred or more huts and shelters and they drew back half a league and pitched their tents on the trodden earth. But the men of Toulouse went back into their town in delight and joy.

Toulousain siege engines attack the Narbonnais castle

Laisse 198
Once back in the town, they sent orders to tell Bernard Parayre and Master Garnier[4] to engage the trebuchets and begin the attack. More than ten thousand tallied on the ropes, and into the slings they put fine large lumps of rock; they demolished, shattered and broke up the Narbonnais castle, its imposing gates, its ramparts, bastions and linking galleries, as well as the high openings in the Ferranda tower.[5] And they shouted,

'Toulouse! Now the fire's blazing, for he's on his way, he's coming, the young count we long for, great and valiant, our rightful lord!'

The Garonne breaks its banks

But very soon their joy ceased, for wind, thunder, storm and tempest brought rain pouring down from the sky during three whole days and nights and the Garonne rose and overflowed the foreshore, the streets and squares, all the orchards and gardens, and came rushing into the cellars in the centre of the

---

1. There were a number of islands near the banks of the Garonne, splitting the river's flow into several channels.
2. On 8 March 1216. The following day Simon de Montfort promised to be their good lord.
3. Goufier of Lastours in the Limousin was a hero of the First Crusade; he is said to have freed a lion from the grip of a snake, and the grateful beast followed him faithfully ever after.
4. Nothing is known of these two except what the *Canso* tells us; see also laisse 213.
5. One of the two great Roman towers of the Narbonnais castle.

town. Not one bridge stood undamaged above the water, nor any of the mills or their conduits, piles or axletrees.

Count Simon's renewed offensive

In the middle of the Garonne where the mountain current flows there were two crenellated towers, manned by good, active men of Toulouse, and when the floods sank and the river went down the mighty count de Montfort, grim and arrogant, filled the whole riverbank, all the shore and meadows, with his massed forces of crusaders and hired men. He stationed his valiant mercenaries, fine companies and crossbowmen, in the hospital;[1] he built strong barricades, steep ditches and walls with arrow-loops; he raised platforms where his standard-bearer and vicious lion could stand; and brought in provisions and supplies by the ton and the hundredweight.[2] He sent swift runners to order good fast boats to come by way of the Agenais. And in the fine sandy open space he built catapults, well shielded, because he wanted to demolish the towers and capture their garrisons.

Dismay in Toulouse

Inside Toulouse there was terror, there was anguish, grief and alarm. Men and women exclaimed,
'Merciful Jesus Christ, defend the rights of your true servants!' Women went barefoot to pray in the churches and took offerings of fine loaves, coins, wax-lights and candles for the candlesticks, and they prayed to the Virgin, source of that rose-tree whose flower was the glorious Son who is light and truth, begging her not to let them be destroyed by their triumphant enemies.

Dalmas of Creixell exhorts his commanders

In addition to this Sir Dalmas of Creixell, an eloquent speaker, sent for the chief captains and spoke to them kindly, saying with gentle reproach,
'My lords, affairs may go badly, may be dangerous and difficult, but do not allow yourselves to be anxious or afraid. Very often a set-back can lead to a great improvement.'

The Toulousains organise their defence

They agreed to defend the town as follows: the ditches, moats and gates should be strongly manned by the count of Comminges and his troops, by Sir Bernard, Sir Roger and the Abbot of Montaut, by Sir Gerald and Sir Pelfort, mounted, and by the townsmen, brave in defence and attack. Also the good and pleasant Roger Bernard immediately sent to inform the Capitol, the commune officials and the other good men, citizens and traders, that the master craftsmen, boatmen and labourers, the good companies and paid sergeants were urgently needed to save the towers.
'Gladly!' they replied. All over the town they collected workmen and put

---

1. There were two hospitals on the west bank of the river, that of La Grava and the new hospital; see plan. The latter is the more likely situation for the crusaders' base.
2. *A moitz e a sestiers*, measures of weight without exact equivalents in English.

carpenters up at the head of the bridge.[1] But they hesitated, for the crossing was very difficult, as sections of the bridge had been broken down into the water.

A hero from Aragon gets supplies to one of the towers

Sir Peron Domingo, however, a brave squire from Aragon, made the venture, and in worse danger than any enemy ever endured, he used a rope to get two large, well laden boats across. A hundred thousand on either side were watching him, and told each other, 'That man's light on his feet!' Next they made a bridge out of ropes and cross-pieces, and the way to the old tower was completed.

But getting any help to the other tower was very difficult for there was no way, no bridge or ladders. Using long double ropes and a container made of reeds, something like a meat-store,[2] they got food and steel quarrels across from one tower to the other.

Hugh of La Mota tries to reach the tower by boat

Meanwhile Sir Hugh of La Mota, a valiant knight, well provided with arms and other necessities, led his fine company onto the river to defend the tower, with the help of members of the Capitol. So great, however, were the waves and so fast the current that he could not reach it and was swept aside, whilst on the further section of the bridge there was fierce fighting and deadly blows were given and taken. But none the less the members of the Capitol, brave and active, thrust into deep water and managed to supply the tower, and then returned to Viviers.[3]

The tower falls to Count Simon's attack

But that stubborn fighter the count de Montfort meant to demolish the tower and its battlements. All night and all day with squared stones and rounded boulders and heavy blows the catapult attacked it, the mangonel smashed into it, till the whole rampart was shattered and its mortar knocked out, wall, gateways, vaults, quoins and all. The defenders saw that there was nothing else to be done; with firm hearts and bitter oaths they had taken wounds and death; now, their breeches red with blood, by force and in anger, in black despair, the survivors abandoned the tower. Into it climbed the standard-bearer of the count de Montfort and his pilgrims and they shouted for joy.

Laisse 199
They shouted for joy together, they shouted 'Montfort!' and, 'Now we'll win back the honour, we'll take Toulouse and drive you out!' But the men in the other tower shouted back:

'Swords, lances and tears will settle it! You're tough and full of talk, but we've got right on our side, we've got the town, courage, and our own lord!'

---

1. On the east bank of the new bridge.
2. *Que recemblec carniers*; a cage in which meat could be hung to keep cool.
3. A name deriving from the Latin *vivarias*, a keep for fish; this was on the east bank by the new bridge.

Yet they were alarmed, and no wonder, for they had neither king nor count,[1] no one to love or help them but God almighty, Jesus Christ. And the count de Montfort and his men raised the oriflamme on the tower in the Garonne.

Now their men and ours drew so close that archers and boatmen fought on the river night and day, and the horses were wounded when they were led down to drink.

Reinforcements for Toulouse

And now a glory shone in the town, a defender bringing back colour and life, for Sir Bernard of Cazenac arrived at the sanctuary.[2] He came to protect Toulouse and brought with him a fine company and his own staunch courage. Never have I seen a more active knight, as fair-minded as he is powerful, renowned for good sense, generosity and the heart of an emperor, a man who rules *paratge* and commands valour. He came as a friend to help Toulouse and its count, to restore justice and banish grief. With him came his kinsman Raymond of Vaux[3] and Vézian of Lomagne,[4] a valiant vavassor. Amid great rejoicing they and their Brabanters rode into the town. The lords of the Capitol and the lords and commons of Toulouse went joyfully to welcome them. Shouting and banners, horns and trumpets shook the town and glittered in the mist.

When the count de Montfort heard the uproar, he took a few men and crossed the water to his own forces, posted men in the hospital and the tower, reached the siege and spoke with them:

'My lords,' said the count, 'your worst enemies are losing the river, the town, the bridge and their courage. I have heard such an uproar in there, you can be sure they are getting away, unless some friend has arrived with help.' Then a messenger came with the facts:

'My lord count, troops have entered Toulouse. Sir Bernard of Cazenac has brought five hundred knights to defend the town, and you will have to fight them.'

'Friend,' said Count Simon, 'they have done a stupid thing. Once I go in, out will go the traitors, for never as long as I live shall I or the Church be afraid of wandering landless men!'

Count Simon complains to his associates

Count, cardinal and counsellors, with Sir Amaury, the bishop and other learned men, consulted together privately.

'My lords,' said Count Simon, 'I make my complaint to you. All my hired troops want to go away because I have no money to pay them and do not know where to find any. I tell you that this town is giving me such trouble that my strength and my reputation decline daily. Of these two choices, God grant me the better: by Saint Mary of Rocamadour, either the town kills me or I will kill them.'

'Count,' said the cardinal, 'the God whom I adore knows well what is right and who the sinners are.'

---

1. 'Neither king nor count', a proverbial expression.
2. *Al santor*, to the place of pilgrimage, says the author sarcastically, where the devout crusaders are coming to destroy Toulouse.
3. Not identified.
4. Viscount of Lomagne and lord of Auvillar.

Battle on the eve of Pentecost, Saturday, 2 June 1218

On the eve of that most holy day when God sent light and glory upon the apostles, Count Simon rose very early at daybreak and rode out with his fine company and his scouts to destroy the vines and other crops. They fanned out through the open areas towards the Oratory Elm.[1] But the men of Toulouse, great and small, strong in attack and staunch in defence - swift did he think himself who outran another to man the trenches and outworks! - the knights, citizens and hard-hitting Brabanters, the brave and active working men, fierce in the field, with resolute sergeants, javelin-men and slingers, occupied the gardens and vineyards, the roads and open places. The fine fighting men of the two sides drew near. Shouting and trumpets, horns and drums, light on the helmets, gold and gleaming white stiffened their courage and gave an edge to their daring. Now together like leaves round a flower came pride, came fierce resolve and spurring knights. Heaven and earth, air and mist shook and sang, mingled steel and fury.

The men of Toulouse saw the movement and in their own defence launched their attack, began the bloody and desperate fight. On the fair open ground before St Salvador[2] tumult broke out, the two sides were engaged, battle began.

Laisse 200
Battle, shouting and bloodshed began again. Across the open ground came Sir Simon's own company; knights on both sides spurred hard. Leading the crusading forces[3] rode Sir Amaury of Craon, Sir Walter of Cambrai,

---

1. This stood on the outskirts of the town near the River Hers, on the boundary between the parishes of St Sernin and St Stephen.
2. Probably north-east of St Sernin, where the present Quartier Marengo stands.
3. Characters included in the following list and not already identified are:
   Walter, either of Chambray or Cambrai, not identified.
   Theobald, from Anjou; fought with great distinction at the battle of Las Navas de Tolosa 1212; later seneschal of Poitou.
   Drogo, younger brother of William of Mello (laisse 196).
   Ralph of Nesle: brother of John, lord of Nesle, a dependency of the county of Vermandois; took part in Louis of France's English campaign 1216-17.
   Albert, not known, perhaps related to Rainier of Chauderon.
   Geoffrey: a Gerard of La Truie also took part in Louis' English campaign; perhaps the same man.
   Renaud, viscount of Aubusson.
   Rainier: possibly Geoffrey of Rancon, lord of Taillebourg in Saintonge.
   Peter: a member of the Scoraille family from the Auvergne.
   Theobald of Orion, from Picardy.
   Gervase 'Le Veautre', a famous French knight from Josas, Montlhéry, whose nickname means 'the boarhound'. See M.-C., ii, p. xix.
   Gilbert: mentioned in a judgment pronounced by the consuls of Toulouse in 1225 as having raided an estate near Toulouse 'in the time of Simon de Montfort'.
   Roger (in the manuscript Robert) of Chinon, a knight of the county of Mortain.
   Gerald, perhaps from Lasson, Calvados, Normandy.
   Renaud: probably a son of John, lord of Trie in the Beauvaisis; fought at Bouvines.
   Guy, held lands of the abbey of Ferrières.
   Bertrand, perhaps related to Robert of Courson, an English cardinal of Norman origin.
   Robert of Chalon, John, and Ralph of Poitiers, not identified.

Sir Theobald of Blaison, Sir Gilbert of Les Roches, Sir Drogo of Mello, Sir Ralph of Nesle, Sir Albert of Chauderon, Sir Geoffrey of La Truie, Sir Renaud of Aubusson, Sir John of Berzy, Sir Rainier of Rancon, Sir Peter of Escorralha, Sir Theobald of Orion, Sir Gervase Le Veautre, Gilbert Maubuisson, Sir Robert of Beaumont, Sir Robert of Chalon, Sir Robert of Picquigny, Sir Roger of Chinon, Sir Ralph of Poitiers, Sir Gerald of Lanson, Sir Renaud of Trie, Sir John of Bouillon, Sir Guy of Mortagne, Sir Rainier the Frisian, Sir Amaury de Lucy and Sir Bertrand of Courson. After them rode the other companies, fierce men and proud. The French and Burgundians charged together, their warhorses trampling the green grass and the sandy ground.

A strong charge bravely received

Unshaken, the defenders held firm and took their charge with steady hearts. Swift Roger Bernard and the other lords, the knights, citizens and commons of Toulouse, the sergeants and foot-soldiers raised the barricade and on it set the Montaigon[1] banner. Sir Elias of Albaroca, a valiant Brabanter, and Sir Bernard Navarra[2] and the men of their company, with Sir Odo of Tarrida, Sir Gerald of Gourdon and brave Sir Amalvis, Sir Hugh of La Mota, Sir Bernard of St Martin,[3] Raymond of Roussillon[4] and Sir Peter of La Isla,[5] (he suffered a lance-thrust from a leader of the assault whose shaft broke and left the stump in his hands), these were the men who bore the first attack.

'Toulouse!' rose the cry, and 'Montfort! Craon!' Trumpets and clarions rang to the skies above. This way and that flashed lances, javelins and pikes; maces, fire-brands and halberds, stones, axes and weights, arrows, quarrels, bolts and darts filled the air; helmets and hauberks, shields and saddles, splendid blazons, fringes and fastenings, horses, straps and goldwork and silk brocades were soaked and red with blood.

The conflict is too fierce for some

So tremendous was the uproar that many of the townsmen slipped away home, up to their chins in water in the moat, but the others stood to it out there on the field, men from the town and citadel, archers and men on foot. They killed William Chauderon[6] among the vines and fought across his body, Sir Sicard of Montaut attacking with fury. Thicker than spines on a hedgehog were clustered shafts, shields, helmets, horses, quarrels, lances and close-ranked pennons, but by sheer force the crusaders carried his body away.

---

1. Montaigon, a large square in the north of Toulouse, now the Place St Georges.
2. Elias and Bernard, mercenary commanders.
3. Bernard of St Martin, a knight from the Lauragais, accused of having helped the Cathar 'bishop' Guilabert of Castres to escape from Castelnaudary when Simon de Montfort was besieging it in 1211; officially reconciled in 1226; excommunicated for involvement in the murder of four inquisitors at Avignonet in 1242; did homage to Alfonse count of Poitiers in 1249.
4. Raymond, not identified.
5. Peter, a dispossessed knight from the viscountcy of Béziers.
6. Various Chauderons are recorded in Champagne at this period, but none called William.

An attempt at fire-raising

Now foreigners came in, Bretons and Flemings. Unarmed, these traitors carried fire, straw, torches and firebrands across the levels and ran for the town with shouts of 'Craon!' But the defenders were ready, sergeants and young noblemen struck and smashed their arms and breastbones. The count and all his forces withdrew.

Count Simon confers with his colleagues

On the day of Pentecost[1] when buds grow green, Count Simon heard mass and then went into a pavilion with the cardinal, the abbot and the wicked bishop,[2] Sir Amaury, Sir Bouchard,[3] the count's brother Sir Guy, Sir Alan, Sir Foucaud and the other barons.

'My lords, 'said Count Simon, 'I have every reason to remind myself and all of you that we are here so that I can recapture Toulouse and its people. I beg God to give me back Toulouse or give me death, for they have made me wretched and furious because I cannot defeat them. How they can hold out, I do not know! But I cannot afford the huge cost any longer.[4] My mercenaries have just told me 'No', and so have the other companies, because I have nothing with which to pay them. But if you'll trust me, I have a good plan to suggest: I am having a cat built, better than any ever made since the days of Solomon. It's not afraid of any trebuchet, mangonel or flying stones, for the platform, sides, beams and rafters, the gateway, vaulting, chain and framework are all reinforced with iron and steel. Into this cat I shall put four hundred knights, the best we have with us, and a hundred and fifty fully equipped archers, and together on foot we shall all of us haul it down into the ditch in front of the town. And when they all come running, every father and son of them, we'll make such a killing with swords and clubs that my lion will bathe in blood and brains! Toulouse shall burn! Either it goes up in flames or I shall die the death.'

'Count,' said the cardinal, 'holy Church orders you to cast aside all anxiety, for she has power to take from you and to give, power to pardon and defend you, and if you serve her well, you will win great reward. Now is the time for it: attack the town!'

The count of Soissons brings reinforcements

A messenger now arrived and said to them:

'My lords, the great count of Soissons[5] is here and he has brought a fine crusade to your help.'

'Good news indeed, friend!' said Count Simon. 'Let us go and welcome them.'

---

1. 3 June 1218.
2. Cardinal Bertrand, the abbot of St Sernin and Bishop Fouquet.
3. Amaury of Craon and Bouchard of Marly.
4. The siege is now in its ninth month.
5. Ralph de Nesle, count of Soissons 1180-1237.

Laisse 201

'Let us go and welcome them, for we need them desperately.' And the count went joyfully to do so, as did his companions Sir Amaury, Sir Bouchard, Sir Guy and Sir Renaud.

As they met each other with fair and pleasant words, the count de Montfort addressed the newcomer courteously:

'My lord count of Soissons, I earnestly request your friendship. You can tell how much I want it, as I have shown more kindness to you than to any knight, for since I saw your letter and the messenger telling me that you and Odo of Angivilliers[1] were coming to my assistance, I have built both cat, castle and mangonel, but so that all the glory should be yours, I have held back from taking Toulouse until you could lead the way. You shall have a fifth or a quarter of the plunder and all the best warhorses, which you can give to those who need them most. In every foreign land it will be reported that a few days ago the great count of Soissons took Toulouse.'

The count laughed aloud and said jokingly,

'My lord count de Montfort, I thank you a hundred times for so promptly making me treasurer of the wealth of Toulouse, giving it me twice over as you have![2] But whether you or I take the town, let everything in it be yours, for I want none of it. If you'll accept my advice, you'll manage this differently and give neither me nor anyone else a penny of it until it has paid all your hired troops. But I'll give you a good return for your offer: if you take Toulouse within a full year from now, once you've conquered it I'll hand over Montpellier as well! For by St Mary, I was told yesterday that they've got everything they need there inside the town, including brave hearts, great strength and their natural lord, and that they are such good fighting men that when you offer them swordplay, what you get back is death. We are new penitents from a foreign land and shall gladly serve the Church for the full forty-day period, up to its last moment, and shall then go home by the way we came.'

So they talked together until they reached the headquarters from which Count Simon was directing his siege.

There was great anxiety inside Toulouse, for so many enemies now hemmed them in and all Christendom was gathering to destroy them.

Young Raymond arrives in Toulouse

But now to comfort them the Virgin's Son sent them joy, sent them an olive branch, a bright star, a glory on the mountains, for the brave young count, daylight, inheritor, rode in through the gateway with cross[3] and steel. And God sent him a marvel, a true sign that he would bind the murderous lion in chains, for from the highest battlement of the bridge tower first captured by the French, the banner fell, the lion tumbled down into water and sand, and this delighted everyone in the city.

Provost, knights and citizens, townsmen and women and noble ladies, all went to welcome the young count they so much longed for. Not a girl stayed at home upstairs or downstairs, but every soul in the town, great and small, ran to gaze at him as at a flowering rose. Tears of pure happiness fell fast in

---

1. Angivilliers, canton of St-Just-en-Chaussée, Oise.
2. *Bis dat qui cito dat* says the proverb: He who gives promptly, gives twice.
3. The cross of the counts of Toulouse.

streets and squares, in palaces and gardens. And young Raymond dismounted in great joy at the abbey church of valiant St Sernin,[1] mighty and merciful, who never wanted or sought for alliance with the French. Trumpets, horns and bugles, standard-bearers and warcries, bells setting bell-towers rocking, re-echoed all across Toulouse, its river and riverbank.

During these celebrations, five thousand men marched out and sergeants and squires manned the levels. Some of these who were light on their feet raced towards the besiegers' camp and shouted,

'Hey, Robin! Hey, Walter! Death to the French, death to the pilgrims! We've doubled the points on the checker-board,[2] for God has given us back our head, the brave young count, the heir, and he's brought us fire and flame!'

Count Simon learns of Raymond's arrival.

The count de Montfort heard these gibes and crossed the river to the sandy shore.[3] His liege lords went to meet him and the count laughed and questioned them.

'My lord count,' said Sir Joris, 'you've got an opponent now who's bringing blood, swords, flame and tempest. We must use iron and steel against him.'

'Joris,' said the count, 'you must not frighten me! The man who can't make a decision when it's needed will never win the hawk at Le Puy.[4] Toulouse and its count will always find me confronting them, for there will be no peace, no truce or agreement until I have conquered them or they have conquered me. Now to help me and hinder them, I shall turn this hospital into a castle complete with battlements, lists and ramparts; outside it a line of squared stakes and a deep ditch all round; on the near side by the river a strong wall on a raised base; and on the Gascon side, a bridge and steps. This will enable me to control the riverbank and the food convoys.'

Now a force of citizens and sailors arrived by boat with sergeants and archers, with banners and warcries, and came ashore shouting 'Toulouse!' The besiegers' sergeants and crossbowmen resumed the attack, the bloodshed and danger. In the towers over the river the garrisons fought night and day.

One of the towers is taken, but recaptured

Laisse 202

All night and all day the besiegers, Count Simon and the French kept up their attack, but the men of Toulouse resisted fiercely. Then de Montfort, evil through and through, brought up some of his best troops by water, and by force and cunning he captured the other tower, tore down part of the bridge and set up his lion banner with its bands of gold. But on land and on the river the men of Toulouse fought back. Knights and citizens, sergeants and commons, struggling hard, managed to set up a mangonel at one end of

---

1. The great abbey where the saint's body lay.
2. See p. 142, n. 4 for this phrase.
3. To the St Cyprian bank, part of which his troops held.
4. Le Puy-en-Velay (Haute-Loire) where tournaments and literary contests took place each year on 15 August to celebrate the Assumption of Our Lady. See Chrétien de Troyes' *Erec et Enide* (lines 559 ff.) for the episode in which Erec, unknown and poorly provided, challenges the established champion, wins the hawk on its silver perch and presents it to Enide.

the bridge; thick and fast with round stones and Turkish bolts they dealt out wounds and death. So many and so fierce were their attacks that they drove the French out of the tower; like it or not, the crusaders left it, first setting it alight. And the town's sailors, good and courteous men, had command of the waterways both up and down river and across it; they sought out and occupied all the landing places, bringing ashore foodstuffs and other supplies.

Toulousain forces attack the crusaders

Meanwhile the townsmen, with some Brabanters and Germans, took their swords, clubs and good Turkish bows and crossed the river, one hundred and sixty-three of them. Knights and men of the crusading army saw them and Sir Joris, who was among the tents, called to Sir Peter of Voisins:
'We're in danger, my lord, the townsmen have crossed the river and are coming fast.' They ran to arms and to horse, they put on hauberks and Pavian helmets and there within La Grava[1] the conflict began. Swiftly on both sides swords, clubs and deadly iron did their work, stones, javelins and arrows flew fast, they shattered crystal and golden bosses, saddles and shields, poitrels and bits.
The townsmen fought fiercely, attacked and wounded the French and hurled them into the river two and three at a time. It was there they brought down Rauli of Champagne.[2] Those who could swim, swam; those who could not, died. Iron hats, javelins, lances, banners and bits sank down into the water and were swept away. Many were left lying dead as the French broke off and in great anger withdrew. Bitterly the count de Montfort addressed them:
'My lords, how right it is to give you horses and palfreys! We must all be delighted that you have overcome the men of Toulouse, but by Saint Mary they are so valiant and so courteous that you have let them keep their ransoms and their armour!'

Count Simon and his allies confer

Next Count Simon crossed the river with Lambert of Cales[3] and held council in the Narbonnais castle. The cardinal and the lord bishop were present, as were the count of Soissons, Sir Aldric the Fleming, Sir Amaury of Craon, Sir Aimery of Blèves,[4] Sir Gilbert of Les Roches, Sir Richard of Fores,[5] Sir Bouchard, Sir Alan and Sir Hugh de Lacy.
'My lords,' said the count, 'you are well aware of the fact that the lord pope granted me the Carcassès, ... that I command this land and hold it lawfully under an agreement which makes it permanently mine. The faith, the cross and I myself took it by force of arms. Now I am in such difficulties that if I do not capture Toulouse within a month I should be better dead or never born, for by St Mary I am so hard pressed that I have no resources, no

---

1. *Grava* means a 'strand' or 'foreshore'. La Grava, part of the west bank of the Garonne, ran from the New Bridge to the hospital.
2. Not identified.
3. Calais, Chalais or Caux? Not identified.
4. A knight from Anjou.
5. Not identified.

gifts, no ransom money, no funds. But if I abandon the siege and fail to take Toulouse, the Church will suffer and the faith be destroyed.'

The count of Soissons is not hopeful

The count of Soissons at once said:

'My lord count de Montfort, if it pleased Jesus Christ that pride should be righteousness and sin compassion, the town would be yours, wealth, weapons and all. But I see no prospect of your taking it now, because Count Raymond, who is duke and marquis, whose integrity we know, claims it by right of inheritance, as does his son the young count, nephew of the English king. Roger Bernard is there too and the count of Comminges, and the men of Toulouse are clearly furious at the deaths and injuries you have caused them. If, however, the pope or the Church wanted an agreement between yourself and your opponents by which you would restore his fief and his inheritance to Count Raymond, this would benefit Rome and Christendom. You would still have the viscount's land[1] - though there is a youngster[2] growing up there who claims it and will try to recover it, whoever may be glad or sorry.'

'My lord,' said the count de Montfort, 'all this is nothing, for I have conquered the Toulousain and the Agenais, Quercy and Bigorre, Comminges and the Albigeois, and if I take Toulouse and the lord there inside it, the scales will go down on my side, mine and that of holy Church. Now tomorrow at first light we shall bring the cat up against the Saracen rampart and get right into the town, as we have planned; we shall spread Greek fire throughout the town and either we shall die together or we shall beat them. It will not be long.'

Laisse 203
'It will not be long before you all see me winning back Toulouse, before you share out its wealth and land among yourselves.'

Amaury of Craon's opinion

'Do not boast, my lord,' said Sir Amaury of Craon, 'for most of the pelt has still to be shaved.[3] And don't be annoyed if I ask how you intend to retake it, for there's no distress in the town, no thirst or hunger, and however often you attack them, you'll find them out of the lists and ready on the battlefield. You will never shut them into the town.'

---

1. Raymond Roger Trencavel, who died held prisoner by Simon de Montfort, 1209.
2. Raymond Trencavel, son of the above, two years old when his father died. In 1223 he besieged Amaury de Montfort in Carcassonne, taking possession of the place when Amaury returned to France in 1224; but Louis VIII captured it in 1226. Trencavel tried again in 1240, but without success. He renounced all his hereditary rights and undertook to go and fight the Saracens in return for an annual pension from Louis IX.
3. *Qu'encara n'es a raire tot lo majer peletz.* A proverbial expression perhaps on a par with advice against selling a lion's skin while the beast still lives.

Cardinal Bertrand rebukes them

But the cardinal said,

'In supporting them, Sir Amaury, you are failing to love holy Church and what is right. For penance I order you to fast tomorrow, to eat and drink nothing but bread and water. And as I love you dearly, I beg you to avoid sin, for Jesus Christ commands you to amend your ways, you and the count of Soissons, and never to speak on their behalf again.'

'My lord,' said Sir Amaury, 'read, and you'll find that you should certainly not accuse me of this fault, for nowhere do scripture or the law say that you should wrongly expel a prince from his land. And if Count Raymond does lose his inheritance now, law and loyalty will give it back to him in time to come. How astonishing it is to see *paratge* brought low, broken and put in danger because of other men's faults![1] If I had known this secret in my own fief, neither I nor my company would be here now.'

'Sir Amaury,' said the count de Montfort, 'you are wrong to argue with my lord the cardinal. It is neither right nor reasonable of you to oppose him in anything. If you love the Church, you will obey him.' And so they talked together until quiet evening fell.

Using his great cat, Count Simon attacks

Next morning as dawn was breaking, the count de Montfort commanded:

'My friends, come here! Never have you served me in a better time! Take hold of the cat, win back Toulouse, crush all my enemies and yours! Conquer Toulouse, do honour to Jesus Christ, make good all my losses and your own!' Trumpets, horns and clarions rang out, and with shouts and whistles they took hold of the cat and brought it lurching along between the castle and the wall. Straight as a hawk stoops on a small bird, a stone came from the trebuchet and struck the upper part of the cat, shattering all the hides and fastenings.

'Lord Jesus, what are you doing?' cried the count de Montfort. 'Any more of this anger and alarm, and you'll bring down myself and holy Church and the cross!' But his men said,

'Don't be distressed, my lord! Turn the cat and it will be out of range.'

'By God,' said Count Simon 'you shall see it done at once.' But no sooner was the cat turned and moved a few paces than the trebuchet took fresh aim and fired again. Its second blow struck, broke and cracked apart the iron and steel, the nails and timbers, pitch and cladding and left many of men who were moving it dead and cold. The rest scattered, and the count was left there alone.

'For God's sake,' he shouted, 'stay here! Move the cat at once, or be killed!' But they answered,

'Anyone you put inside it would be better off with wounds, disease or fever!'

Count Raymond and his men consider the cat

The count of Toulouse and his close vassals discussed matters with the Capitol, as you shall hear. Together they said,

---

1. Other men's faults - those of heretics.

'Jesus Christ, now we most urgently need your advice!' The count of Comminges said,

'My lord, listen to me. Whatever harm the cat may do, you will be the gainer. It is saving your vines and your corn, for while they are busy protecting the cat they can't be cutting those down. Don't let it alarm you, none of their devices can keep you out.'[1]

'Don't worry, my lord,' said Roger Bernard. 'You'll never lose the town because of a cat. If they bring it here, you can destroy it here. How we shall fight them! With swords and maces and cutting steel we'll glove our hands in brains and blood!'

'Do that indeed, my lords,' said Sir Bernard of Cazenac, 'and don't let anything you're seeing now disturb you. Here comes the cat with its castle and carriage - the nearer they drag it, the better you can capture it, and if it gets as far as the lists, you can burn cat and men together.'

Sir Estolt of Linars[2] said,

'My lords, take my advice and it won't mislead you: let us build good walls inside these lists, big, high walls well crenellated, which will command the ditches and the palisades, and then you can defend yourselves at any time and need not fear any sort of trick they may try. If they make an assault, you can kill them all.'

'Take his advice,' said Dalmas of Creixell, 'for it is right and sensible and you won't go wrong with it. It is essential that you all work together.'

Under fire, the Toulousains build fresh defences

Then they blew horns and clarions, ran to the ropes and wound the trebuchets. Members of the Capitol bearing staves distributed food and fine gifts and presents, and the people brought picks, shovels and tools. Nothing was left behind, not a wedge, a hammer, bucket or cooking pot, not a tub or stake. They began the outworks, the doors and hatches. Knights and citizens handled the stones, as did noble ladies and their daughters, young men, little girls and boys, everyone, great and small, and they sang songs and ballads as they worked. Thick and fast the besiegers' mangonels shot at them, archers and slingers loosed bolts and stones, knocked the bowls and pitchers off their heads, smashed handles and head-pads and pierced their legs, their hands and fingers. But so firm and strong was their courage, not one of them took fright.

Laisse 204
Not one of them took fright, far from it. They were delighted to be building shelters to protect the ditches, and the whole community worked with great joy. But the besiegers' mangonels and bent bows poured stones and feathered bolts into the thick of them and from the side too, piercing legs, chests and arms and shattering beams, posts and timbers. But the Virgin's Son kept them safe and there was almost no damage done in the town.

---

1. *Que re no vos pot toldre c'ab ela no us n'intretz* - this seems to mean 'for nothing can prevent you entering with it', but it is hard to see how this makes sense. Dr Simon Gaunt suggests that one might take *intretz* in a generalised sense of 'being victorious'.
2. From Lias, a fief of La Isla Jordan.

Count Simon presses on his attack

Now the count de Montfort summoned his bravest and most experienced knights. He had good shelters built with latticed fronts, and filled them with his companies and his armed knights with their fine weapons and laced helms. Swiftly and handsomely they brought the cat forward.

Inside Toulouse the wise defenders wound and aimed the trebuchets, put good dressed stones into the slings, then released the ropes. The stones came flying fast and hit the cat on its chest and flanks, on the doors, roofing and recesses, so that pieces flew off in all directions and many of the men moving it were struck down. All over the town rose the cry: 'By God, madam cat, traitress, you won't catch any rats!' In a frenzy of rage the count de Montfort cried out,

'God, why do you hate me? My lords,' he said, 'knights, look at this disastrous luck, see how I am bewitched! The Church is no help to me, nor the wisdom of learned men, the bishop and legate are useless, my valour and competence are of no avail, weapons, intelligence, and generosity make no difference, I am thwarted by wood and stone! I was sure I would have good luck and with this cat I would take the town. Now I don't know what to say or what to do.'

'My lord,' said Sir Foucaud, 'try some other way, for this cat is never going to be worth three dice. Indeed I never thought it wise of you to take it so far forward. You'll lose it before it can be turned back, I'm sure you will.'

'Sir Foucaud,' said the count, 'believe me when I tell you by holy Mary of whom Christ was born, either I shall take Toulouse before a week is out or I shall die in the attempt.'

'Not so, please God!' said Sir Hugh de Lacy.

Discussion and exhortation in Toulouse

Inside Toulouse the council met, lords of the town and other important men, knights and citizens, wise and sensible persons, who told each other:

'Now's the time to settle it for good and all, the whole inheritance must be ours or theirs.' Master Bernard, an eloquent speaker, addressed the assembly. He was born in Toulouse and is a learned man.

'My lords, free knights, be pleased to listen to me. I am one of the Capitol and our consuls are ready day and night to do all you can wish. Friendship is flourishing, it is bearing fruit, for together you and we are defending the count, defending *paratge*, and therefore I want to tell you this story, so that in your inmost hearts you may understand where it points:

Christendom held Acre besieged and closely blockaded on every side. But very soon our forces' wine and corn ran short and King Saladin, a very determined man, laid siege to the besiegers.[1] But it pleased the most holy Lord, third Person of the Trinity, that the lord king of France, greatest of crowned heads, should bring food and plenty and he came ashore at the siege

---

1. The Christians besieging Acre were themselves held under close siege by Saladin. Famine began in their camp in October 1189 and persisted all through the following terrible winter and early spring. It was not relieved until Philip Augustus king of France arrived with supplies in April 1191. Richard I of England joined the siege in June 1191, shortly before the Moslems made a successful attack on the crusaders' camp.

of Acre, where he was so much needed. There was joy in all the tents, tapers and candles were lit, and such a blaze of light shone over land and sea that Saladin asked his interpreters what the host of Christendom was celebrating.

'Truly, my lord king,' they answered, 'it is the arrival of the mighty king of France.'

Now Saladin forced his way forward and encamped less than a third of a league away from the crusaders. Then very soon their situation improved still more, for amid scenes of great delight the king of England arrived and very gladly joined the siege of Acre, and joy was redoubled throughout the camp. But King Saladin drew nearer still, only a crossbow-shot away, and his scouts could hear all the talk and laughter. At daybreak the lords of France, England and the other realms gathered, and everyone was astonished to see King Saladin there beside them. But an archbishop, a wise and well-read man, demonstrated from scripture and holy writings

....

A knight called Robert of Salventina[1] exclaimed aloud in the hearing of all the assembled lords,

"Good my lord archbishop, change your argument and let us beg Jesus Christ to save us from the arrival of any more great men! If one more king joins us, you can be sure that the unbaptised king will quarter himself, his troops and all his emirs right inside our camp!"

My lords, I have told you this riposte because our position is like that of the besiegers at Acre - the stronger we become, the more they triumph over us! When my lord Count Raymond, Sir Roger Bernard, the count of Comminges and my lord Sir Dalmas were here quietly in the town with us, the mighty and arrogant count de Montfort stayed in his tents, so well fenced in that as long as we did not trouble him, he did not trouble us. But when my lord Sir Bernard came from Cazenac, bringing wisdom, generosity and a fine troop of men, the count de Montfort turned to and built so many shelters near our position that he kept us busy night and day. And when the young count, our light and glory, arrived, Count Simon built that fortress right under our eyes, and then he brought those shelters so near that a single leap will take him into the ditches. If one more count arrives, Simon will triumph and will quarter himself and his crusaders here amongst us!'

Master Bernard announces an attack on the cat

'Free and distinguished knights,[2] agree to this: the game is set out on the table, besiegers and besieged, and it must be played out till death checkmates either us or them. By the holy Virgin, flower of chastity, may the fief and the county now become theirs or ours! By the most holy Cross I tell you that whether it's sense or folly, we are now going to attack the cat. Whether you join us or not, all of us in the town and citadel are determined on this. What blows will be struck for the sake of this cat, what blood and brains will lie thick on the battlefield! We shall all die together or else live in honour, for death with honour is better than life in wretchedness.'

'Look at us,' answered the knights, 'we are all ready. The best of good luck go with us, and together you and we, please Christ, will go and burn the cat.'

---

1. Not identified.
2. Master Bernard is appealing to the knights who have come from other districts, to help him and the local forces.

Laisse 205

'We'll go and attack the cat, for that must be done. Together we shall take it, and Toulouse and *paratge* will never be parted again.'

All night long they grew more eager, and as day[1] was breaking Sir Arnold of Villemur, a determined man and fine warrior, went through their quarters and made the best knights, the good companies and brave mercenaries take arms and prepare. They placed crossbows, good handbows, quarrels, arrows and linen-workers' combs[2] ready for the defence of lists, ditches and platforms. Outside on the left flank Sir Estolt of Linars, careful and thorough, had ladders placed, and garrisoned the approaches, paths, lanes and cross-passages. When they were all assembled, the townsmen and the commanders agreed to capture the cat together.

Advice offered

Sir Bernard of Cazenac, an excellent speaker, laid it all before them, talking like a man of sense:

'My lords, men of Toulouse, those enemies you see there have killed your sons and your brothers and caused you great grief. If you can kill them, it will do you good. I know how these showy Frenchmen behave - they'll wear fine double armour on their bodies, but down below on their legs they'll have nothing on but their hose. Keep hitting hard at the backs of their knees and when the fight is over, they'll be carrion.'

'And they deserve it!' answered the men, and said to each other, 'There are plenty of us here.'

'Plenty at the moment,' said Sir Hugh of La Mota, 'but when it comes to hitting and being hit, it will be more even.'

The attack begins

Out they went down the ladders, deployed onto open ground and occupied the levels, shouting,

'Toulouse! Now the fire's alight! Kill them, kill them, it's the only way!'

The French and the men of Berry received their attack, shouting,

'Montfort! Montfort! Now we'll show up your lies!' Fierce was the struggle wherever they could meet; with swords, lances and sharpened steel they fought and struck on helmets from Bavaria.

Twice Sir Arnold of Lomagne[3] cried out to them:

'Strike, sweet comrades, remember freedom! Today sets *paratge* free from the powers of hell!'

'Yes,' they answered him, 'yes, and so it shall!' And the outcry, the din and clash of arms of citizens and men of the Capitol broke out afresh.

Present were: brave and active Sir Raymond of Lasbordes,[4] Bernard of St Martin, who is swift and alert, fierce William Peter of Montlaur,[5] Sir Peter of La Isla who can take blows and give them, and Sir Bernard of

---

1. Dawn on 25 June 1218.
2. The sharp steel teeth of combs used for dressing linen; these were used as arrows.
3. Eldest son of Vézian, viscount of Lomagne (laisse 199).
4. Raymond of Villeneuve of Lasbordes in the Lauragais, whose son Arnold testified in 1243 that his father had sheltered heretics at Lasbordes.
5. Probably a dispossessed lord from the Carcassès.

Comminges, ever fast and keen, with William Bernard of Luzenac,[1] always alert, Sir Gaudin and Sir Ferrando, courageous and agile, Godfrey, Sir Arbois, Sir Henry Campanier[2] and the men of Toulouse, impatient to come to blows.

'Have at these drunkards!' shouted Sir Raymond Isarn.[3] 'To arms, knights, and remember Sir Bernard's advice!' With swords and lances and great stones the struggle began again. The townsmen did very well, they forced their way inside the fences and fought them there, hacking the gold and crystal off their helmets. Under this pressure the crusaders gave way and abandoned the shelters. Once they remounted their chargers, however, the bloodshed began again with such fury that feet, fists and arms flew off and the ground was red with blood and brains. And on the river sergeants and sailors fought. Outside at Montoulieu the engagement was general and Sir Bartas[4] spurred his charger right up to the approach to the gates.

Count Simon urgently called from mass

At this point a squire came up to the count shouting,
'My lord count de Montfort, you are too slow! This piety is disastrous! The men of Toulouse have killed your knights, your troops and your best mercenaries. William is dead, so are Thomas, Garnier and Sir Simon of Le Caire, Walter is wounded.[5] Sir Peter of Voisins, Sir Aimery and Sir Rainier[6] are holding the attack, they're defending the men behind the shields.[7] If we have to stand this slaughter any longer, you'll never keep the fief!' The count shook and sighed, his face black with grief, and at the moment of the elevation[8] said,
'Jesus Christ the righteous, now give me death on the field or victory!'

Count Simon leads his charge

Immediately after this he ordered all his troops, his mercenaries and the barons of France to assemble with their Arab chargers. At once a good sixty thousand of them gathered. Then the count rode out fast at the head of them all, followed by Sir Sicard of Montaut and his standard-bearer, by Sir John of Berzy, Sir Foucaud, Sir Richard[9] and the whole mass of pilgrims. Their shouts, trumpets, horns and warcries, death flying from the slings and stones clattering from the mangonels came like a snowstorm, like thunder and tempest, and shook the town, the river and the riverbank. Fear struck the men of Toulouse and many fell into the ditches as they ran. But very soon they recovered, they made a sally across the orchards and gardens, and sergeants and javelin-men filled the area. Slender arrows and double quarrels,

1. A knight from Foix.
2. None of these are identified. Ferrando may have been from Aragon.
3. Two men of this name are known, one from Toulouse, another from Fanjeaux.
4. Peter William Bartas; his name occurs in a list of southern knights who in 1243 promised obedience to the Peace of Paris of 1229.
5. None of these are identified, except that Walter may be Walter Langton.
6. Probably Aimery of Blèves and Rainier of Aubusson.
7. The archers and crossbowmen firing from behind shelters.
8. Count Simon is at mass: the elevation of the sacred host.
9. Not identified.

round stones and fast strong blows came flashing like flame from either side, like wind and rain, like a rushing torrent.

Guy de Montfort wounded

Now from the left-hand parapet an archer let fly and his bolt hit Count Guy's horse on the head and drove half its length into its brain. As the horse turned, another crossbowman with a bow fully wound and ready shot at Sir Guy from the side and struck him in the left side of the groin, leaving the steel deep in his flesh; his side and breeches were red with blood. Guy rode up to his brother, his good friend, dismounted and said, as a devil might:

'Brother, God has thrown me and my comrades to the ground, it's the robbers he's helping. This wound will make me an Hospitaller!'[1]

Death of Count Simon, 25 June 1218

As Sir Guy was speaking and beginning to shout and yell, there was in the town a mangonel built by a carpenter and dragged with its platform from St Sernin. This was worked by noblewomen, by little girls and men's wives, and now a stone arrived just where it was needed and struck Count Simon on his steel helmet, shattering his eyes, brains, back teeth, forehead and jaw. Bleeding and black, the count dropped dead on the ground. Jocelyn and Sir Aimery[2] galloped to him at once and hurriedly covered him with a blue cape; but panic spread. How many knights and barons you would have heard lamenting, weeping under their helmets and crying out in anger! Aloud they exclaimed,

'God, it is not right to let the count be killed! How stupid to serve you, to fight for you, when the count who was kind and daring, is killed by a stone like a criminal! Since you strike and slay your own servants, there's no work for us here any more!'

Then they carried the count to the clergy and learned men, and the cardinal, the abbot and Bishop Fouquet received him sorrowfully with cross and censer.

Joy in Toulouse

But a messenger brought the news into Toulouse and such was the joy that all over the town they ran to the churches and lit candles in all the candlesticks and cried out,

'Rejoice! God is merciful and *paratge* shines forth, victorious for ever! The cruel and murderous count is dead, dead unshriven because he was a man of blood!' Trumpets, horns and universal joy, chimes and peals and clamouring bells in belfries, drums, tabors and slender clarions rang through the town till every paving-stone re-echoed.

Siege of Toulouse abandoned

The siege was then abandoned and the men across the river and holding the foreshore went away along every track. Behind them they left a great deal of

---

1. A black joke: Hospitallers were vowed to chastity.
2. Jocelyn, not known; Aimery, perhaps of Blèves.

property, pack-beasts, pavilions, tents, armour and money; and the townsmen took many of them prisoner. But the men of Toulouse lost one man they could ill spare, and that was young Sir Aimery,[1] courteous and pleasant. This was a great grief to the whole town.

Celebration in Toulouse

Laisse 206
The whole town was filled with such joy at Sir Simon's death that darkness shone like the day, light blazed and flowered, it raised up *paratge* and buried arrogance. Resounding trumpets, horns, bells and clarions and joy at the deadly stone brought new strength to hearts and minds and wills. Every man seized his weapons and went out into the open to burn the cat, a fire that nothing could quench. All night long and all day too the city celebrated, and outside it the besiegers groaned and shook.

Anxiety in the Narbonnais castle

Very early as dawn was breaking the cardinal from Rome and the other great lords, the bishop and the abbot carrying the crucifix, met on the ancient paved floor to consult each other. The cardinal spoke so that all could hear him:
'My lords, barons of France, hear what I have to say! This town and our enemies have done us great harm, great loss, grief and distress, for the count's death strips away our whole strength, grain and ear together. I cannot understand how God could let it happen and did not keep him safe for holy Church and for us! But dead he is, and we must act at once. Here and now let us make his son Amaury[2] count, for he is brave and wise and has a noble heart. Let us give him the fief his father conquered, and so let us die here together as the count has died! Preachers and speakers must go to every land and we must send to France, to our good friend the king, and ask him to send his son Louis to us next year, so that he may raze this town and lay it so flat that no one ever builds here again!'
'My lords,' said the bishop, 'there is nothing to prevent this. And the lord pope who approved and chose Count Simon will place him in the consistory where he interred St Paul;[3] let him become a most holy relic, for he obeyed the Church, he is a saint and martyr. This is so, I tell you, for no count in this world ever did less sin, nor since God died on the cross has he ever granted a greater death than the count's. Neither God nor holy Church had a better friend.'
'My lords,' said the count of Soissons, 'I strongly advise you not to describe him as most holy, or holy Church itself will ring false. Count Simon, holy? No one ever told a more thorough lie, for he died unshriven. But if he gave love and good service to holy Church, ask Jesus Christ not to punish his soul.'

---

1. Probably one of the Castelnau family (laisse 174).
2. Amaury was knighted in 1213, and so was probably not much more than eighteen at this period.
3. M.-C. suggests that Fouquet had seen Innocent III's restoration of the chapel of St Lawrence in the Lateran palace, with an altar containing the heads of St Peter and St Paul; M.-C., iii, p. 215, n. 4.

Amaury de Montfort is chosen as count

Everyone welcomed the recommendation and Sir Amaury took possession of the whole fief. The cardinal granted it him and gave him his blessing.

The lord of La Isla returns to his allegiance

Brave young Count Raymond now left Toulouse, for Sir Bernard Jordan sent word and found enough courage to become his friend; he made La Isla over to him and garrisoned it on his behalf.[1]

And the crusaders, bitter at heart, stayed in safety for four days, none of them venturing out till the Sunday.[2]

Laisse 207
Sunday brought appalling weather, storms raged across the whole country and shook everything that grew.

But the men of Toulouse and its joyful people posted guards in the defences and went back together into the town to eat.

The crusaders try again to take Toulouse

Outside the town the besiegers discussed the position and felt sure they could capture the place. They began at once by loading up vine-trimmings, wood, fire and burning torches onto carts and running them fast towards the town as far as the ditches and barricades, where the straw began to blaze and the fire took hold. The guards cried out in horror, and panic spread through the town. All ran to arms at once, not a father or son hung back, no fighting man, knight or count, cousin or kinsman. Out through the gates they poured by hundreds and thousands and occupied the levels and adjacent works. Women, ladies and elegant girls carried water and stones, calling on Our Lady and exclaiming, 'Holy Mary, lady, defend us now!' The men with the carts turned back and ran.

Meanwhile the townsmen found the besiegers and the French waiting for them, armed, arrayed and ready. The two sides met and clashed. With swords, lances and slashing blades, with javelins, stones and flung cobbles, they fought both hand to hand and at a distance. Bolts and arrows flew thick as small rain when it comes soaking down from the sky. Danger and distress, bloodshed and bitter struggle raged out there at Montoulieu, and the fire and flames, the dust and wind blew about amongst them as they fought.

Outside in the besiegers' camp it was agreed that the knights should all arm at once, clothing themselves and their swift chargers in strong mail. Onto the field they spurred, a deadly force, shouting 'Montfort! Soissons!' and 'Brittany!' But the townsmen's courage rose, battle-joy grew, their eagerness increased, not one of them flinched but all stood fast, watched, waited and patiently endured as the enemy ranks approached. 'Toulouse, who restores and conquers!' they cried, and 'Comminges!' for the count because he is worthy and brave, 'Cazenac! Creixell!' and 'Fighting Villemur!' because his

---

1. Although married to Raymond VI's sister, Bernard Jordan of La Isla made terms with the crusaders, so as not to lose his fief. Simon's death, however, cancelled all commitments, and Bernard Jordan at once recognised Count Raymond's suzerainty.
2. 1 July 1218.

banner was there blowing in their teeth. The bright shining helmets, the silver and fine gold, the red and white, the different hues and colours, the silk banners that flapped and gleamed, the shrill clarions and blaring trumpets strengthened their hearts and hardened their resolve. Wherever they could find an enemy, there they fought. With scythe-blades, axes, sharp-pointed pikes, halberds and arrows, with sharp quarrels, glittering shields and shining blades they struck and struggled so obstinately that they hacked off and cut away both armour and flesh. Thick on the ground lay feet, legs, arms, brain-matter and blood; every path and all the open ground was red and bloody.

So fierce was the fighting, such their fury that they grappled and held each other with hands and teeth. Attackers and attacked, both were determined that no limb or body should feel fear.

The Toulousains are victorious

But the townsmen conquered. Cutting and slashing with steel and sword, heaping blows upon their enemies, they drove them through all the passages and broke up their formations at the first entrance near the defences by the besiegers' gates.

This conflict, this loss and destruction continued until dark night parted the poor wretches. Never since God chose to die has any living man seen such a battle fought by so few men! As they broke off, those turned away in sorrow, these in joy. There you would have heard the wounded moan and complain, asking for doctors, wanting ointments, shrieking 'God help me!' because their wounds hurt so much.

The crusaders discuss plans.

Several days then passed peacefully and neither side made any attack on the other. It was not long before a meeting was held secretly between the cardinal from Rome, the bishop and the other lords. Guy de Montfort spoke privately, saying:

'My lords, barons, this siege is nothing but a loss to us. From now on I neither like nor approve it, for we are losing our horses, our kinsmen and ourselves. They were afraid of my brother, but now that he is dead, we are out of our minds if we do not give up the siege.'

'My lords,' said Sir Amaury, 'you have just made me count, think about me! If I abandon the siege so shamefully, it will harm the Church and will make me as nothing. In every land they'll say I surrendered while I still lived, and had forgotten my father's death.'

'Sir Amaury,' said Sir Alan, 'you misjudge this. All your barons can see that the shame will be worse if you continue the siege. You must realise that the defeated are winning! No one ever saw a town triumph through being beaten, yet every day these people are using their corn and wheat, their meat and firewood, which keep them in fighting trim, while we have to endure more and more danger and distress. And in my opinion you haven't the supplies to keep up the siege or to remain here long.'

'My lords,' said the bishop, 'this makes me so wretched that I shall never be happy again as long as I live.'

In grief and anger the cardinal spoke:

'My lords, let us raise the siege. But I promise you that word shall be preached all over the world, that the son of the king of France will certainly come here at Pentecost and we shall have such ample forces that the fruit, flowers and growing grass .... and they will think Garonne water sweet as hippocras. We shall destroy the town, and every one in it shall be put to the sword. Sentence is given!'

25 July 1218, the crusaders depart

Then they raised the siege in such urgent haste that on St James' day, which was fine, good and holy, they set fire to all their buildings, including the wonderful castle. But the townsmen promptly put all the fires out.

The French went away, leaving a great deal behind them - many dead and slaughtered, including their count who had ceased to exist. His body, however, they removed, having no other gifts to take away, and bore it straight to Carcassonne.

Count Simon's burial and epitaph

Laisse 208
Straight to Carcassonne they carried it and buried it with masses and offerings in the church of St Nazaire.[1] The epitaph says, for those who can read it, that he is a saint and martyr who shall breathe again and shall in wondrous joy inherit and flourish, shall wear a crown and be seated in the kingdom. And I have heard it said that this must be so - if by killing men and shedding blood, by damning souls and causing deaths, by trusting evil counsels, by setting fires, destroying men, dishonouring *paratge*, seizing lands and encouraging pride, by kindling evil and quenching good, by killing women and slaughtering children, a man can in this world win Jesus Christ, certainly Count Simon wears a crown and shines in heaven above.

Count Amaury de Montfort continues the struggle

The Virgin's Son glorifies what is right, he gave his body and precious blood to destroy pride - may he now protect law and reason in their peril, may he make the right blaze forth between these two contenders! For Montfort and Toulouse are renewing the conflict. Because of his father's death the son is seeking to strengthen his position and has summoned his barons and his fiefs. He holds a plenary court to establish his right. He talks, takes counsel and begins by saying:

'My lords, my father who loved you is dead, and as I cannot take Toulouse by siege, help me to hold and defend the fiefs!'

Cardinal Bertrand sends Bishop Fouquet to France

'Count,' said the cardinal, 'listen to me. What I want you to do is this: fortify your towns and castles and garrison them with men who can stand firm. And you, my lord bishop, go quickly and ask the lord king of France not to let us

---

1. It was buried in the cathedral of St Nazaire, then exhumed in 1224 and reburied in a priory church near Chevreuse (Seine-et-Oise). The epitaph described by our poet is lost. An unnamed tombstone, however, was found in 1845 and placed on the wall. It showed a thirteenth-century knight whose armorial bearings included both the Montfort lion and the cross of Toulouse.

be wiped out. Let him come on the first of May - let them not fail! - and restore her lordship to the Church. Let his crown and his son give us their help, so that we can destroy Toulouse, which has killed our count and is causing us such grief.'

Bertrand himself will write to the pope

'And I will send sealed letters to be read to the lord pope telling him he must make every effort to defend the Church and increase his own power, now that the once blazing st ir is dead. And, to make him hate it more, I will tell him about Toulouse, that neither the Church nor anything else can tame it, that it is so savage, so obstinate and reluctant to convert that no fire, sword or slaughter can subdue it. Let him have the summons preached in every land, and he should call on the prelates of the Church to provide for the war, to kindle hearts and polish tongues; let preachers go over the whole world, let them shake all Christendom and set it ablaze. We must rouse all the peoples and stir their courage, so that no man who can bear arms stays at home but all take up cross and sword to follow the king. And at Pentecost I promise you faithfully you will see such crusades and such crowds arriving that the earth will do well to bear them. With these we shall be well able to crush Toulouse and we shall do such works there that when we leave none will dare murmur or oppose us.'

'My lord,' said the bishop, 'I earnestly wish to accomplish this mission. But it is hard, strange and terrible to hear, I am amazed that God could agree to the death of this excellent son of his, who always served him. Indeed, I think a human father would suffer to see his son die, but God appears quite unmoved by the count's death! It is them he ought to be killing, but it is us whose defeat he orders! As Toulouse is causing us such pain, let us go and find a doctor who can heal us. God is paying no attention, so we must do all we can. If they somehow manage to elude us and escape into heaven or on earth, neither we nor the Church will ever recover.'

'My lords,' said Count Amaury, 'I owe you sincere thanks for wishing to pay such a price for my father's death.'

The count of Soissons offers his opinion

'My lords,' said the count of Soissons, 'I am going away and shall take my whole company with me. But, to do what is right, I can and will tell you, if you'll trust my opinion, how to get out of your great trouble: if the Church would be kinder and use mercy, mercy and the town could reach agreement. But if the Church uses pride where she should be gentle, mercy will take offence and regret her obedience. And if you do not compel the Church and Toulouse to join hands, many will die who could have lived happy lives.'

'Count,' said the cardinal, 'it is not going to end like that! We would let ourselves be cut to pieces rather than fail to make them sorry they killed Count Simon. Upon my honest word, one thing I promise you: they are not such warriors nor so skilled in battle but that at Pentecost we shall raise such a storm of war, there will not be an archangel who does not weep to see it!'

'My lords,' said the count of Soissons, 'may God keep those in joy who support what is right and make the rest repent!'

The crusade disperses; young Raymond campaigns in the Agenais

The cross is broken in two and parts in hatred. Now it is time to attack, time for Toulouse to triumph and save *paratge* and worth. Now the brave young count, who paints the darkness with gold and brings green back to a dead world, must ride to regain his fiefs and fly his flag, must take Condom, Marmande and Clairac, must seize Aiguillon and conquer and kill the French.

Sir Joris invades Comminges

Sir Bernard of Comminges must bestir himself, for Sir Joris is riding against him, he has summoned him to battle and is laying waste his land.[1]

Laisse 209
Sir Joris laid waste the land and made himself master, he threatened and hunted down the dispossessed knights; with his fine weapons and good Arab mounts he conquered and entered St Gaudens. Sir Bernard of Comminges, handsome, good and much liked, was inside Salies[2] castle with a small force; the sight of the invaders' banners angered them all. Sir Bernard sent urgently to the staunch men of Toulouse and to that fine man his father, the count of Comminges, and asked him to send help, as he could very easily do.

Sir Bernard pursues Sir Joris

Sir Joris rode joyfully out and along the riverbank,[3] his banners displayed. Sir Bernard chose the best, most intelligent and strongest of his men, well equipped and well armed, and when daylight returned and the morning brightened they rode after them on the track by the river, banners raised and standards flying. But when they reached Martres, Joris had already left, and when they failed to find him at St Elix, they stopped in its wide square to talk it over and told each other,

'That's the end of our pursuit'. But then Sir Inard of Pointis,[4] a brave and sensible man, spoke out before them all and said,

'My lord Sir Bernard, I am sure if you let them go now, you'll be burying yourself and us alive. But if you'll do as I suggest, you won't lose them: let us ride on all day until we catch them up. If they'll wait for us, let there be battle till one or other side quits the field. Even if we never find them but someone tells them you are pursuing them to give battle, they will be in a constant state of alarm and you will have saved us.'

'My lords,' said Marestaing,[5] 'let my nephew's plan be followed!' And they set off at once along the well-trodden roads.

When they reached Paumès a man there said to them:

---

1. Once the siege of Toulouse was raised, Joris, ally of the crusaders, was free to make war elsewhere.
2. The chief stronghold of the counts of Comminges, 22 km east of St Gaudens on the River Salat which runs into the Garonne.
3. Eastwards along the Garonne.
4. Lord of Pointis-Inard, St Gaudens, Haute-Garonne.
5. Bernard, lord of Marestaing and Clermont-Savès (Gers).

'My lords, look, there's Sir Joris, he has just set off. If you don't go and help them at Meilhan, he'll kill and destroy them all.'

'God be praised!' exclaimed Sir Odo of St Béat. 'Sir Joris is always bragging that he has challenged us to a fight. Now, trust me, we'll give him the lie!'

'Before they hear us coming,' said Raymond At of Aspet, 'let's plan our attack. If they get away undefeated, we and all our kin will be disgraced for ever.'

'My lords,' said Sir Espanel,[1] 'once it's over, whatever happens to the rest, Joris must be taken, so that Sir Roger of Aspet can be released safe and sound.'

Sir Bernard exhorts his men

While they were talking together, Sir Bernard of Comminges addressed them. He spoke well and greatly encouraged them, saying:

'My lords, free knights, Jesus Christ, true God, loves and guides us, and see how kind he is to us, delivering these enemies who have done us so much harm into our hands! We shall have battle, no doubt of that, and we shall win, I know it in my heart. My lords, remember how they oppressed us! They intruded false lords into all our fiefs, they killed fathers and small children, they slew gentlewomen and murdered husbands, they overthrew *paratge* and puffed themselves up, they drove us out grieving into the dangers of the world and daily they hunted us down in the flowering woodlands. But by Saint Mary, Virgin Empress, I would rather die by the sword and shining steel than let them keep us crushed and helpless! If today they find us fierce and resolute, *paratge* will always be honoured and obeyed. Believe me, we have now got them in our grip, and their business and ours shall be so settled as to fill hell and paradise with souls, for an honourable death is better than life in shame. As for any plunder we may win, it must be properly shared out between us all.'

'Well said, well said!' they all shouted. 'Into battle, ride! God will lead us!' And they rode on together until they could hear and see the others.

Sir Bernard surprises his quarry at Meilhan

Meanwhile, quite unperturbed, the castellan,[2] Sir Joris and Sir Anselm[3] together with the tough and courageous French were attacking the town and its keep. Now suddenly Sir Bernard and his men charged, shouting their warcries. When the French saw the bright blazons, the cross, hackle and bull, the sheep[4] and the brave knights' other devices, when they saw the good companies which had pursued them so doggedly, they were appalled, and no wonder. They gathered into the barbican, manning its passages and

---

1. Probably Espan, younger son of Vézian of Lomagne.
2. No doubt the crusader in charge of Meilhan; his name is not known. M.-C. supposes that the inhabitants had rebelled on hearing of Simon's death, and that Joris had been sent in response to an appeal for help; M.-C., iii, p. 244, n. 3.
3. Not identified.
4. Comminges bore the cross pattée gules (laisse 187); Espan of Lomagne a sheep or ram; a bull is a common heraldic symbol; the hackle or hemp-brake was a linen-worker's tool.

openings. Hoping to prevent this, Sir Bernard of Comminges charged full tilt faster than the rest, closely followed at a swift gallop by Sir Inard of Pointis and Sir Odo of St Béat, who thrust well ahead.

Now Sir Bernard of Seysses[1] struck and overthrew Sir Anselm, but he escaped injury. Sir Roger of Montaut leapt from his horse to attack them with strong and repeated blows. Meanwhile Sir William of Seysses, daring and brave, spurred and attacked and was himself struck and his horse thrown down, but got to his feet. Loudly Sir Roger of Montaut cried,

'Hit them hard, keep hitting them, usurpers, murderers!' At that they spurred their Arab chargers and drove home the attack on every side. Joris' men had sharp steel and used it well; both sides fought strongly. Stones, javelins, lances, brandished spears, bolts, arrows and twice-tempered quarrels struck through the chainmail, and the red blood ran down and soaked their samite surcoats.

Now too the men of Meilhan saw what was happening and hurled stones and rocks at Joris' men. But the castellan raged in fury, he turned and twisted like a wounded boar, he smashed, shattered and hacked whatever came near, so that a hedge of lance-stumps bristled round him. Sir Anselm and Sir Joris fought hard, as did Sir Roger of Lignières,[2] till they were exhausted. Sir Inard shouted to them,

'Now you're paying for all the harm you've done us! If you want to live, surrender before we cut you to pieces!' But they replied,

'And who'd guarantee us?'

Together and fiercely the attackers spurred and forced their way through all the openings and right into the barbican among Joris' men. Hand to hand they fought amid noise and uproar; swords, maces and keen-edged blades cracked and cut open the shining green helmets. It was no wonder they defeated them, for so heavy were the blows both given and taken that their bones were shattered inside their armour.

Defeat and slaughter of the French

Now Sir Joris remounted and sallied out, and was again struck and felled to the ground. Wherever they could find them, they hacked and dismembered them, so that feet and fists, arms, brain-matter, fingers, heads, jawbones, scalps and skulls littered the battlefield and encrusted the reddened ground. A scene of war indeed, you would have said, before the place was cleared.

Laisse 210

A scene of war indeed, when the killing was done - blood, brain-matter, eyes and limbs, feet, legs and arms lay strewn about, filling the roads and open ground. The castellan, Sir Joris and Sir Anselm were made prisoner, and all the rest were delivered up to torment there on the killing ground, where they lost both lives and armour.

Sir Bernard of Comminges and Sir William of Touges[3] ....

And when the great count of Comminges heard the news, I do not think he was at all displeased.

---

1. Co-suzerain of Fousseret, Muret.
2. His name occurs in a list of those swearing fealty to Alfonse of Poitiers and his wife Jeanne of Toulouse in 1249.
3. Held land in Pouy-de-Touges and Savères (Haute-Garonne).

Young Raymond returns to Toulouse

Then the brave young count arrived in Toulouse to defend his fief and recover his inheritance.

Amaury de Montfort besieges Marmande

Count Amaury went away into the Agenais, taking with him knights and clerks, the feudal levies, crusaders and the French. The lord abbot who holds Rocamadour[1] went with him, accompanied by men from Quercy and from Clermont; and so did Sir Amanieu d'Albret[2] of the Armagnac family, lord of Seyches, rich, daring and delightful, ungrudgingly lavish, one of the best men in the Bazadais. And with many lords from other areas and local men too, Count Amaury sat down before Marmande[3] - an action he will regret if the king[4] fails to arrive, for the place is defended by Centule of Astarac,[5] a young and valorous count, skilful and daring.

He and good Amanieu,[6] with bold Araimfres, Sir Arnold of Blanchafort, Vézian of Lomagne, Sir Amanieu of Bouglon, Sir Gaston, Sir Sicre, Sir William Amanieu and the two men from Pamplona, with the townsmen, sergeants, commons, young noblemen and archers, Brabanters and Germans took swords, lances and good Turkish bows and manned the town from moat to towers.

Now Count Amaury made a vigorous assault and the fighting spread across land and water.[7] Resistance was strong; attackers and attacked used maces, swords and sharp steel from Cologne to give and take such blows that the blood, flesh and bodies left strewn about provided rich feeding for birds and dogs.

The count of Foix campaigns in the Lauragais

Now let us leave this savage and deadly siege and speak of the good count who is lord of Sabartès,[8] of Roger Bernard and the Wolf of Foix, these three.

---

1. The abbot of Tulle held the lordship of Rocamadour; the present abbot's name was Bernard of Ventadour.
2. The lords of Albret (Labrit, Landes) held fiefs in the Bazadais and the Agenais.
3. Marmande (Lot-et-Garonne); no authorities give a date for the setting of this siege, but it was probably after Countess Alice and Bouchard of Marly brought reinforcements at Christmas 1218.
4. In fact, the prince, who symbolises and brings with him the power of the French crown.
5. Son-in-law of the count of Comminges, fought at Las Navas de Tolosa and Muret.
6. In the following list, knights not previously identified are:
   Amanieu, probably Pons Amanieu, ousted from Montastruc (Monclar-d'Agenais);
   Arnold, either from Fumel (Lot-et-Garonne) or the Gers;
   Amanieu, lord of Bouglon, Gironde;
   Gaston, probably son of the lord of Gontaud;
   Sicre, not identified;
   two knights from Pamplona, mercenaries from Navarre.
7. Marmande stands on a height above the Garonne; at this period the river flowed immediately beneath the town.
8. The count of Foix.

With them were Bernard Amiel lord of Pailhès,[1] William Bernard of Arnave and Sir Isarn Jordan, Sir Robert of Tinhes with men from the Carcassès, Raymond Arnold of Le Pech, and Sir Aimery too, as well as Sir William of Niort and Jordan of Cabaret. All these rode with the count of Foix into the Lauragais, where they seized cows and oxen, villeins and peasants. Then they reached Bazière[2] and quartered themselves there.

Crusaders ride to attack the count of Foix

But Sir Foucaud of Berzy, a hard man, valiant, clever, daring and tough, rode out with his kinsmen, with Sir John,[3] Sir Theobald and the viscount of Lautrec, with Sir John of Bouillon, Sir Amaury de Lucy, Sir Evrard of Torletz, Sir Aubry, Sir James, Sir John of Mozencs, Sir John Lomagne, well-armed and lion-hearted every one of them, to find and attack the count of Foix.

Young Raymond leads men to support the count of Foix

And when daylight and fair weather returned, out from Toulouse rode the young count and marquis, of the lineage of France and of the good English king. In his company were many men of Toulouse, Sir Arnold of Villemur and Sir Bertrand Jordan, also Gerald Unaud, Rodrigo and Sir Hugh,[4] Sir Bertrand of Gourdon and the Abbot of Montaut; William Unaud was there, Sir Raymond Unaud, Sir Amalvis, daring Sir Hugh of La Mota, Garcias

---

1. Some of those listed here are:
   Bernard Amiel, a principal vassal of the count of Foix.
   William Bernard, another Foix vassal.
   Isarn Jordan, a dispossessed lord; fought alongside Trencavel in the latter's attempt to regain his inheritance.
   Robert of Tinhes, not identified.
   Raymond Arnold, dispossessed, had held lands in Alzonne, Aude; fought for Trencavel; castellan of Carcassonne in 1226.
   Aimery, probably from Clermont-sur-Lauquet (Aude), dispossessed; excommunicated 1242 for helping Trencavel.
   William of Niort, related to the lords of Niort, several of whom were found guilty of heresy. In 1237 a William of Niort was sentenced to life imprisonment for this offence.
   Jordan; the lords of Cabaret, high up in the Montagne Noire north of Carcassonne, had been driven out by the crusaders in 1211. Another Trencavel supporter.
2. The date of the battle of Bazière is not known, except that it took place in winter, most probably in 1218-19.
3. Knights who rode with Foucaud include:
   his brother John;
   Theobald of Nouvila;
   Sicard, viscount of Lautrec (Castres, Tarn);
   Amaury, who may be related to Guy de Lucy;
   Evrard, not identified;
   Aubry, not identified;
   James, possibly Jacques d'Etalle (Ardennes);
   John of 'Mozencs' perhaps an error for Monceaux;
   John, relative or vassal of the viscount of Lomagne.
4. Rodrigo, not identified; Hugh of Alfaro; Garcias Sabolera, below, was probably a mercenary from Spain like Peter Navarra.

Sabolera and Sir Peter Navarra and the knights and citizens of Toulouse. These and many men from other lands came with enthusiasm to join the count,[1] as had been agreed.

They anticipate the battle with pleasure

As soon as they met, before others arrived to increase their numbers, the mighty count of Foix said to young Raymond,

'My lord count, I feel sure your renown is increasing, for we shall certainly do battle with the French, I recognise their banners, their blazons and orfrays. It looks as if Sir Foucaud, Sir Alan, Sir Hugh de Lacy, Sir Sicard of Montaut[2] and the men of this neighbourhood intend to attack us. Never have I seen a battle which would give me more pleasure, for never since I first bore arms can I remember to have seen a force as fine as ours today! Ill faith and arrogance will go down if we fight now, I am sure of that.'

Sir Roger Bernard, rich in all virtues, said,

'My lords, free knights, today will show who can fight! My heart fills with joy, for I can see here the flower of this land and of the whole Carcassès.' And the young count began to laugh and like a courteous man said,

'God save me my lady[3] and the Narbonnais castle! My standard shall not swerve aside till I have killed or taken them. If all France and every Montfort were there, they should all have battle till one side or the other is beaten!' Then straight away he shouted so that they could all hear: 'To arms, knights, while we have the chance! And let us do this so well that no one can reproach us, for by holy Mary in whom Jesus Christ took flesh, if they will only wait for us, today, like it or not, they shall have battle!'

Laisse 211
'Today, God willing, they shall have battle and when it is done we'll see who holds the dice! How near us they are, how dearly we can make them pay for our inheritance! You can be sure God hates them, he has brought them here for us to slaughter!'

An attempt to keep young Raymond out of the battle

'My lord count,' said Sir Arnold of Villemur, 'excuse me, but you could win no honour in this battle. Your rank is too great, you should not fight them unless they had Sir Amaury with them, or some other count or great noble. Sir Foucaud is a brave and intelligent man, but he has not the wealth or power for you to put yourself at risk. If you captured him, you would gain nothing, it would bring you no land, no peace or agreement. But if you want to fight, you will find me beside you on your right hand and on your left.'

Young Raymond rejects this advice

'Sir Arnold,' said the count, 'why do you lecture me? Today I shall fight, and

---

1. Of Foix.
2. Sicard and the brothers Bernard, Roger, Odo and Isarn 'the Abbot' belonged to two unconnected families both called Montaut.
3. Sancha of Aragon, sister of Peter II king of Aragon. Some months later in 1220 she gave birth to Jeanne, last countess of Toulouse, who married Alfonse of Poitiers.

with your good will, I hope, for any who fail me now will be disgraced for ever. Any man, whoever he is, even a crowned king, must risk his life and all he possesses to destroy his enemies, until he has overthrown them. Now let us give all our attention to helping this land.'

The battle is planned and posts allotted

'My lord count,' said the count of Foix, 'give me the front rank and the most active men.'

'You and Sir Roger Bernard,' said the count, 'with the men from the Carcassès, as I know they are well armed and can hit hard and take risks, with the men of your own fief whom you most trust and your own company just as it is, you make the assault, and I beg you to hit them hard. Spearhead our attack, and then the moment you're engaged, I'll charge to support you, I and the men of my own fief whom I've tested so often, my company and my friends, my trusted men of Toulouse, and my brother Bertrand[1] who is well prepared. And when the fighting's done, the field and the glory will be ours.'

....

'No fear of that, my lords,' said the young count. 'Live or die, whatever you do there, you'll find me beside you whether I'm dead or alive, for I am determined to win glory in this battle or else die in it. May the Virgin's Son who died in agony behold what is right and perceive their sins!'

'Well and nobly spoken!' said the count of Foix. 'But let us get our attack started. The men with the best horses must lead it.' Roger Bernard said,

'Have it proclaimed that anyone who disobeys your orders will lose his lands for the rest of his life.'

'My lords,' said Peter Navarra, 'knights, guard the young count all of you, don't let him be wounded! Worth and *paratge* return in him, valour would perish if he were injured.' But the Wolf of Foix exclaimed,

'Sir count, move on! Into battle, ride, the moment has passed!'

Allies and troops of Foix charge the crusaders

Out ahead of them all rode Sir Arnold of Villemur, with Sir Gerald of Gourdon, Sir Hugh of Alfaro and the Abbot, Sir Bertrand of La Isla, Sir Garcias Coriadats,[2] Sir William and Sir Raymond Unaud, well equipped, Raymond Arnold of Le Pech and Le Tinhos of the Jurats,[3] Rodrigo and the rest, all spurring hard. After their commanders came the knights at full gallop, banners lowered and pennons flying.

Sir Foucaud of Berzy observed them carefully, recognised their blazons, and riding onto the riverbank[4] he said to his men:

'Stand firm!' Nobly and well he addressed them, saying, 'My lords, barons of France, my own mighty kinsmen, God, the Church and I all promise you that you need have no fear, no worry, no anxiety. Here comes the young

---

1. Illegitimate son of Raymond VI.
2. Probably from Navarre or Aragon.
3. Lord of Castillon-en-Couserans (Ariège). The nickname *Tinhos* means 'Scabby', and *Jurats* 'the sworn', i.e. the six lords who in 1197 promised on oath to support the count of Comminges. See M.-C., iii, p. 270, n. 5 for detective work on this.
4. The River Hers and two tributaries flow across the Baziège plain.

count who hates us, here comes the valiant count of Foix, a hard man and crafty, here's Roger Bernard and the assembled barons, and they have brought hired captains and the dispossessed men. But if they are good in battle, we are much better! Here is the whole of France, here is stubborn Montfort, with the pick of the southerners and the flower of the crusade. And if any one of us is killed, the bishop of Toulouse and the lord legate have forgiven us all our sins.'

'Brother,' said John, 'make sure you hit hard, for judging by the miracles done for us and the crusaders, the battle today is between holiness and sin.'

'Listen, my lords,' said the viscount of Lautrec. 'I have had a good look at these captains and their men, and I think it's madness to wait for them here.'

'Viscount,' said Theobald, 'go away if you like. We shall wait for the count, and then we'll see who's mad.'

Talking and preparation done and courage high, the ranks of armed horsemen drew nearer. The two forces came closer till nothing divided them, no bridge or plank, nothing but a little ditch. When the count of Foix and his brave men crossed it, the two sides formed two halves of a whole.

Sir Foucaud of Berzy waited for them, his ranks well arrayed, ready and resolute. Trumpets spoke each to each, they rang across riverbank, meadows and open land. 'Foix!' and 'Toulouse!' rose the shouts and 'Montfort!' and 'Berzy!' came the replies. As the leaders met, light glanced from banners and coloured shields; with lance-points and fringed pennons lowered, they rode to break their lances on gold-inlaid hauberks. After them came the massed knights, well armed, spurring full tilt at the men who waited for them and galloping around their defences.

'Make for the young count, barons, all of you!' shouted Sir Peter William of Séguret.[1] 'I fear nothing but his knighthood and skill, his pride and prowess. Bring him down before they beat us, or he'll make us all suffer before the end.'

Young Raymond's feats of arms

Then like a lion or leopard loosed from its chains the young count raced on before them all. How well his black charger bore him! Lance lowered, head bent, he drove into the thickest of the fight. He struck John of Berzy who rode to meet him, and hit him so hard with his inlaid spear that he pierced surcoat, mail and gambeson,[2] flung him from his horse and rode on. 'Toulouse!' he cried. 'Free knights, have at these foreigners! Thrust deep, cut hard!' On every side he twisted, turned and struck, the men of his household close by to protect him and Sir Arnold bearing the banner ahead of them. Sir John of Berzy got to his feet, he thrust and cut till his steel blade broke.

Now Peter William of Séguret rode up fast and struck the young count as he could reach him, full on the straps that grip the hauberk, so that he cut his belt and made the chainmail fly. 'Montfort! Montfort!' he shouted. 'Free knights, have at him!' But the count kept his seat unshaken. All around there was shouting and uproar, and stubborn conflict. With swords, maces and tempered blades, with blows to the neck from gilt scabbards, they

---

1. Séguret in the Venaissin was part of the marquisate of Provence, so that its lord Peter William is guilty of treason in supporting the crusaders against his overlord.
2. Armour was worn over a padded or quilted undergarment; the surcoat of thick silk was worn outside the hauberk.

struggled and struck at chests and sides, they hacked at strong-rimmed green helmets, at hauberks, mailshirts and studded shields.

The count of Foix prepares another charge; Foucaud of Berzy is ready for it

Now the count of Foix shouted: 'Rein in! Rein in!' and Sir Foucaud of Berzy: 'Free knights, stand firm!' Sir Evrard, Sir Amaury and Sir Theobald rode together, Sir John of Bouillon and Sir James knee to knee. With the viscount of Lautrec who had entered the mêlée and the French, these took their stand on the field.

Chatbert,[1] Sir Aimery and good Roger Bernard, the Wolf of Foix and Sir William of Niort (now wounded), Bernard Amiel, young William Bernard, and Sir Amalvis with famous Sir Hugh of La Mota and the men of Toulouse, fired by their anger - all these and the count's own men united to make a single charge and with sharp steel they cut deep into the French array. They rode around and outflanked them, they struck and wounded them on chests and sides and down they flung the Frenchmen and unhorsed them two at a time.

Foot-soldiers finish off the fallen

Now all together sergeants entered the battle to kill the fallen. Steel flashed on steel, on overthrown and beaten men; knights and sergeants struggled, and they slashed, slew and finished them. Eyes, brain-matter, hands, arms, scalps and jaw-bones, bits of limbs, livers and guts sliced up and tossed about, blood, flesh and carrion lay everywhere. Red was the battlefield and red the riverbank, heaped with dead Frenchmen. The viscount of Lautrec, however, escaped with his life. Sir Foucaud, Sir John and Sir Theobald surrendered and were kept, but the rest lay slaughtered on the battlefield.

It was a miracle of the holy Trinity that none of the count's men were hurt in this affair, except one squire who rode too far ahead. The battle won and the field stripped, the count rode back in great joy. Peter William of Séguret was hanged then and there.[2]

Count Amaury learns of the defeat at Baziège

Count Amaury did not feel like laughing, you can be sure of that, when his swift messenger brought him the news at the siege of Marmande.

Laisse 212
At the siege of Marmande the messenger reported that the brave young count had beaten the French, taken Sir Foucaud, Sir John and Sir Theobald prisoner and slaughtered the rest. This roused Count Amaury to such fury that he mounted a sharp attack by land and water, but the townsmen faced him outside on the open ground and fought back with vigour. Men on both sides took such blows from swords, lances and sharpened steel that many were left lying dead, both men and horses. Bravely they held their own and fought night and day.

---

1. Chatbert of Barbaira (Capendu, Aude), a dispossessed knight.
2. As a traitor.

Another crusading force reaches Marmande

But soon trouble came upon them from which they could never recover, for the bishop of Saintes[1] who was leading the crusade, and the much feared seneschal Sir William of Les Roches,[2] bringing troops, provisions and baggage trains, set up their tents and pavilions all round where the highway runs, and filled the river with their boats.

June 1219, Prince Louis of France brings an army

After that it was not long before their courage and folly brought them all to grief, for now the son of the king of France appeared. He brought with him twenty five thousand lances,[3] splendid knights astride bright-maned horses, ten thousand of them clad in shining iron and steel, horses as well as men. As for foot-soldiers, they were past counting. They brought cartloads of weapons and supplies and occupied all the open ground, the gardens and orchards.

And the king[4] dismounted with great joy at his own tent. It is no wonder the townsmen despaired when they saw who it was, and each in his heart wished he had never been born.

Marmande's commanders arrange a surrender

In their first attack the French captured the ditches and lists and broke down the bridges and barricades. After this they held discussions which gave the townspeople some hope, for by deliberate and public agreement Count Centule and the others surrendered themselves to the king.

Inside the grand pavilion adorned with beaten gold the prelates of the Church attended upon the king and the barons of France took their seats before him. The king sat on a silken cushion and folded his right glove, rich with gold embroidery. Everyone listened for the others to speak, and the king seemed dumb.

Bishop Pons demands the death of Centule of Astarac

But the bishop of Saintes, a clever man, spoke out before them all and was heard:

'Great king, joy, honour and salvation be to you this day! You have left the realm of France to lead the Church and her powers, and as you are her guide, she now commands you, a command you must in no way alter, to give back to Count Amaury the count who has surrendered to you, for it is his duty to burn or hang him, and yours to help him do so. Give Amaury the town and its heretics too, for death and the sword have reached them.'

---

1. Pons, son of the lord of Pons (Charente-Maritime), became bishop of Saintes in 1216.
2. A poor but valiant knight who married an heiress; became seneschal of Anjou; transferred Anjou, Maine and part of Poitou from English to French rule; married one of his daughters to Amaury of Craon.
3. 'Lances' translates *escutz* (literally, 'shields'); these were military units consisting of a knight and his three, four or five subordinates.
4. Prince Louis.

Crusading nobles reject the bishop's demand

Angered by this, the count of St Pol[1] said,

'By God, my lord bishop, you won't be obeyed! If the king hands over Count Centule and he comes to any harm, the nobles of France will be disgraced for ever.'

'The count was accepted,' said the count of Brittany.[2] 'The crown cannot in justice surrender him.'

'My lord,' said the bishop of Béziers,[3] 'if anyone reproached the king, he would say that holy Church had claimed them.'

Louis supports the bishops

'Barons,' said the king, 'since it is the Church who brought me here, her law shall not be challenged. The count is in dispute with the Church, so she may do what she likes with her justiciables.'

The archbishop of Auch defends his flock

But very promptly the archbishop of Auch[4] said:

'By God, good my lord king, if we are to go by the law, neither the count nor his household should suffer death or injury, for he is no heretic, no traitor or miscreant. No, he followed the cross and upheld his rights. He has behaved badly towards the Church, but he is not a heretic nor accused of wrong beliefs, and it is the Church's duty to receive a defeated sinner in such a way that his soul is not lost nor himself harmed. In Toulouse they are holding Sir Foucaud prisoner, and if the count is condemned, Sir Foucaud will hang.'

'Good my lord archbishop,' said William of Les Roches, 'your advice will be taken. The count shall not be killed but released in exchange for Sir Foucaud.'[5]

In this way Count Centule and four other lords were saved.

Massacre in Marmande

But clamour and shouting arose, men[6] ran into the town with sharpened steel; terror and massacre began. Lords, ladies and their little children, women and men stripped naked, all these men slashed and cut to pieces with keen-edged swords. Flesh, blood and brains, trunks, limbs and faces hacked in two, lungs, livers and guts torn out and tossed aside lay on the open ground as if they had rained

---

1. Gaucher of Châtillon, distinguished at the siege of Acre, at Bouvines and in the Albigensian crusades of 1209 and 1215.
2. Peter of Dreux, great-grandson of Louis VI, count of Brittany by marriage to its heiress.
3. Bernard 'de Coxiaco', bishop of Béziers from 1215.
4. Garcias de l'Ort, appointed archbishop in 1215.
5. Centule of Astarac. Foucaud of Berzy was released, but during the winter of 1220 he and his brother John resumed their warfare in the Toulousain, and were captured and beheaded by young Count Raymond.
6. No subject is expressed with this verb, simply *corron*; in fact the massacre, inspired by a loathing of heresy, was committed by crusading troops while their commanders were finishing their conference.

down from the sky. Marshland and good ground, all was red with blood. Not a man or a woman was left alive, neither old nor young, no living creature, unless any had managed to hide. Marmande was razed and set alight.

Very soon after that the king left to go to Toulouse.

Louis rides for Toulouse

Laisse 213
To go to Toulouse, that was what the son of the king of France now meant to do, and so his standard-bearer rode out ahead of the rest. Such crowds accompanied the king that the hills and plains, the roads and paths were crammed and swarming with men and women. The whole country was filled with people from France, from Berry, with Flemings and English, Normans, Champenois, Bretons and Poitevins, with Germans and Bavarians. So huge was this throng of murderers that the full host numbered thirteen hundred thousand. They brought carts, mules and pack-beasts, tents, pavilions, victuals and money, and travelled in short stages to let those at the rear keep up.

The cardinal[1] from Rome and prelates of the churches, bishops, archbishops, abbots, Templars, monks and canons both black and white, were present in the host, five thousand of them, men who could speak and read. They preached and commanded that the sword should lead the way.

Alarm in Toulouse

It is no wonder that fear fell on all the inhabitants of Toulouse when they saw the messengers.[2] In urgent haste the consuls sent their best and fastest couriers to the feudal levies and to all fighting men: let none stay behind, no sergeant or archer, no magnificent knight or hired mercenary, no landless man from the forest or any active man, no one who longed for worth and *paratge*, longed to recover his heritage, to defend himself and live once more in joy. Anyone who came to Toulouse would earn the right to a permanent share in all its wealth.

Discussions in Toulouse

A thousand good knights came to the town's help, tough fighters all of them, and five hundred javelin men as well. When they were all gathered in a full meeting of the townsmen and their commanders, Pelfort addressed them, as he is a fine speaker, and explained the situation and what they should do:

'Barons, men of Toulouse, today you need wisdom, experience, good sense and a practical way forward. This matter of the king of France is immensely important to us. He is bringing foreigners here, men who know how to kill. But before the king encamps outside in the vineyards, my lord the young count,

1. The legate Bertrand.
2. Reporting the army's approach.

being his vassal[1] and his close relative, should send him brave and courteous messengers to tell him that he has done him no wrong, is not false or untrue; that if the king wants to claim his rights he will be happy to pay them to him, to the Church and to others who have claims on him. Or if the king will come to Toulouse with a small retinue, the count will receive his fief from him as his vassal, will yield him the town and let him garrison its towers. Law he offers him, and law is supreme, so that the king ought not to destroy him because of reports spread by slanderers. But if he speaks with their voice and as an enemy, then let Jesus Christ our standard-bearer lead and defend us!'

'This is excellent advice,' said the barons.

Young Raymond refuses to be cautious

'My lords,' said the young count, always venturesome, 'it is very good advice, but we shall not take it. The king was my lord; if he had treated me justly I would have been true to him for ever. But he is my enemy, he is violent and tyrannical. It was he who began the bloodshed, he who took my town of Marmande and killed my knights, and therefore as long as I remember the injury and suffering he has caused, as long as he rides against me with those pilgrims of his, I shall send him no messengers, do him no courtesy. His servants are arrogant, they give him dishonest advice, so that it would do no good for us to be courteous, it would only double our hardship and disgrace. But when the king's son confronts me face to face, when blood is flowing and men are dying night and day, when knights and horses fall on the battlefield and we withstand their attack, then if we send him word, he will answer kindly! Trust me, the flames must blaze higher before the king becomes our lord, or our equal! We are well matched, his men and ours, and we shall see how Toulouse stands up to the slashing steel, whether the mortar will hold the wine or water or whether it will break under the blows of the pestle. If we can defend it, the rose tree will flower and *paratge*, merriment and joy will return to us!'

Hostilities are agreed on, and supplies assured

All agreed to the young count's words. Then the consuls said:

'We shall be happy to supply everything the feudal levies and the hired troops can need, they shall have good food and kind hosts. We will have it proclaimed throughout the town that all the squires are to come and take free and plentiful delivery of bread, meat and wine from our cellars, of oats and barley by the hundredweight and the ton, and of pepper and cinnamon too, and fruit from the fruit trees, quite without payment. All anyone need ask is, "Mouth, what do you want?" And if my lord the king intends to attack us, we can certainly hold out for a good five years.'

---

1. The feudal bond between Toulouse and the French crown was broken when Philip Augustus accepted homage from Simon de Montfort for the fiefs hitherto held of him by Raymond VI. But Simon's death broke that link and left the way open for young Raymond to re-establish the former connection.

They call St Exupéry to their help; and build siege engines

The first thing they did after the meeting broke up was to place St Exupéry in the main vault under the noble bell-tower and surround him with lights and candles. He was bishop of Toulouse, a good and holy man, who defends and cherishes all his heirs. [1] After that they ordered all the carpenters in their ground-floor workshops in the town to make catapults, engines and mangonels; and Sir Bernard Parayre and Master Garnier were to manage the trebuchets as they were accustomed to this work.

Posts are allocated and work begun

Commune officials were now chosen in all quarters of the town, knights, citizens and the best merchants, to garrison the gates and command the workmen, and everyone laboured cheerfully - working people, noble sons and daughters, women and ladies, boys and girls and little children, singing ballads and cheerful songs. They constructed barriers, ditches, levels, bridges, barricades, walls and stairs, and built galleries, round-walks, doorways and platforms, lists, arrow-loops and crenellations as well as openings, shelters and cross-hatchways, trenches, covered lanes and side passages. All the barbicans, including those along the river's edge, they entrusted to the counts and to experienced commanders. Thoroughly fortified, the town stands well defended against the pride of France.

Laisse 214
Against the pride of France they make ready, so that the young count can defend himself and his people. Orders are given in Toulouse so that together throughout the town .... with the brave young count in command. The feudal levies must work together and prepare, sharing guard duty and labour, not laying aside their armour day or night. The town's consuls and respected men, knights and citizens, making thorough preparations, entrust the city gates to the best and wisest of its inhabitants, and then they hand the barbicans and new defences over to these counts and barons, who accept their charge.

Officers in charge of the different barbicans

Sir Dorde Barasc,[2] who is young and well esteemed, Sir Arnold of Montégut, courageous and valiant, Bernard of Rocafort and noble Sir Arnold Barasc defend the Bazacle[3] barbican with their fine and daring troops.
Sir William of Minerve, who has great experience, William of Belafar, brave and intelligent, and Sir Arnold Feda, these in good heart garrison the count's barbican.

---

1. Fifth bishop of Toulouse, praised by St Jerome who said that 'his merits had preserved Toulouse from ruin'; reputed to have saved the city from Vandal attack, but no facts are known.
2. Dorde and Arnold Barasc, father and son, from Quercy.
3. For the location of this and the other barbicans, see plan of Toulouse. Some of the locations are disputed; see M.-C., iii, pp. 304 ff. and nn.

The Baussana barbican is in the firm and cheerful hold of able Sir Frotard Peter,[1] a noble and competent commander, of open-handed Sir Bernard of Penne,[2] of William Frotier[3] and Sir Bertrand of Monestiès.[4]

Good Sir Roger Bernard, a man of sense, valour, and knowledge, who brings comfort to those who suffer loss, he with Sir Bernard Amiel, always in the lead, Jordan of Cabaret and Sir Chatbert, strong in defence, and Sir Aimery of Roca Negada,[5] is the noble keeper of the Crosses barbican.

Sir Arnold of Villemur, who is strength and courage itself, a mighty man, cheerful and wise, generous in word and deed, keeps strong hold of Sir Arnold Bernard's barbican, aided by his nephew William Unaud, by William Bernard of Arnave, and by Sir William Arnold, swift and capable, the man who made *genhs* and *brocidas* at the time of the first dispossessions.[6]

Sir Espan of Lomagne, a true friend who has come fast to Toulouse with his fine troops, holds the barbican where trouble is expected. With him are Sir Amalvis who hits hard, good Sir Hugh of La Mota who fights and does not give up, and Bertrand of Pestillac. Fierce and vigorous, these hold the Pozamila barbican, enduring assault, danger, and distress.

Pelfort, who is valiant, wise, clever and pleasant, and Sir Ratier of Caussade,[7] grim, ferocious and effective, with Sir Ratier of Bosna[8] and active John Martin[9] faithfully defend the Matabiau barbican.

The Gaillarde Gate, centre of conflict, out of which every day the knights and sergeants of Toulouse sally to make shrewd attacks, to fight and struggle and stain the fields with blood, is held by men of the town who come and go, protecting those who pass in and out.

And my lord the young count, bravery itself, who lifts up *paratge* and vanquishes the proud, who brings colour and gold to defeated and suffering men, he and Sir Bertrand[10] of Toulouse with well-armed Sir Hugh of Alfaro garrison the Vilanova barbican.

Sir Bernard of Comminges,[11] handsome, good and kind, mighty, valiant, wise, generous and a conqueror, with his cousin Sir Bernard of Comminges, Sir Arnold Raymond of Aspet[12] and the good knights from Montaigon,[13] staunch and resolute, hold the newly built barbican.

The Pertus barbican is nobly held by good Sir Inard of Pointis, worthy and

---

1. From Cahuzac-sur-Vère, Gaillac, Tarn.
2. Penne, Gaillac, a towering fortress which withstood Simon de Montfort's siege in 1212. Bernard and his brother Oliver in 1230 ceded Penne to Alfonse of Poitiers in return for other property.
3. Connected with Albi, and possibly with Cordes, Gaillac, Tarn.
4. Monestiès, not far from Cordes and Penne.
5. A dispossessed lord from the viscountcy of Carcassonne.
6. William Arnold of Tantalon (laisse 185); his achievements have been left untranslated, as *genhs* can mean either 'tricks, stratagems' or 'siege weapons' and the meaning of *brocidas* is not known. Meyer suggests 'incendie', *Chanson*, i, p. 394.
7. Viscount of Caussade, probably a son-in-law of Jordan of La Isla.
8. Or Raynier of Bona, not identified.
9. A mercenary who had long served Raymond VI.
10. His natural brother.
11. This Bernard is the son of Bernard IV, count of Comminges; the next one is son of Guy, lord of St Foy, Bernard IV's brother.
12. Arnold Raymond, another cousin, son of Fortanier, Count Bernard's brother.
13. Montaigon, a square in Toulouse; see laisse 200.

brave, by his uncle Sir Marestaing whom everyone respects, by Sir Roger of Montaut, strong in command and defence, and by Sir Roger of Noé,[1] handsome and well behaved.

Gerald Unaud, wise, good and patient, Sir Raymond Unaud, clever and well liked, and the staunch and resolute Sir Jordan of Lanta[2] hold the St Stephen barbican.

Active Sir Sicard, lord of Puylaurens, and Sir Hugh of Monteils[3] together with Sir Padern,[4] are glad to command the Montoulieu barbican. The Montgaillard barbican is firmly held by Bernard Meuder[5] with none but his own men, soldiers of fortune who seek and take.

And Viscount Bertrand,[6] a young man learning his trade, together with Sir Bartas, keeps wise and determined hold of the castle barbican.

Sir Bernard of Montaut, a true fighting man, with Sir Gilbert[7] and the Abbot and dogged Sir Frézoul[8] and their fine companies of friends and kinsmen, keep the barbican by the old bridge and will not be shifted.

The barbican by the new bridge is strongly held by brave Bernard Jordan, lord of La Isla, together with Sir Bertrand Jordan and experienced Sir Odo,[9] working closely with Sir Gerald of Gourdon, generous Sir Bernard Beynac,[10] Sir Estolt, who commands the shelters and siege engines, and by their fine companies, who can both endure attacks and launch them.

On the newly built Bazacle bridge are posted excellent archers to keep up a rapid fire and defend the shore and watering places so that no boat or enemy can reach them.

The defenders of Toulouse swear to stand firm

All the barons have sworn together upon holy relics that for no alarm or for any attack, for no blows, wounds or terror, not for death or the sword, while they still have life will any of them quit their posts. And the men of Toulouse unanimously agree to reserve a force of knights, citizens and sergeants, some of the town's best and strongest fighters, to gather where they are most needed. The town is strongly garrisoned by the barons, by the men of Toulouse and by the glorious martyr and the other holy bodies.

God, St Sernin and the blessed Virgin will defend Toulouse

Now may the Virgin's Son, full of light and glory, who gave his precious blood for mercy's victory, defend reason and law, may he cause the guilt of wrongdoing to fall on those who purpose sin! For now the son of the king of France comes in pride bringing thirty or forty counts and so many troops that no man alive

---

1. Descended from the lords of Noé, as were the Montauts.
2. Related to the Unaud family.
3. Monteils, Caussade, Tarn-et-Garonne.
4. Perhaps from the Corbières district.
5. A mercenary commander, perhaps Catalan.
6. Probably one of the co-suzerains of Lautrec; still alive in 1277.
7. Gilbert, son of Bernard of Montaut.
8. Not identified.
9. Bertrand Jordan, lord of Launac, and Odo of Tarrida, viscount of Gimoès, were younger brothers of Bernard Jordan, lord of La Isla.
10. From Périgord, more likely called Gaillard or Mainard.

can reckon up their thousands and hundreds. The cardinal from Rome too, he comes proclaiming that death and slaughter must lead the way, that in and around Toulouse there shall remain no living man, neither noble lady, girl nor pregnant woman, no created thing, no child at the breast, but all must die in fire and flames.

But the Virgin Mary will save them from this, she who puts right all that is wrong, so that innocent blood will not be shed. They will not be afraid, for St Sernin leads them, and God, justice, strength, the young count and the saints will defend Toulouse for them.

Amen.

7 Simon de Montfort attacks Toulouse

Drawing by Caroline Metcalfe-Gibson based on manuscript no. 25425 fonds français in the Bibliothèque Nationale, Paris.

Chronology

1179 Lateran Council: stronger measures proclaimed against heresy in the districts of Carcassonne, Toulouse, Albi and in Gascony.

1180 Philip Augustus (1165-1223) becomes king of France.

1191 Celestine III elected pope.

1194 Raymond VI (1156-1222) becomes count of Toulouse.

1196 Peter II (1174-1213) becomes king of Aragon.

1198 Innocent III elected pope.

1199 John (1167-1216) becomes king of England.

1204 Peter of Castelnau and Arnold Amauri, abbot of Cîteaux, appointed papal legates in Languedoc.

1206 Fouquet of Marseille becomes bishop of Toulouse.
Dominic and others preach against heresy in Languedoc.

1207 Peter of Castelnau excommunicates Raymond VI as 'a protector of heretics'.

1208 Raymond VI says he will obey the Church; meets Peter of Castelnau at St Gilles; Peter is murdered.
Innocent summons a crusade against the Cathars.

1209 A crusading army descends the Rhône valley.
Raymond VI takes the cross.
Otto IV of Brunswick (1174-1218) becomes emperor.
Crusaders take and sack Béziers, massacre inhabitants.
Siege and surrender of Carcassonne.
Imprisonment and death of Raymond Roger Trencavel.

1210 Minerve falls to the crusaders.
Fall of Termes to the crusaders.

1211 Council of Montpellier: Raymond VI is excommunicated again.
Cabaret surrenders to the crusaders.
Crusaders take Lavaur.
Crusaders overrun the Albigeois.
Simon de Montfort is defeated outside Toulouse.
Crusaders overrun Foix.
Siege of Castelnaudary; Toulousains defeated.
The Albigeois rises against the crusaders; Raymond VI recovers his fiefs.

1212 More crusaders arrive; Simon counterattacks.
Crusaders take St Antonin, Montcuq, Penne, Castelsarrasin, Moissac.
Battle of Las Navas de Tolosa, Spain: the kings of Aragon, Castile and
Navarre, led by Arnold Amaury, defeat the emir of Morocco.
Crusaders conquer Gascony and Béarn.
Arnold Amaury becomes archbishop of Narbonne.
Statutes of Pamiers: northern laws are to replace those of the south.

1213 Peter II king of Aragon goes to war against Simon de Montfort;
Peter is defeated and killed at Muret.

1214 Simon de Montfort devastates Foix.

1215 Lateran Council: Raymond VI is stripped of his lands and titles.
Simon de Montfort becomes duke of Narbonne and count of Toulouse.

1216 Death of Innocent III, election of Honorius III.
Raymond VI and his son raise Provence against Simon.
Raymond VI goes to Spain to seek reinforcements.
Simon lays siege to Beaucaire.
He abandons siege and returns to Toulouse.
Revolt in Toulouse, suppressed.

1217 Simon devastates Ariège; goes to make war in Provence.
Raymond VI returns to Toulouse.
Simon leaves Provence and besieges Toulouse.

1218 Death of Simon de Montfort. Amaury chosen to succeed him.
Prince Louis of France takes the cross.

1219 Louis' crusading army marches south. Marmande surrenders.
Louis approaches Toulouse.

(The narrative of *The Song of the Cathar Wars* ends here.)

After two months, Louis returns to France.
Young Raymond and the dispossessed lords capture a number of strongholds.

1222 Raymond VI dies in Toulouse.
Raymond VII continues the struggle; and writes to the king of France to
demand his inheritance.

1223 Raymond Roger, count of Foix, dies, succeeded by Roger Bernard.
Philip Augustus, king of France, dies, succeeded by Louis VIII.

1224 Amaury de Montfort leaves Carcassonne; he makes over all his rights in the
south to the king of France.
Young Trencavel recovers Carcassonne.
Conference of Montpellier: Raymond VII asks the pope to recognise him as
count of Toulouse. He promises to expel heretics; so do the count of Foix and
the viscount of Carcassonne.

1225 Council of Bourges: Raymond VII again asks the pope to grant him his inheritance. Amaury de Montfort claims to be sole heir to the counts of Toulouse.

1226 In Paris the Church declares that Raymond VII cannot prove his orthodoxy, and grants his lands to the king of France.
Louis VIII takes the cross and leads an army down the Rhône. Only Avignon resists, but surrenders after a three-month siege. Louis takes all the great towns of the south, but avoids Toulouse.
Death of Louis VIII at Montpensier.
Imbert de Beaujeu, French captain-general, continues the war.

1227 The archbishop of Narbonne excommunicates Raymond VII, the count of Foix and the 'so-called' viscount of Béziers.
Guy de Montfort, Simon's brother, dies besieging Varilhes, Ariège.
French forces devastate the south.

1229 The Treaty of Paris: Raymond VII submits to the Church and to the king of France. He keeps his title.

1230 The Inquisition established.

1240 Raymond Roger, exiled viscount of Béziers and Carcassonne, returns from Spain; he and other dispossessed lords try to throw off the French yoke, but fail.

1244 Fall of Montségur.

1271 Deaths of Jeanne of Toulouse, daughter of Raymond VII, and of her husband Alfonse of Poitiers, leaving no children. The French crown inherits the County of Toulouse.

Index